T0341512

THE JEWS IN MEDIEVAL BRITAIN

THE JEWS IN MEDIEVAL BRITAIN

HISTORICAL, LITERARY AND ARCHAEOLOGICAL PERSPECTIVES

EDITED BY

Patricia Skinner

THE BOYDELL PRESS

First published 2003
The Boydell Press, Woodbridge
Reprinted in paperback and transferred to digital printing 2012

ISBN 978 0 85115 931 7 hardback
ISBN 978 1 84383 733 6 paperback

The Boydell Press is an imprint of Boydell & Brewer Ltd
PO Box 9, Woodbridge, Suffolk IP12 3DF, UK
and of Boydell & Brewer Inc,
668 Mt Hope Avenue, Rochester, NY 14620, USA
website: www.boydellandbrewer.com

A CIP catalogue record for this book is available
from the British Library

Library of Congress Catalog Card Number: 2002152647

Papers used by Boydell & Brewer Ltd are natural, recycled products
Made from wood grown in sustainable forests

Printed and bound in Great Britain by
CPI Group (UK) Ltd, Croydon CR0 4YY

Contents

Preface and Editorial Note

This book arose from a meeting held at the University of Southampton in December 2000, co-hosted by the Wessex Medieval Centre and the Parkes Centre for the Study of Jewish/non-Jewish Relations. Some of the papers given that day were published in a special issue of the journal *Jewish Culture and History*, 3 (2000); they included Barrie Dobson's chapter in this volume, which is reprinted by kind permission of the journal's editor, Dr Nadia Valman, and publisher, Frank Cass. However, the vibrancy of the day demanded publication of its remaining papers, within a volume that would both provide an introduction to the history of the Jews in medieval Britain, and reflect upon recent research in the field. It is testimony to the enthusiasm that the subject provokes that three of those whose papers had appeared in *JCH* wrote further chapters for this book, and that three other invited contributors agreed to write new chapters covering areas not addressed by the colloquium. The result is a book that we all hope will provide a guide for the reader to work already done, and encourage new research into the social life of Britain's Jews during the twelfth and thirteenth centuries.

The editorial process has been a genuine pleasure, and I thank all of the contributors for their good-natured co-operation, and Caroline Palmer and the staff at Boydell & Brewer for seeing it into print. The support of the Director of the Wessex Medieval Centre, Professor Tim Reuter, led to this project coming to fruition. I was financially aided by a Leverhulme Trust Research Fellowship. A final editorial note: much previous work on the British Jewish community appeared in the *Transactions of the Jewish Historical Society of England*; this became *Jewish Historical Studies* from volume 29 (1982–6). In all cases, volumes are cited by the date of the transactions: the date of publication is usually one or two years later.

Patricia Skinner, University of Southampton

Abbreviations

AHR	*American Historical Review*
Anglo-Jewish Exhibition	*Anglo-Jewish Historical Exhibition Catalogue* (London, 1887)
ANS	*Anglo-Norman Studies*
Benedict	*Chronicle of the Reigns of Henry II and Richard I (attributed to Abbot Benedict of Peterborough)*, 2 vols, ed. W. Stubbs (RS 49, London, 1867)
BIHR	*Bulletin of the Institute of Historical Research*
CBA	Council for British Archaeology
CCR [and year/s]	*Calendar of the Close Rolls of the Reign of Edward I, 1272–9* (London, 1900); *1279–88* (London, 1902); *1288–96* (London, 1904)
CChR (and vol.)	*Calendar of Charter Rolls, I: Henry III 1226–57* (London, 1903); *II: Henry III and Edward I 1257–1300* (London, 1906)
CFR	*Calendar of Fine Rolls, 1272–1307* (London, 1911)
Close Rolls [and year/s]	*Close Rolls of the Reign of Henry III, 1227–31* (London, 1902); *1231–4* (London, 1905); *1234–7* (London, 1908); *1237–42* (London, 1911); *1242–7* (London, 1916); *1247–51* (London, 1922); *1251–3* (London, 1927); *1253–4* (London, 1929); *1254–6* (London, 1931); *1256–9* (London, 1932); *1259–61* (London, 1934); *1261–4* (London, 1936); *1264–8* (London, 1937); *1268–72* (London, 1938)
CLR [and vol.]	*Calendar of the Liberate Rolls, I: Henry III, 1226–1240* (London, 1916); *II: Henry III, 1240–5* (London, 1930); *III: Henry III, 1245–51* (London, 1937); *IV: Henry III, 1251–60* (London, 1959); *V: Henry III, 1260–7* (London, 1961); *VI: Henry III, 1267–72* (London, 1964)
CPR [and year/s]	*Calendar of the Patent Rolls of the Reign of Henry III, 1232–47* (London, 1906); *1247–58* (London, 1908); *1258–66* (London, 1910); *1266–72* (London, 1913); *Calendar of the Patent Rolls of the Reign of Edward I, 1272–81* (London, 1901); *1281–1292* (London, 1893)
CPREJ [and vol.]	*Calendar of the Plea Rolls of the Exchequer of the Jews*, I (London, 1905), II (Edinburgh, 1910), III (London, 1929), IV (London, 1972), V (London, 1992)

Davis, *Deeds*	Davis, M.D., *Hebrew Deeds of English Jews before 1290* (London, 1888)
Diceto	*Ralph de Diceto: Historical Works*, ed. W. Stubbs, 2 vols (RS 68, London, 1876)
EHR	*English Historical Review*
Gervase	*Gervase of Canterbury: Historical Works*, ed. W. Stubbs, 2 vols (RS 73, London, 1879–80)
Gesta Stephani	*Gesta Stephani*, tr. K.R. Potter (London, 1955)
Howden	*Roger de Howden: Chronicle*, ed. W. Stubbs, 4 vols (RS 51, London, 1868–71)
HUCA	*Hebrew Union College Annual*
Jacobs, *Jews*	Jacobs, Joseph, *The Jews of Angevin England: Documents and Records from Latin and Hebrew Sources* (London, 1893)
JCH	*Jewish Culture and History*
JEH	*Journal of Ecclesiastical History*
JH	*Jewish History* (published Haifa)
JHS	*Jewish Historical Studies*
JMH	*Journal of Medieval History*
JQR	*Jewish Quarterly Review*
Lipman, *Norwich*	Vivian Lipman, *The Jews of Medieval Norwich* (London, 1967)
MJHSE	*Miscellanea of the Jewish Historical Society of England*
Mundill, *Solution*	Robin R. Mundill, *England's Jewish Solution: Experiment and Expulsion, 1262–1290* (Cambridge, 1998)
Newburgh	*William of Newburgh*, in R. Howlett, ed., *Chronicles of the Reigns of Stephen, Henry II and Richard I*, 4 vols (RS 82, London, 1884–9).
Patent Rolls [and years]	*Patent Rolls of the Reign of Henry III, 1216–25* (London, 1901); *1225–32* (London, 1903)
PpR [and regnal year and king]	Pipe Rolls volumes: see Bibliography, section 2
PRO	Public Record Office
Prynne, *Demurrer*	Prynne, William, *A Short Demurrer to the Jewes long discontinued barred remitter into England, comprising an exact and chronological relation of their first admission into, their ill deportment, oppressions, and their final banishment out of England, collected out of the best historians and records. With reasons against their readmission to England* (2nd edn, London, 1656)
RCHM	Royal Commission for Historic Monuments
REJ	*Revue des Études Juives*
Richardson, *English Jewry*	Richardson, Henry G., *The English Jewry under the Angevin Kings* (London, 1960)
Rigg, *Select Pleas*	Rigg, J.M., ed., *Select Pleas, Starrs and other*

	Records from the Rolls of the Exchequer of the Jews A.D. 1220–1284 (London, 1902)
Rot. Chart.	*Rotuli Chartarum, 1199–1216*, ed. T.D. Hardy, vol. Ii (London, Record Commission, 1837).
Rot. Litt. Claus.	*Rotuli Litterarum Clausarum in Turri Londiniensi asservati*, ed. T.D. Hardy, vols I (1204–24); II (1224–27) (London, 1833 and 1844)
Rot. Litt. Pat.	*Rotuli Litterarum Patentium in Turri Londiniensi asservati, 1201–1216*, ed. T.D. Hardy, 2 vols (London, Record Commission, 1835)
Roth, *History*[2] and	Cecil Roth, *History of the Jews in England* (2nd edn,
History[3]	Oxford, 1948, 3rd edn, Oxford, 1964)
RS	Rolls Series
SCH	*Studies in Church History*
Starrs	*Starrs and Jewish Charters preserved in the British Museum*, ed. I. Abrahams, A.P. Stokes and H. Loewe, 3 vols (London, 1930–2)
Stat. Realm	*The Statutes of the Realm*, I (London, 1810)
TJHSE	*Transactions of the Jewish Historical Society of England*
Torigni	*Robert de Torigni: Chronicle*, ed. R. Howlett (RS 82, London, 1889)
TWNFC	*Transactions of the Woolhope Naturalist Field Club*
WAM	Westminster Abbey Muniments

Introduction: Jews in Medieval Britain and Europe[1]

PATRICIA SKINNER

The date 1066 has an indelible and pre-eminent position in the history of Britain, as an immigrant group arrived from across the Channel and fought its way into power; the date 1290 rather less so. Yet these two points traditionally mark the beginning and the end of the medieval Jewish presence in Britain, starting with a tiny group accompanying (or following) the Normans and ending with the shockwave of expulsion. Its compressed history, into just over two centuries from the time of the Norman conquest, is both an attraction and a trap for the unwary. For its apparently neat chronological edges, coupled with a collection of sources that for other purposes has been described as the most systematic in medieval Europe, can lead to assumptions being made about the completeness of the picture that emerges. Compared with other national Jewries, the British Jewish community has been studied more than anywhere else except, perhaps, that of medieval Spain.[2] And yet it has been studied far more frequently as *Jewish* history, rather than as an integral aspect of *British* history in this period, a point made most eloquently by Colin Richmond.[3] Even in the most recent histories of medieval Britain, the Jews have been notably under-represented.[4] The study of the Jewish community, however, is vital to an understanding of the political and social history of the region. Although numerically the community was a tiny minority within the population, its economic life concerned the government and affected the lives of the host majority, and its presence posed a religious problem for the Church; in addition, a close examination of contemporary attitudes to the Jewry here inform and deepen our understanding of the twelfth- and thirteenth-century intellectual world. A study of the Jewry of medieval Britain should need little justification at the start of the twenty-first century, and yet, for some reason, it remains a specialist area not entirely embraced by the 'mainstream'.

What was particularly exceptional about the British Jewish community apart from the brevity of its presence? An easy answer would be, very little: its

[1] I am grateful to Robin Mundill for his helpful input, and to Elizabeth Ewan for advice on points of Scottish history. Any errors remaining are entirely my own.
[2] C. Roth, *The Jews of Medieval Oxford* (Oxford, Oxford Historical Society new series no. 9, 1945–6), p. iii.
[3] Colin Richmond, 'Englishness and medieval Anglo-Jewry', in Tony Kushner, ed., *The Jewish Heritage in British History: Englishness and Jewishness* (London, 1992), pp. 42–59.
[4] E.g., John Hatcher and Mark Bailey, *Modelling the Middle Ages: the History and Theory of England's Economic Development* (Oxford, 2001); Barbara Harvey, *The Short Oxford History of the British Isles: the Twelfth and Thirteenth Centuries* (Oxford, 2001).

position as a corporate body, subject only to the ruler, was one which would have been just as familiar to the Jews of medieval France (where local magnates supplanted the king as the 'protectors' of the Jews outside the royal demesne), Germany (where the emperor is credited with the first explicit statement of the Jews' position as fiscal property) or Italy (where each autonomous city-state and its territory negotiated its own relationship of power over the Jews).[5] Like the Jewish communities of the Rhineland in the eleventh and twelfth centuries,[6] the medieval Anglo-Jewry suffered a catastrophic outbreak of Christian fury, resulting in deliberate attacks on individual communities after Richard I's coronation in 1190. Finally, like their co-religionists in parts of France, Germany, Italy and Spain, the Jews of Britain eventually found themselves being forced into exile from the land of their settlement and, for at least two generations, birth.[7] The really exceptional feature of the history of the Jews in England, it seems, is how intensively they were recorded by the state: in no other country was a separate government department set up to control specifically Jewish affairs in the way the Jewish Exchequer did in England. And had English rule spread faster to Wales, Scotland and Ireland, then the remit of the Jewish Exchequer might well have extended to those territories too.

This raises the issue of the rather ambitious title of the present book. In fact, there is some fragmentary evidence for a Welsh and Irish presence or involvement by Jews before their departure, and acknowledging and documenting this fact represents something of a departure from previous studies focusing solely on Anglo-Jewry. Nonetheless, the majority of chapters have dealt only with England, for lack of evidence elsewhere. As for Scotland, it is tempting to speculate that Jews fleeing England in 1290 might have looked northwards rather than across the Channel, but the combined factors of their distribution prior to that date (none further north than York, apparently, Newcastle having

[5] Robin R. Mundill, 'The medieval Anglo-Jewish community: organization and royal control', in *Proceedings of Christliche und jüdische Gemeinden in kulturräumlich vergleichender Betrachtung.* Trier, 1999 (forthcoming); France: W.C. Jordan, *The French Monarchy and the Jews: from Philip Augustus to the Last Capetians* (Philadelphia, 1989); Germany: G. Kisch, *The Jews in Medieval Germany: a Study of their Legal and Social Status* (Chicago, 1949); Italy: M. Botticini, 'A tale of "benevolent" governments: private credit markets, public finance and the role of Jewish lenders in medieval and renaissance Italy', *JEH*, 60 (2000), 164–89.

[6] Sources: S. Eidelberg, tr., *The Jews and the Crusaders: the Hebrew Chronicles of the First and Second Crusades* (Madison, 1977); discussion in Robert Chazan, *European Jewry and the First Crusade* (Berkeley, 1987) and id., *In the Year 1096 . . . The First Crusade and the Jews* (Berkeley, 1996).

[7] Expulsions took place in France under Philip II Augustus (banning Jews from royal territories) in 1182, reversed in 1198; in Gascony in 1287 (repeated in 1305, 1310/11 and 1313–17); England in 1290; in the royal domain in France definitively in 1306 and 1322 (although a Jewish presence is documented later in the south); Germany was a fragmented region, and each area expelled its Jews at a different time between 1196 and 1476; Spain famously expelled its Jews in 1492. England, see below, note 16; France: Sophia Menache, 'The king, the Church and the Jews: some considerations on the expulsions from England and France', *JMH*, 13 (1987), 223–36; Gerd Mentgen, 'Die Vertreibungen der Juden aus England und Frankreich im Mittelalter', *Aschkenas*, 7 (1997), 11–53; W.C. Jordan, 'Princely identity and the Jews in medieval Europe', in Jeremy Cohen, ed., *From Witness to Witchcraft: Jews and Judaism in Medieval Christian Thought* (Wiesbaden, 1996), pp. 259–73; Gascony: Richardson, *English Jewry* (see Abbreviations), p. 232; Germany: R. Po-Chia Hsia and H. Lehmann, eds, *In and Out of the Ghetto: Jewish–Gentile Relations in Late-Medieval and Early-Modern Germany* (Cambridge, 1995). The literature on the Spanish expulsion of 1492 is vast: recent contributions include Haim Beinart, 'The expulsion from Spain: causes and results', in id., ed., *The Sephardi Legacy*, 2 vols (Jerusalem, 1992), II, pp. 11–42; Edward Peters, 'Jewish history and Gentile memory: the expulsion of 1492', *JH*, 9 (1995), 9–34.

expelled its community in 1234), and Edward I's invasion of Scotland in 1296, massacring the inhabitants of Berwick before ruling the country until 1306, render the likelihood of a post-1290 Scottish Jewish community somewhat remote. A Thomas fil Isaac, recorded in Aberdeen in the fourteenth century, is unlikely to have been Jewish as he married the king's daughter.[8] If Jews remained in Britain after 1290, it was purely in the literary imagination: the Scottish *Ballad of the Jew's Daughter* is but one manifestation of the lingering of the Jewish presence in British literary culture.[9] A post-1290 Jewish presence in England is unlikely: the fact that the expulsion edict was not repeated (unlike, for instance, the situation in the French royal territory) is itself a strong indicator that it was effective, and local studies have found no evidence to support a continuing physical presence.[10] I shall return to this point below.

What is not in dispute is the recent and welcome upsurge in interest in Britain's medieval Jewish community after almost a century of relative neglect. Fuelled by the wider popularity of the study of medieval minority groups, the belated resumption of publication of the documents of the Jewish Exchequer, and the series of events in 1990 commemorating the massacre of 1190 and the Expulsion a century later, historians looked at long-published sources with new research questions. Alongside reassessments of the Church's attitude towards the community,[11] and legal situation,[12] the economic life of the Jewish community has been investigated in greater detail and, crucially, its social and cultural life has also begun to be studied, using these externally created sources.[13] Most recently, there has been a revival of interest in, and reassessment of, sources created and left by the Jews themselves.[14] The violence of the year 1190, perhaps neglected by historians because the British Jewish community did not produce extensive commemorative texts as their continental co-religionists did (the English disaster was recorded only by Christian clerics, and the sole Jewish source to mention it was the work of Ephraim of Bonn), was belatedly studied and, if not atoned for, at least recognised as a catastrophe in English as well as Jewish history.[15] The

[8] Wales and Ireland: see Joe Hillaby's chapter, below, pp. 36–40. A threat to banish the Jews to Ireland in 1244 does not appear to have been carried out: *Close Rolls, 1242–7*, p. 275. Scotland: M. Haskell, 'Breaking the stalemate: the Scottish campaigns of Edward I, 1303–4', in M. Prestwich et al., eds, *Thirteenth-Century England VII* (Woodbridge, 1999), pp. 223–41.

[9] Bishop Percy's *Reliques of Ancient Poetry* includes the Scottish 'Ballad of the Jew's daughter': J. Kinsley, ed., *Oxford Book of Ballads* (Oxford, 1982); the story resembles Chaucer's Princess' Tale but could also be related to the Trent blood libel of 1475, on which see R. Po-Chia Hsia, *The Myth of Ritual Murder: Jews and Magic in Reformation Germany* (New Haven and London, 1988). Richardson, *English Jewry* (see Abbreviations), p. 232, comments on the memory of the Jews remaining after 1290.

[10] Cecil Roth, 'Jews in Oxford after 1290', *Oxoniensia*, 15 (1950), 63–80.

[11] Menache, 'King, Church and the Jews'; J.A. Watt, 'The English episcopate, the state and the Jews: the evidence of the thirteenth-century conciliar decrees', in P.R. Coss and S.D. Lloyd, eds, *Thirteenth Century England II: Proceedings of the Newcastle upon Tyne Conference* (Woodbridge, 1988), pp. 137–47.

[12] Paul Brand, 'Jews and the law in England, 1275–90', *EHR*, 115 (2000), 1138–58.

[13] Zefira Entin Rokeah, ed., *Medieval English Jews and Royal Officials: Entries of Jewish Interest in the English Memoranda Rolls, 1266–1293* (Jerusalem, 2000).

[14] See, e.g., Susan Einbinder, 'Meir ben Elijah of Norwich: persecution and poetry among medieval English Jews, *JMH*, 26 (2000), 145–62; and below, p. 5.

[15] A. Haberman, ed., *Gezeirot Ashkenaz ve-Zorfat* (Jerusalem, 1971), p. 127; Robert Chazan, 'Ephraim ben Jacob's compilation of twelfth-century persecutions', *JQR*, 84 (1994), 397–416; on the commemoration at York, see Dobson's chapter, below, pp. 145–56. That the fate of the

years leading up to and including the Expulsion have also received renewed attention.[16]

A new synthesis of the state of research seemed timely, therefore. Many of the authors in this volume acknowledge the debt owed to those nineteenth-century scholars whose efforts saw the first substantial publication of documents relating to the Anglo-Jewish community: the compilations made by Joseph Jacobs and Meyr Davis, still heavily cited and not yet satisfactorily replaced.[17] The contemporary campaign to publish the holdings of the Public Record Office also revealed more information.[18] And with the availability of sources much improved, the Anglo-Jewish community found its historians: Lionel Abrahams, A.M. Hyamson and, pre-eminently, Cecil Roth, whose figure bestrides most of the twentieth-century historiography and whose interests extended far further afield than the British Isles.[19] It is from Roth's writings that we gain clues as to the origins of the neglect of the Jewish contribution to medieval British history: post-Holocaust, it is all too easy to forget that scholars of medieval Jewry faced a barrier of antisemitism for decades before the Second World War. Many early works are frankly apologist in tone, and Roth himself was not immune to this tendency. He sums up the difficulties eloquently in an essay of 1928: Jewish history, partly through its own emphasis on rabbinical study, was 'an outcast in the universities'. 'Until a man's academic position is assured', he added, 'he cannot dare to let it be known that he is seriously interested in questions relating to Jewish scholarship.'[20] The difficulties facing historians of the Jewry may have eased after 1945, but Roth remained a relatively lone figure in the field until the early 1960s.

Thereafter the picture was patchy: the growth of interest in the modern catastrophe of the Jews led to centres for Jewish history beginning to emerge in universities across the world. In some, precedents were sought to the Holocaust,

---

Jewish community is beginning to become a mainstream topic after years of neglect is suggested by its inclusion in Simon Schama's recent *History of Britain* television series and accompanying book, *The History of Britain: at the Edge of the World? 3000B.C.–A.D.1603* (London, 2000).

[16] Mundill, *Solution* (see Abbreviations); Robert C. Stacey, 'Parliamentary negotiation and the Expulsion of the Jews from England', in R.H. Britnell, R. Frame and M. Prestwich, eds, *Thirteenth-Century England VI* (Woodbridge, 1997), pp. 77–101; Mentgen, 'Die Vertreibungen der Juden'; Yosef Kaplan and David Katz, eds, *The Expulsion of the Jews from England in 1290 and its Aftermath* (Jerusalem, 1992); Schama, *History of Britain*, p. 199, calls the expulsion 'ethnic cleansing'.

[17] Jacobs, *Jews* (see Abbreviations); Davis, *Deeds* (see Abbreviations).

[18] See below, Bibliography, section 2 for those sources relating specifically to the Jewish community.

[19] B. Lionel Abrahams, 'The debts and houses of the Jews of Hereford in 1290', *TJHSE*, 1 (1893–4), 136–59; id., 'The expulsion of the Jews from England in 1290', *JQR*, 7 (1894), 75–100, 236–58, 428–58 (also published as a single volume, Oxford, 1895); id., 'Condition of the Jews of England at the time of their expulsion in 1290', *TJHSE*, 2 (1894–5), 76–105; id., 'The economic and financial position of the Jews in medieval England', *TJHSE*, 8 (1915–17), 171–89; J.M. Rigg, 'The Jews of England in the 13th century', *JQR*, o.s., 15 (1903), 5–22; A.M. Hyamson, *A History of the Jews in England* (London, 1908, 2nd edn, 1928). See below, Bibliography, p. 166, for Roth's extensive output, and Lloyd. P. Gartner, 'Cecil Roth, historian of Anglo-Jewry', in Dov Noy and Issacher ben-Ami, eds, *Studies in the Cultural Life of the Jews of England* (Jerusalem, 1975), pp. 69–86.

[20] See, e.g., the heavily apologist preface to H.S.Q. Henriques, *The Jews and the English Law* (London, 1908); Cecil Roth, 'Jewish history for our own needs', *The Menorah Journal*, 14 (1928), 419–33, quotes from 432–3.

and the medieval period was discussed most frequently in relation to, and as a possible precursor of, the Fascist regimes. Scholars disagreed fiercely, however, on the linkage between the two.[21] In other regions, particularly in the new state of Israel, the initial thrust of study was into the heroic, biblical and state-building period rather than the middle ages,[22] and subsequent work on the latter period has focused on continental Europe rather than Britain, the notable exception being the research of Zefira Entin Rokeah, whose studies have been influential on some of the essays in the present volume.[23]

The neglect of the British situation is explicable largely on the grounds that, compared with other northern, Ashkenazic communities, the Anglo-Jewish community was not perceived to have produced the scholarly superstars so evident in France and Germany, a significant lack given that the thrust of much Jewish history has been grounded in the study of the development of Jewish law. Indeed, as is pointed out in the chapters by Robert Stacey and Sue Bartlet below, contentious matters of rabbinic law might be referred across the Channel for resolution. Does this mean that the British community lacked its own experts? Did the British Jews lean on the knowledge of their brethren on the continent? Certainly the argument in favour of this depressing statement finds support in the fact that very few of the surviving Hebrew manuscripts in Britain can securely be identified as locally produced. Those manuscripts in Jewish ownership, listed by Stokes, were not necessarily written by local scribes. We must remember, however, that the massacres of 1190 led also to manuscripts

---

[21] Bernard S. Bachrach, *Early Medieval Jewish Policy in Western Europe* (Minneapolis, 1977), p. vii, comments, 'Among our contemporaries modern parallels – Nazi Germany, Fascist Italy, Communist Russia – are often evoked to bring to the reader the full impact of the medieval debacle. In discussions of anti-Jewish legislation enacted by either secular or religious powers during the middle ages, it is not uncommon to see the Nuremberg Laws introduced as the ineluctable finale to a centuries-long process.' David Biale, *Power and Powerlessness in Jewish History* (New York, 1986), pp. 8 and 142, adds that we see 'all of Jewish history through the lens of the Holocaust . . . as if the history of the Jews in the Diaspora culminates in Auschwitz', and claims that the Nazis appropriated medieval symbols of repression when they repealed German citizenship for the Jews, drove them out of the professions, introduced the yellow badge and enclosed them in ghettos. Guido Kisch, 'The yellow badge in history', *Historia Judaica*, 4 (1942), 95–144, at 122, says that the Nazis 'studied systematically and carefully' the oppressive measures of the middle ages. Salo Baron, however, was opposed to the prevailing view: 'Any comparison with the contemporary legislation of Nazi Germany and Fascist Italy, however, will reveal that we are maligning the middle ages when we call the Nuremberg laws a reversal to medieval status': Salo W. Baron, 'The Jewish factor in medieval civilisation' [1941], reprinted in Robert Chazan, ed., *Medieval Jewish Life* (New York, 1976), pp. 3–50, at p. 37. But Raul Hilberg, *The Destruction of the European Jews* (revised and definitive edition, New York and London, 1985), pp. 5–28, does seek precedents for Nazi actions and, at pp. 11–12, explicitly links medieval canon law to Nazi legislation.

[22] David N. Myers, 'Between Diaspora and Zion: history, memory and the Jerusalem scholars', in id. and David B. Ruderman, eds, *The Jewish Past Revisited: Reflections on Modern Jewish Historians* (New Haven and London, 1998), pp. 88–103, at p. 98. Salo Baron, 'Who is a Jew?' [1960], reprinted in A. Hertzberg and L.A. Feldman, eds, *History and Jewish Historians* (Philadelphia, 1964) pp. 5–22, at p. 19, said that the young Israeli, 'in his eagerness to start a new life . . . is prepared to consider the history of his people as relevant only insofar as it relates to the First and Second Jewish Commonwealths, and then start it over again in 1948'. Thus Jewish histories of the 1960s, he argued, privileged the heroic fighter for Israel over the religious martyr, and heroes of ancient Israel over figures of medieval and early modern times: 'Newer emphases in Jewish history' [1963], reprinted in *ibid.*, pp. 90–106, at p. 99.

[23] See below, Bibliography, p. 166 for Rokeah's extensive output.

being looted and sold to the Jewish communities abroad: Ephraim of Bonn records their purchase by the Cologne Jewry.[24] It is equally obvious that a community whose ritual life centred on the texts in the home and the synagogue would not have abandoned such treasures during periods of violence or at the time of the Expulsion. And the chapters below reveal considerable evidence of the respect with which Anglo-Jewish community leaders were regarded. It might well be the case that future research into this issue should focus on continental, rather than English, libraries and archives. Indeed, those texts that remained on English soil are far more likely to have formed a part of a Christian cleric's library by the thirteenth century, as interest in studying Hebrew as a means to biblical study gained ground.[25]

The fact that the vast bulk of our information about the Jewish community in medieval Britain comes from fiscal sources produced by the Christian administration has also hampered research, in that it offers a one-dimensional picture of its subject. Even if medieval Anglo-Jewry had a vibrant intellectual and cultural life, we are not going to find it in this source. The state was concerned to record residence and payment of taxes, and the often very terse entries in the rolls bear this out. As Paul Brand explains in his chapter, the records give us a detailed picture of legal procedure and the interaction between royal officials and individual Jews. But unlike, for example, contemporary coroners' records, where explaining the circumstances of a death can often provide substantial additional information about the social circumstances of the deceased and his/ her family, the fiscal records at best give a patchy and partial history of an individual's business transactions. A separate chapter on the economic life of the British Jewish community in this volume would have been a superfluous exercise, in that *all* of the thematic chapters presented here are in some way inextricably concerned with the subject, a picture that is perhaps unique among European Jewish communities. The nature of the records, however, prompted Henry Richardson to produce in 1960 what was more than simply a survey work on the position of the Jews under the Angevins.[26] The comprehensive nature of his work, commented upon by several of the contributors to the present volume, may ironically have stemmed the impetus towards a better understanding of this minority: although Gavin Langmuir published a much-cited article, and Roth published a third and revised edition of his own history of Anglo-Jewry in 1964,[27] both presumably in response to Richardson's findings, the historiography then became fitful and confined to specialist journals,[28] a state from which it has only recently begun to emerge.

[24] H.P. Stokes, 'Records of mss and documents possessed by the Jews in England before the expulsion', *TJHSE*, 8 (1915–17), 78–97; M. Beit-Arié, *The Only Dated Medieval Hebrew Manuscript written in England (1189 C.E.) and the Problem of pre-Expulsion Anglo-Hebrew Manuscripts* (London, 1985); on Ephraim's evidence, see Haberman, ed., *Gezeirot Ashkenaz*, p. 127.

[25] See, e.g., Lee M. Friedman, *Robert Grosseteste and the Jews* (Cambridge, MA, 1934); Raphael Loewe, 'The mediaeval Christian Hebraists of England: the *Superscriptio Lincolniensis*', *HUCA*, 28 (1957), 205–52; *Christian Hebraism: the Study of Jewish Culture by Christian Scholars in Medieval and Early Modern Times* (Cambridge, MA, 1988); and Roth, 'Jews in Oxford'.

[26] Richardson, *English Jewry* (see Abbreviations).

[27] Gavin Langmuir, 'The Jews and the archives of Angevin England: reflections on medieval antisemitism', *Traditio*, 19 (1962), 183–244; Roth, *History*[3] (see Abbreviations).

[28] E.g., P. Hyams, 'The Jewish minority in medieval England', *JJS*, 25 (1974), 270–93.

It might be objected at this point that, since the vast bulk of the source material has been available to scholars for almost a century, there is little that is new to be said about the history of the Jewry. This ignores the fact that since the 1960s (and, in Jewish historiography, since the 1980s), new questions have been asked of existing sources. The explosion of social and cultural history, and the inroads made by gender historians into the mainstream, have meant that even distinctly unpromising or limited records can be coaxed into telling a different story. Much of the best work of the late twentieth century has revolved around identifying and tracing local family connections and acknowledging (belatedly) the significant role played by Jewish women in the business affairs of the community, although as Sue Bartlet comments in her chapter, only a small proportion of the work done thus far on Jewish women addresses the British situation directly.[29] Prosopographical work, the tracing of individuals and the study of naming practices, is also opening up new lines of information.[30] In-depth local studies, such as the early and pioneering study of the Jews of Norwich by Vivian Lipman (1967), the remarkable work done by Joe Hillaby for the Midlands and Robin Mundill's painstaking reconstructions of rural communities, the latter in his book and in his chapter for this volume,[31] offer the real possibility of connecting lesser-known families and beginning to compare the relative wealth and well-being of each individual Jewish settlement. The work of Robert Stacey has also demonstrated how the fiscal records can be made to tell us something of the social structure of the community.[32] As Hillaby himself points out in the first chapter of this book, however, there is a distinction to be made between the twelfth and thirteenth centuries as regards the evidence available. We may never be able to truly document the social life of post-conquest Jewry in the same way as we are beginning to understand that of the pre-expulsion generations.

Indeed, the social life of medieval British Jewish communities is largely hidden from view: we can with an effort trace individuals and their families, and we can get some sense of community leaders through their substantial contributions to communally raised tallages. But we cannot satisfactorily answer questions about everyday life for the Jewish residents and their neighbours; if Richmond is right about the proportion of Jews recorded in the fiscal records,[33] then our view is very limited, confined to the wealthiest and those active in dealing. Jewish law might provide us with a framework for determining familial relationships and the rhythms of ritual life, but as in any prescriptive source, we cannot be sure that its provisions were closely followed. The legal position of Jewish women is a case in point here: Avraham Grossman

---

[29] See also Dobson's chapter, below, pp. 145–56. J.R. Baskin, 'Jewish women in the middle ages', in ead., ed., *Jewish Women in Historical Perspective* (Detroit, 1991), pp. 94–114; R.B. Dobson, 'The role of Jewish women in medieval England', in D. Wood, ed., *Christianity and Judaism* (= *SCH* 29, Oxford, 1992), pp. 145–68; id., 'A minority within a minority: the Jewesses of thirteenth-century England', in S.J. Ridyard and R.G. Benson, eds, *Minorities and Barbarians in Medieval Life and Thought* (*Sewanee Medieval Studies*, 7, 1996), pp. 27–48. Cheryl Tallan has compiled a downloadable bibliographic guide at http://www.brandeis.edu/hirjw/pdf/tallan.pdf.

[30] Simon Seror, 'Les noms des femmes juives en Angleterre au moyen age', *REJ*, 154 (1995), 295–325.

[31] Lipman, *Norwich* (see Abbreviations); see below, Bibliography, p. 163 for work by Joe Hillaby; Mundill, *Solution.*

[32] See Stacey's chapter and the Bibliography, below.

[33] Richmond, 'Englishness', p. 53.

has convincingly argued that the Gentile environment profoundly affected women's status within each Jewish community across Europe,[34] and we know, for example, that northern and southern European rabbis differed on their interpretations of certain legal points. Thus, although it is useful to draw upon European examples to fill in the gaps in our knowledge of the British Jewry, such extrapolation must be done with an eye to the methodological pitfalls involved.

That said, the studies in this volume show that some communication did happen between Jews based in Britain and those on the continent. Hillaby points out the family links between London and Rouen in the twelfth century; Bartlet and Stacey both highlight the referral of a thirteenth-century divorce case to the Paris *Beth Din*, or rabbinical court; and Bartlet mentions that items from Rouen feature among Jewish women's moveable goods, even if they may have reached England via an indirect route. Jewish merchants were itinerant, and must have been crossing the Channel regularly, especially from southern enclaves such as London, Winchester and Canterbury, or the burgeoning East Anglian trade centres. Continental toponyms also indicate (at the very least) that Jews did business there. Again, however, information about the nature of their business, or the frequency of travel or its pitfalls, is almost entirely lacking. The current Cambridge University collaborative project on Jewish migration may well provide some answers, but northern Europe has nothing to compare with the treasures of the Cairo Genizah, preserving letters from Jewish merchants across the Mediterranean.[35]

What prospect, then, of new evidence becoming available? Medieval historians are now well-used to turning to other types of material, most notably archaeology. But as David Hinton points out in his chapter on archaeological evidence for the Jewish community, actually identifying an ethnic group by its material culture is fraught with methodological hazards. Even a well-excavated and well-published site like the medieval Jewish cemetery at York can only provide fragmentary additional information about diet and health. Such information is not unimportant, of course – the relative longevity of the Jewish females found there raises important questions about fertility and diet – but it essentially remains another piece in a far-from-complete jigsaw, as Barrie Dobson's chapter acknowledges. The identification of Jewish buildings from archaeological evidence is also a highly contentious issue: can we be sure that often far better-preserved continental models were replicated in the British Isles? On what criteria does a room in a house become a private synagogue, or a pit capable of holding water turn into a *mikveh*, or ritual bath? Such questions remain open at present, and may only be more fully resolved as additional sites are identified and excavated.

Similarly limited, as Anthony Bale reminds us, are literary sources. Historians taking a literary turn and students of literature embracing the New Historicism have effectively muddied the distinction between literary and

---

[34] Avraham Grossman, 'Medieval rabbinic views of wife-beating, 800–1300', *JH*, 5 (1991), 53–62, at 53.

[35] S.D. Goitein, 'What would Jewish and general history benefit by a systematic publication of the documentary Geniza papers?', *Proceedings of the American Academy for Jewish Research*, 23 (1954), 29–39, first highlighted the richness of the source, and Goitein himself went on to be its most distinguished scholar.

historical works in a mutually beneficial way. But historians still need to be wary of trying to find the literal in the literary: Christian and Jewish writers in the middle ages both borrowed heavily from precedents, fitting their contemporary observations into well-established genres.[36] As Bale highlights, we are far better advised to unpick the ways in which texts are constructed around models than to search for the truth about Jewish life.

Nevertheless, the lasting images in contemporary and later narrative sources provide some sense of how their educated, elite authors had received and transmitted ideas about their Jewish neighbours.[37] Such ideas, ultimately, derived from early patristic works. All were basically hostile to the Jewish community, yet viewed its survival and preservation as an important aid to Christian faith. The writings of Pope Gregory I formed the basis of early medieval legislation about the Jews: they were to be protected, but they were not to proselytise nor were they to extend their places of worship.[38] This situation of preserving the status quo lasted until precisely the period covered in this book: crusading enthusiasm in the eleventh and twelfth, and increasing ecclesiastical hostility to heretical sects in the twelfth and thirteenth, centuries led to new forms of attack on Jewish communities, both directly through violence and, more subtly, through sustained efforts to convert them to Christianity.[39] Both trends affected the British Jewish communities as seriously as their continental counterparts. Whether the negative images of the Jews were based on genuinely religious grounds is highly debatable: outbreaks of hostility owed as much to economic competition as to religious zeal. Nevertheless, John Edwards's survey in this volume takes up the worsening story of Christian–Jewish relations between the twelfth and thirteenth centuries which, while affected across Europe by the same papal measures, found particular expression in England. It is notable, for example, that the earliest and most frequent accusations of ritual child murder occurred in English settings. Much work has been done on the accusations in England, but this has again largely centred on the Jewish communities involved, or on the authors who disseminated the myth; its impact on the wider community, or its place in the specific context of ecclesiastical foundations competing for a decreasing number of benefactors, would reward further research.[40]

---

[36] Nancy Partner, *Serious Entertainment: the Writing of History in Twelfth-Century England* (Chicago, 1977).

[37] B. Glassman, *Antisemitic Stereotypes without Jews: Images of the Jews in England 1290–1700* (Detroit, 1975).

[38] S. Grayzel, 'The papal bull *Sicut Judeis*', in Jeremy Cohen, ed., *Essential Papers on Judaism and Christianity in Conflict* (New York, 1991), pp. 231–59. See also S. Katz, 'Pope Gregory the Great and the Jews', *JQR*, n.s., 24 (1933–4), pp. 113–36.

[39] R.I. Moore, *The Formation of a Persecuting Society* (Oxford, 1987); see also Valerie Flint, 'Anti-Jewish literature and attitudes in the twelfth century', *JJS*, 37 (1986), 39–57 and 183–205; Anna Sapir Abulafia, *Christians and Jews in the Twelfth Century Renaissance* (London, 1995); Jeremy Cohen, *The Friars and the Jews* (Ithaca, NY, 1982).

[40] On the legend, see Alan Dundes, *The Blood Libel Legend: a Casebook in Antisemitic Folklore* (Madison, 1991); Reiner Erb, ed., *Die Legende vom Ritualmord: zur Geschichte der Blutbeschuldigungen gegen Juden* (Berlin, 1993); J. McCulloh, 'Jewish ritual murder and medieval Christian hostility and anti-semitism in western Europe: William of Malmesbury, Thomas of Monmouth and the early dissemination of the myth', *Speculum*, 72 (1997), 698–740; a recent attempt to shift the origins of these and of the associated blood libel back to the period of the crusades appears not to have found universal acceptance: see Bale's chapter below, p. 130, note 5. Gavin Langmuir

But the Church was not responsible for the expulsion of the Jews from Britain or anywhere else (except the papal territories themselves and late medieval Spain and Portugal).[41] Returning to a point made above, the presence of the Jewish community in Britain was wholly a matter of their dependence on the king, and their value to him lay in their ability to provide a source of liquid wealth. Successive rulers, however, failed to ensure that the resource they had at their disposal was prudently managed, and as a result the hugely wealthy lenders of the late twelfth century were soon impoverished by waves of special taxation known as tallages, with little time in between to recover their financial position.[42] As William Jordan has demonstrated for France, an expulsion of a group whose fiscal value was entirely diminished, set against the background of dissatisfaction with the ruler and/or papal pressure to force the Jews into conversion, could be an astute political move.[43]

How effective were measures to expel whole peoples from medieval states and territories? Are we right to end this survey in 1290? Anthony Bale thinks not, from the perspective of the literary historian, and David Hinton rightly points out that iconographical depictions of the Jews also continued long after their supposed departure. Even the devotee of English constitutional history would be hard pressed to state unequivocally that Edward I's administrative machinery in that year was entirely capable of wiping out the Jewish presence. Is it possible to posit a crypto-Jewish presence in England, at least, until the formal readmission of Jews to the country in the seventeenth century? Probably not: unlike their co-religionists in later medieval Spain, where crypto-Judaism was a possibility as well as an Inquisitorial invention, the Jews of medieval Britain would have found it more difficult to vanish into their communities and continue practising. Cecil Roth, for example, has dismissed the idea of a crypto-Jewish presence after 1290 in Oxford. Another subject that would reward study, however, is the status of those who converted to Christianity in the last, difficult years before 1290 and who were supported in some way by alms or in the London 'House of Converts'.[44] We can only speculate as to the sincerity of their change of faith – and genuine conversions clearly did happen,

---

treats accusations as part of his history of antisemitism: 'Thomas of Monmouth: detector of ritual murder', *Speculum*, 59 (1984), 822–47; an interesting attempt to dissociate the ritual murder accusation from a specifically Jewish context is Magdelene Schulz, 'The blood libel: a motif in the history of childhood', *Journal of Psychohistory*, 14 (1986), 1–24.

[41] I. Baumgartner, 'The other Rome: national minority groups and the Jewish community between the middle ages and the renaissance', *Historisches Jahrbuch*, 118 (1998); Kenneth Stow, ed., *The Jews in Rome*, 2 vols (Leiden, 1995–7); Y. Baer, *A History of the Jews in Christian Spain*, 2 vols (Philadelphia, 1961); E.H. Lindo, *The History of the Jews of Spain and Portugal* (London, 1848).

[42] Y. Barzel, 'Confiscation by the ruler: the rise and fall of Jewish lending in the Middle Ages', *Journal of Law and Economics*, 35 (1992), 1–13.

[43] Jordan, 'Princely identity'.

[44] G.F. Abbott, *Israel in Europe* (London, 1907), pp. 254–8, suggests that the expulsion was not as thorough as supposed, but cites only a 'Jewish legend' to support the idea that a remnant remained until 1358. Roth, 'Jews in Oxford', p. 63, dismisses the legend of a crypto-Jewish community in Penny Farthing (now Pembroke) St in Oxford. On the 'House of Converts', see below, pp. 51, 63, 74, 92–3; also Michael Adler, 'History of the "Domus Conversorum"', *TJHSE*, 4 (1899–1901), 16–75; Joan Greatrex, 'Monastic charity for Jewish converts: the requisition of corrodies by Henry III', in D. Wood, ed., *Christianity and Judaism* (= *SCH* 29, Oxford, 1992), pp. 133–45.

both ways, in medieval Europe – but the change of name that accompanied baptism effectively conceals the individual from view in the records.[45] The methodological issues surrounding the history of converts are ripe for assessment. Paradoxically, then, we may never be able to state categorically that the Jewish presence ended in 1290; there is even some debate as to whether we can say that 1066 was the start point. The chapters that follow, however, try to tell the fullest possible story of the years between those dates: their gaps point to the areas still awaiting research.

---

[45] The best-known examples are all continental: A. Cabaniss, 'Bodo-Eleazar: a famous Jewish convert', *JQR*, 42 (1952–3), 313–28; Joshua Starr, 'The mass conversion of the Jews in southern Italy, 1290–1293', *Speculum*, 21 (1946), 203–11; A. Büchler, 'Obadyah the proselyte and the Roman liturgy', *Medieval Encounters*, 7 (2001), 165–73; Jeremy Cohen, 'Between martyrdom and apostasy: doubt and self-definition in twelfth-century Ashkenaz', *Journal of Medieval and Early Modern Studies*, 29 (1999), 431–71. Roth, 'Jews in Oxford', p. 63, highlights the case of a convert to Christianity who taught Hebrew and Greek at the university in 1321. He appears, however, only because arrangements had to be made to support him financially.

PART I

The History of the Jews in Britain

Map 1. Jewish communities in the twelfth century

1

Jewish Colonisation in the Twelfth Century

JOE HILLABY

The twelfth century witnessed the Jewish colonisation of England, that is the establishment not only of the London but also, by 1189, of twenty-four provincial Jewries (see Map 1).[1] This, the first of the two centuries of the medieval Anglo-Jewry, has suffered neglect owing to the paucity of the sources. The great series of public records that furnish such rich details of England's medieval Jewry begins only with the turn of the century: the Charter, Fine, Patent and Close Rolls between 1194 and 1204 and the Plea Rolls of the Exchequer of the Jews in 1218 (see Paul Brand's chapter, below, pp. 73–82). For the twelfth century there are occasional references in ecclesiastical sources, especially the chronicles, and elsewhere, but only one series of public records, the Pipe Rolls, annual audits of the shrieval accounts at the Michaelmas exchequer. For Henry I's reign there is but one roll, for 1130–1. The extant series begins only in 1155, the second year of Henry II's reign, and this recorded only royal borrowings and repayments, which anticipated current revenue. However, the Rolls provide two fundamental documents, in 1130–1 describing the role and key personnel of the London Jewry, and in 1159 identifying the first ten provincial Jewries (Table 1), with their tax burdens. Finally, the 1194 Receipt Roll, the Northampton *Donum*, lists twenty such Jewries (Table 2), naming their tax payers.[2]

The publication in 1893 of Joseph Jacobs's *The Jews of Angevin England: Documents and Records from Latin and Hebrew Sources* was a rich beginning in making these sources more widely known. It is particularly appropriate that an appreciation of our debt to Jacobs who, with 'no claim to be a professed medievalist, made accessible so much that was new and true', should have been expressed by H.G. Richardson in his own study of 1960, a book that has thrown a penetrating light on the position of the Jewry in its first century.[3] In 1896 came Jessopp and James's translation and commentary on Thomas of Monmouth's *Life and Miracles of St William of Norwich*. The ritual child murder accusation that this contained has provoked more discussion than any other aspect of the history of the twelfth-century Jewry.[4] In terms of the

---

[1] Colonisation in this context is 'a number of people of a particular ethnic group residing in a foreign city or country, especially in one quarter or district'.

[2] H.G. Richardson, 'The Chamber under Henry II', *EHR*, 69 (1954), 596–611, at 608–9. *PpR 31 Henry I*, pp. 53, 146–9; *PpR 5 Henry II*, pp. 3, 12, 17, 24, 28, 35, 46, 53, 65; PRO, E101/2.

[3] Jacobs, *Jews* (see Abbreviations); Richardson, *English Jewry* (see Abbreviations); M.R. James and Augustus Jessop, eds, *Thomas of Monmouth, The Life and Miracles of St William of Norwich* (Cambridge, 1895).

[4] G. Langmuir, 'Thomas of Monmouth: detector of ritual murder', *Speculum*, 59 (1984), 820–46, at 822–6. For miracles wrought, see B. Ward, *Miracles and the Medieval Mind: Theory, Record and*

provincial Jewries, Vivian Lipman has provided a portrait of Jurnet of Norwich, the twelfth-century magnate, and Barrie Dobson has analysed the Jews of York. Otherwise there is but one study devoted to a twelfth-century Jewry, of London from William I to John.[5]

Foundation and growth of the London community to 1135

The London community was the child of the Rouen Jewry. William of Malmesbury tells us that it was the Conqueror who had transferred the London Jews from Rouen. The wealth of the latter community in the late eleventh and early twelfth centuries is reflected in the size, and the quality of the workmanship, of the synagogue or *yeshiva* walls, which still stand to some 5 metres.[6] Measuring some 14 by 9½ metres, it compares well with contemporary synagogues of the great Jewries of Speyer, Worms and Cologne.[7] Natives of Rouen, Rabbi Josce and his family played a major role in London's Jewry for well over a century, until 1236. To the rear of their house at the north-east end of Old Jewry, they built the great synagogue, *magna scola*, its design strongly influenced, no doubt, by that at Rouen.[8]

The London Jewry was strengthened in the late eleventh century by the arrival of a number of wealthy Rouennais seeking refuge from events at home. In November 1090 the forces of Duke Robert, having defeated those of William Rufus, looted, ransomed and slaughtered the citizenry. Guibert, abbot of Nogent sous Coucy, writing some thirty years later, tells of 'crusaders' herding Rouen Jews into what is evidently their synagogue, giving them the choice of conversion or death. As Guibert gives us neither dates nor names, nor is there confirmation in the martyrologies or other sources, Runciman is probably justified in his doubts that the massacre, as described by Nogent, ever took

Event, 1000–1215 (rev. edn, Aldershot, 1987), pp. 67–76. The story is also examined by J. Trachtenberg, *The Devil and the Jew* (New Haven, 1943) and M.D. Anderson, *A Saint at the Stake: the Strange Death of William of Norwich, 1144* (London, 1964). On how such stories spread: J. Hillaby, 'The ritual child murder accusation: its dissemination and Harold of Gloucester', *JHS*, 34 (1994–6), 69–109. See also the discussion by Anthony Bale below, pp. 130–5.

[5] Lipman, *Norwich* (see Abbreviations); R.B. Dobson, *The Jews of Medieval York and the Massacre of March 1190* (York, 1974; rev. edn, York, 1996), reviewed by Dobson's chapter below, pp. 145–56; J. Hillaby, 'The London Jewry: William I to John', *JHS*, 33 (1992–4), 1–44.

[6] R.A.B. Mynors, R.M. Thomson and M. Winterbottom, eds and tr., *William of Malmesbury: The History of the English Kings*, I (Oxford, 1998), pp. 562–3 TA; D. Halbout-Bertin, G. Duval, M. Baylé and B. Blumenkranz, 'La synagogue de Rouen', in *Art et archéologie des juifs en France médiévale* (Toulouse, 1980), pp. 229–303 – the questions raised by Blumenkranz in pp. 290–302 of this study are not answered by N. Golb, *The Jews in Medieval Normandy: a Social and Intellectual History* (Cambridge, 1998), pp. 146–67; J. Tanguy, *Le monument juif du Palais de Justice de Rouen* (Rouen, 1990); M. de Bouard, 'L'affaire de la synagogue de Rouen', *L'Histoire*, 48 (1982), 80–4, suggests that it was a first-floor hall-house 'chers à nos amis britanniques'.

[7] R. Krautheimer, *Mittelalterlicher Synagogen* (Berlin, 1927), pp. 145–6 and 151; O. Böcher, *Die alte Synagoge zu Worms* (Worms, 1960); O. Doppelfeld, 'Die Ausgrabungen im Kölner Judenviertel', in Z. Asaria, ed., *Die Juden in Köln* (Köln, 1959); M. Gechter and S. Schütte, 'Ursprünge und Voraussetzungen der Rathausumgebung', in W. Greis and U. Krings, eds, *Das historische Rathaus und seine Umgebung* (Köln, 2000).

[8] J. Hillaby, 'London: the thirteenth-century Jewry revisited', *JHS*, 32 (1990–2), 89–158, at 98, 100–2 and 129; id., 'London Jewry', pp. 36–9; id., 'Beth miqdash me'at: the synagogues of medieval England', *JEH*, 44 (1993), 182–98, at 189–90.

place. However, the leaders of the French communities were 'gripped by fear' on the appearance of Peter the Hermit, demanding letters of commendation for his followers to the Jewries of the Rhineland and beyond. Resorting 'to the customs of their ancestors they wrote letters and dispatched messengers to all the Rhenish communities', warning them of the impending danger.[9]

A century later the rabbi's elder son, Isaac, returned to Rouen after the disastrous attack on London's Jewry during Richard I's coronation in September 1189. There he lived in the family property, on its prestigious site in the *rue des juifs*, a stone's throw from the synagogue, the remains of which can be seen beneath the court of the present *palais de justice*. It was he who in 1195 negotiated, on behalf of the Norman and English Jewries, the renewal by Richard I of Henry II's charter. His son, called Josce after his grandfather, sold the family's Rouen house in 1203. In 1207 he was appointed presbyter of the English Jewry by John, an office he held until 1236. The conquest of Normandy by the French king in 1204 broke up irreparably what had been no mere Anglo-Jewry but 'something considerably more involved and much closer to a single Anglo-Norman community'.[10]

Suggestions as to William the Conqueror's motives for bringing Jews from Rouen are put forward by Stacey: he was interested in coin to pay his troops, and assistance in keeping an ear to the mood of London's resolutely hostile citizens. Perhaps William of Malmesbury himself gives us a clue when, in his character sketch of the Conqueror, he tells us that the only thing for which he could deservedly be blamed was 'his hoarding of money which he sought on all opportunities to scrape together – provided he could allege that they were . . . not unbecoming the royal dignity'. William further refers to the Jews giving 'proof of their insolence towards God in [William Rufus's] reign'.[11] The first firm date for a Jewish presence comes from the *Disputation of a Jew and a Christian*, between Gilbert Crispin, abbot of Westminster c.1085–1117, and Jacob, a French Jew educated at Mainz. This took place before March 1093, for Crispin presented a copy to Anselm while he was still abbot of Bec. The disputants probably became acquainted as a result of business visits Jacob made to the abbey concerning loans for the construction of the Romanesque cloister, refectory and dormitory.[12]

The so-called 'Charter of Liberties', issued by John in 1201, states that the Jews 'may have all their liberties and customs as well and peaceably and

[9] Edmond-René Labande, ed. and tr., *Guibert de Nogent: Autobiographie* (Paris, 1981), pp. 246–7; English translation in J. Benton, ed., *Self and Society in Medieval France: the Memoirs of Abbot Guibert of Nogent* (New York, 1970), pp. 134–5. F. Barlow, *William Rufus* (London, 1983), pp. 274–5; S. Runciman, *A History of the Crusades*, I (London, 1965), pp. 135–6, quoting A. Neubauer and M. Stern, *Quellen zur Geschichte der Juden in Deutschland* (Berlin, 1892), pp. 25, 131 and 169.

[10] T. Rymer, *Foedera* (London, 1816), I.i, p. 51; Golb, *Jews in Medieval Normandy*, pp. 367–71; Hillaby, 'London Jewry', pp. 36–9, fig. 4; *Rot. Chart.*, I.i (see Abbreviations), p. 105; P.R. Hyams, 'The Jews in medieval England, 1066–1299', in A. Haverkamp and H. Wollrath, eds, *England and Germany in the High Middle Ages* (Oxford, 1986), pp. 174–92, at p. 177.

[11] R.C. Stacey, 'Jewish lending and the medieval English economy', in R. Britnell and B.M.S. Campbell, eds, *A Commercialising Economy: England 1086 to c. 1300* (Manchester, 1995), pp. 78–101, at p. 82; *William of Malmesbury, Gesta Regum*, pp. 508–9 TA and CB and 562–3 TA and CB.

[12] A. Sapir Abulafia and G.R. Evans, eds, *The Works of Gilbert Crispin, Abbot of Westminster* (London, 1986), pp. xxi–xxxii and 1–54; R.W. Southern, 'St Anselm and Gilbert Crispin, abbot of Westminster', *Medieval and Renaissance Studies*, 3 (1954), 78–99. Cf. Bale in this volume, p. 140.

honourably as they had them in the time of the aforesaid King Henry, our father's grandfather'.[13] There is no reference to Jews in the *Leges Henrici Primi* but their 'liberties and customs' are mentioned in the later *Leges Edwardi Confessoris*. Compiled in Henry I's reign, probably between 1120 and 1130, it purports to be an expression of the Confessor's laws as observed in William II's reign. Chapter 25 summarises these customs and privileges as acknowledged at the time, with the categoric statement, *Iudei enim et omnia sua regis sunt* ('The Jews certainly and all they have are the king's'), from which it follows that 'if anyone withholds them or their money the king, if he wishes, can recover it as his own property'. Further, 'all Jews wherever they are in the realm ought to be under the defence and protection of the king's lieges' and 'no Jew, without royal licence, may subject himself to any magnate'. The relationship is clear: the king permitted the Jews to reside in his kingdom and granted them his protection; in return they and their wealth were at his disposal.[14]

The site of the London Jewry is first referred to in a survey of the property of the dean and chapter of St Paul's, c.1127. In *vicus judeorum* Lusbert, a Christian, held three plots. The first was 32 feet (10 metres) wide on the front, the western side, and 95 feet (29 metres) long '*versus* (i.e., towards, against, alongside) St Olave's church'. The second was 13 feet (4 metres) wide and 65 feet (20 metres) long 'again towards St Olave's'. The third measured 73 feet (22 metres) in front and 41 feet (12½ metres) long.[15] This apparently indicates a site on the west side of Old Jewry, close to St Olave's.

The use of the term *vicus*, as quarter or district, may throw further light on the Jewry's status at this time. The St Paul's survey, the earliest and only twelfth-century list of the London wards, mentions only twenty, all except Cheap and Aldgate identified by the name of their aldermen. Three areas are not described as wards: Aldermansbury, *in vico judeorum* and beyond the fleet. These, it has been argued, were outside the ward system: Aldermansbury may have been the official residence or *burh* of the king's officer, the king's Jews were certainly outside ward jurisdiction and the area beyond fleet was outside the walls. Probably the surveyor, in using the term *vicus judeorum*, was seeking to express a legal concept that, by the century's end, was clearly defined as *in Judaismo*.[16] As the Jews belonged to the king they lay outside the jurisdiction of the city courts, at either ward or Hustings level. Thus citizens had in such cases to seek redress in the royal courts, which, in London, meant principally that of the Constable of the Tower, who was responsible to the Crown for law and order within the Jewry and whose agent was his serjeant of the Jewry.[17] The

---

[13] *Rot. Chart.*, I.i, p. 93; Rigg, *Select Pleas* (see Abbreviations), p. 1.

[14] F. Liebermann, ed., *Gesetze der Angelsachsen*, I (Halle, 1894), p. 650.

[15] London, St Paul's Cathedral Library, Liber L(WD.4), ff. 47r–50v, cited in H.W.C. Davis, 'London lands and liberties of St Paul's, 1066–1135', in A.J. Little and F.M. Powicke, eds, *Essays in Medieval History presented to Thomas Frederick Tout* (Manchester, 1925), pp. 45–59. For map, see Hillaby, 'London', p. 92.

[16] J. Tait, 'Two unknown names of early London wards', *London Topographical Record*, 15 (1931), 1–3; cf. C. Brooke and G. Keir, *London 800–1216: the Shaping of a City* (London, 1975), pp. 162–70; D. Dawe, *11 Ironmonger Lane* (London, 1952), pp. 20–2; D. Keene and V. Harding, *Historical Gazetteer of London before the Great Fire: Cheapside* (London, 1987, only available as microfiche, copy in London Guildhall Library), pp. 134–5.

[17] H.M. Chew and M. Weinbaum, eds, *The London Eyre of 1244* (London, 1970), p. 277; Richardson, *English Jewry*, pp. 155–60.

term *vicus* also had a topographical context. It referred to settlement principally in five city parishes: St Olave Old Jewry, St Martin Pomary, St Laurence Jewry, St Mary Magdalen Milk Street and St Michael Wood Street. In the thirteenth century there was some movement into four further parishes: St Margaret Lothbury, St Stephen Colman Street, St Michael Bassishaw and St Peter Westcheap. The Jewry thus lay north of the great market in Cheapside: in Colechurch Lane, which became Old Jewry after 1290, Ironmonger Lane, Milk and Wood Streets, Catte, now Gresham, Street and at the southern end of Bassishaw and Colman Street.[18]

The solitary extant pipe roll of Henry I's reign, for the financial year 1130–1, provides firm evidence of the extraordinary wealth of London's Jewry. It names five of the leaders, with indications of their clientele, and identifies some of their financial activities. For 'the sick man they killed' the community was fined £2,000. Given that the Crown's combined annual income from the vacant sees of Canterbury and Salisbury and the abbacies of the ancient monasteries of St Augustine's, Canterbury, Newminster at Winchester, Malmesbury, Ely and Chertsey in the reign of William Rufus was £2,385, we get a sense of the size of the fine. However, in 1130 the Jews paid in total only £833 6s 8d of which £600 was towards that fine; as usual, the sum outstanding was carried forward.[19]

Among the clientele listed as in debt to five of London's wealthiest Jews were Ranulf II de Gernons, earl of Chester, Richard fitz Gilbert, lord of Ceredigion, and Osbert of Leicester. By 1130 loans were being made to the monasteries as well as the laity. A certain Jacob paid 60 marks for royal support in recovering money lent to 'the men of the abbot of Westminster'. Notably Jacob's wife was a partner in the deal. The sums proffered give little idea of the amounts outstanding. The Jewry was also lending money to the Crown. Some 180 marks were due to Rabbi Josce (Rubigotsce), 85 marks to Manasser and a sum, no longer legible, to Jacob, '*in soltis*', as repayments for such loans. Jews were also playing an important part in the market in gold and silver. The pipe roll records Abraham sold two silver cups to the Crown for £10 5s 10d. Linked activities, on which the pipe rolls throw no light, were pawnbroking and exchange, not only of foreign coins but also of precious metals and silver plate for coin of the realm.[20]

Benefits to Henry I from his Jewry were both direct and indirect. It was a source of ready cash in the form of fines, 'gifts' or loans but it also provided fluidity, by which tenants-in-chief, and others, could meet his financial demands. Wealth was used as an expression of status, whether by ostentation, security or charity, and, even for kings, hoarding money was held to be dishonourable. The greatest in the realm had few easily realisable assets other than plate, jewels, armour and furs. Increasing royal demands relating to inheritance, wardship and marriage were difficult to meet without credit facilities. In 1131 Ranulf II, earl of Chester, owed the Crown £2,000, of which £1,000 was outstanding from his father, Ranulf I, for his 'succession to the lands of earl Hugh' in 1121. A further 500 marks was due from his

---

[18] Hillaby, 'London', pp. 90–6 and map 1.
[19] *PpR 31 Henry I*, pp. 146–9; Barlow, *William Rufus*, pp. 238–9.
[20] The mark was the money of account: £6 equals one gold or nine silver marks; unless otherwise stated marks referred to in the text were silver. For the term *in soltis*, see Richardson, *English Jewry*, p. 54, n. 4; further discussion in Hillaby, 'London Jewry', pp. 8–12.

mother, the dowager countess Lucy, for excuse, for five years, from marriage (a fourth time). Osbert of Leicester, who had fallen foul of Henry I in a big way, owed 1,000 marks for relaxation of *malevolentia regis* (literally: the ill-will of the king).[21] The Jews provided the means, through loans secured on land, by which instalments on such levies could be raised quickly. However, land used as security was, in case of default, lost. This was to cause major social tensions which, at the outset of Richard I's reign sixty years later, would find expression in the attack on the London Jewry and the York massacre.

Stephen and the foundation of the provincial Jewry, 1135–1154

Evidence of Jewish colonisation outside London comes only after Henry I's death. By 1141 there were Jews at Oxford. Anthony Wood quotes a late, possibly fifteenth-century, and corrupt source, the chronicle of Nigel of Rewley, but its reference to 'exchanges of pennies', otherwise little recorded, gives it credibility. A premium of about 10 per cent was charged for the exchange of old for newly minted pennies. Such exchanges of money were a profitable business for moneyers and Jews alike. On this occasion they were merely a veil for an arbitrary levy. In September 1139 Matilda landed at Arundel, opening up eight years of civil war. In 1141, holding her Easter court at Oxford, she imposed one such 'exchange of pennies'. In mid-December 1142 Stephen, after taking the town by siege, demanded three and a half such 'exchanges' in retribution, with threats to burn the Jews' houses about their ears if payment was not made forthwith.[22] As the case of the twelve-year-old William, whom the Norwich Jews were accused of crucifying, shows, there was a Jewry there, and at Cambridge, prior to 1144. At Winchester a survey of 1148 refers to the properties of two Jews, Urselino and Deulecresse, in *Scowrtene*, now Jewry, Street.[23]

Certainly Stephen was protective towards the English Jewry, which was spared the horrors inflicted at the time of the Second Crusade on those of Germany and France, in 1146–7. Ephraim of Bonn, in the *Sefer Zekhirah*, reports that in 1146 'the Most High King rescued them through the instrument of the king of England, putting it into his heart to protect them and save their lives and property. Blessed be He Who aids Israel.' Certainly, during the St William crisis in 1144, the Norwich Jews were protected by Stephen's castellan, John de Chesney. At the diocesan synod, when the priest Godwin proposed trial by ordeal, Chesney removed the Jews from the

---

[21] *William of Malmesbury, Gesta Regum*, pp. 508–9 TA; *PpR 31 Henry I*, pp. 82, 110 and 114.

[22] Bodley Twyne MS xxii, 106, quoted in C. Roth, *The Jews of Medieval Oxford* (Oxford Historical Society, n.s. 9, 1945), p. 3, n. 1; Roth, *History²* (see Abbreviations), pp. 2–3 and 8; id., *Jews of Medieval Oxford*, pp. 2, 3 and n. 1. On exchange D.F. Allen, *A Catalogue of English Coins in the British Museum: the Cross and Crosslets (Tealby) Type of Henry II* (London, 1951), pp. lxxxii and xcii–xciv; also P. Nightingale, 'Some London moneyers and reflections on the organisation of the English mints in the eleventh and twelfth centuries', *Numismatic Chronicle*, 142 (1982), 34–50, at 47–8; Stacey, 'Jewish lending', pp. 79 and 83–5.

[23] *Thomas of Monmouth, Life and Miracles of St William*, pp. lxxi and 93–4; M. Biddle, ed., *Winchester in the Early Middle Ages: an Edition and Discussion of the Winton Domesday* (Oxford, 1976), p. 101.

Table 1: The *Donum* of 1159. Contributions of Jewish communities

Community	Sheriff	Marks	%	Rank
London	London	200	37	1
Norwich	Norfolk and Suffolk	66.5	12	2
Lincoln	Lincolnshire	60	11	3
Cambridge	Cambridgeshire	50	9	4=
Winchester	Hampshire	50	9	4=
Thetford	Norfolk and Suffolk	45	8	6
Northampton	Northamptonshire	22.5	4	7=
Bungay	Norfolk and Suffolk	22.5	4	7=
Oxford	Oxfordshire	20	3.7	9
Gloucester	Gloucestershire	5	1	10
Worcester	Worcestershire	2	0.4	11
Total		**543.5 (£362 6s 8d)**		

Source: *PpR 5 Henry II*, pp. 3, 12, 17, 24, 28, 35, 46, 53, 65.

hearing to his castle, under armed guard. At the trial of Simon de Nover for Eleazer's murder Stephen himself presided and, rejecting Bishop Turbe's plea that the Jews themselves should be on trial, adjourned the proceedings *sine die*.[24]

At London Stephen had been warmly welcomed by the ruling oligarchs who, in Matilda's own words, 'made very large contributions . . . lavishing their wealth on strengthening him'. Even after his capture at Lincoln in 1141 they remained loyal. Gervase of Cornhill, the city's justiciar from 1135 to 1147, lent money to Stephen's queen, Maud. Later he was to have close financial ties with Aaron, from whom he borrowed considerable sums to develop property about Lothbury and Old Jewry and selling him land on which to build his London house. It is thus highly probable that the system operating in 1130, of local loans repaid (*in soltis*) by the Crown to the London Jews, remained in place at least for the early years of Stephen's reign and may explain the origins, as London outposts, of at least some of the provincial Jewries, such as Oxford, Winchester and Lincoln.[25]

Some Jewries already in existence in this period may have gone unrecorded. Only in 1159 does the extent of the colonisation become clear, when the third pipe roll of Henry II's reign identifies sums collected from ten provincial Jewries (Table 1). All except Bungay shared significant characteristics. They were boroughs of early foundation with good land and water communication. South-west of Watling Street Winchester, Oxford, Worcester and Gloucester had been major Anglo-Saxon *burhs*. To the north-east, Lincoln, Northampton

[24] S. Eidelberg, tr., *The Jews and the Crusaders: Hebrew Chronicles of the First and Second Crusades* (Madison, 1977), p. 131; *Thomas of Monmouth, Life and Miracles of St William*, pp. 43–9 and 97–112.

[25] *Gesta Stephani* (see Abbreviations), pp. 121–7; H. Round, *Geoffrey de Mandeville* (London, 1892), pp. 120 and 302–12; Richardson, *English Jewry*, pp. 47–8, 58–9 and 237–9.

and Cambridge were Anglo-Danish *burhs*. Lincoln was a major port by 1020, trading via the Witham with north-east Europe, and by 1086 much the largest town in the East Midlands. Northampton on the Nene already had by the ninth century a massive stone hall. Norwich, on the Wensum, like Thetford, was a major Danish trading centre. By 1086 it was one of the largest English towns, with a population of over 5,000, served by some fifty churches with a new Norman town and cathedral. All nine were Anglo-Saxon mint towns. When Henry I closed twenty-nine of his fifty-one mints, only Cambridge was not retained.[26]

Castles of all nine boroughs formed part of the early Norman defence network. Major fairs were held nearby: St Giles, Winchester, All Saints, Northampton and St Ives were of international standing. Purchases, especially of cloth, were made here and at Stamford and Bury for the royal household.[27] The reason for the early Jewry at Cambridge, ten miles from St Ives, rather than at Huntingdon, may have been political. Cambridge was the dower town of Constance, wife of Stephen's eldest son, Eustace, but Huntingdon honour had been held until 1141 by David I of Scotland's heir, earl Henry, who supported Matilda.[28] Stamford, also an Anglo-Danish borough, had all the advantages to attract a Jewry: its great fair, royal purchasers, a mint and the protection of Gilbert de Gant's royal castle. The only onslaught, in 1153 when it fell to Duke Henry, may well have led to the Jews' dispersal. Bury Jewry was within the Liberty of the abbot of St Edmunds. Situated in Hethenman Lane, now Hatter Street, just south-east of the Cornmarket, it probably postdates abbot Hugh I's election in 1157. In 1160 Deulecresse was lending money at Canterbury, which by 1194 was the second wealthiest of all twenty provincial Jewries.[29]

Stephen had powerful financial reasons for protecting the Jews, given his financial burdens. After the campaigns of his first three years had exhausted the treasure laid up by Henry I, Stephen, as Crouch explains, 'shrugged off the mantle carefully tailored for him out of his uncle's wardrobe'. The unprecedented creation of earls now began: only six in 1135, by 1154 there were twenty-two. Henry I's tight control of both mints and Jewry was relaxed. Stephen, responding to pressure from his earls, and others, reopened nineteen of Henry I's mints 'as a general measure rather than on an ad hoc basis'. Later he reopened six more and authorised at least six new mints.[30] It is likely that a similar, more liberal, policy was adopted towards the Jewry, but to attribute the

[26] J.W.F. Hill, *Medieval Lincoln* (Cambridge, 1948), pp. 24–63; J.H. Williams, 'From "palace" to "town": Northampton and urban origins', *Anglo-Saxon England*, 13 (1984), 113–36; J. Campbell, 'Norwich', in M.D. Lobel, ed., *The Atlas of Historic Towns*, II (London, 1975), pp. 2–3.

[27] S. Reynolds, *An Introduction to the History of English Medieval Towns* (Oxford, 1977), p. 47.

[28] D. Crouch, *The Reign of King Stephen, 1135–1154* (London, 2000), p. 133; R.H.C. Davis, *King Stephen* (London, 1967), p. 134; A.O. Anderson, tr., *Early Sources of Scottish History, A.D. 500–1206* (Edinburgh, 1922), pp. 150–1.

[29] *RCHM Stamford* (London, 1977), pp. xxxix–xli; M. Blackburn, 'Coinage and currency', in E. King, ed., *The Anarchy of King Stephen's Reign* (Oxford, 1994), pp. 180–1; *Gesta Stephani*, pp. 234–7; D. Knowles et al., *Heads of Religious Houses: England and Wales, 940–1216* (Cambridge, 1972), p. 32; F. Palgrave, *The Rise and Progress of the English Commonwealth*, II (1st edn, London, 1832), pp. xxiv–xxvii (2nd edn, London, 1922), pp. 117–18.

[30] Crouch, *Reign of King Stephen*, pp. 84–9; Davis, *King Stephen*, pp. 129–45; Blackburn, 'Coinage', p. 158.

growth of provincial Jewries merely to a royal policy of maintaining control of such key centres of trade is to overestimate Stephen's power.[31]

Bungay and Thetford were seigneurial in origin. If the other new communities were royal foundations, given the breakdown of royal authority and with it 'the shift in executive power from the centre to the provinces', to what extent did they become seigneurial?[32] Who gave protection, who derived benefit? Simon II of Senlis, earl of Northampton and lord of Cambridge, was a major ally of Stephen, but on the death of Henry I he seized the royal castle and borough at Northampton. Royal control was only re-established, by Henry II, on Simon's death in 1154. Independent baronial coins were issued from both Northampton and Cambridge, where the mint was otherwise inoperative during this period. Both Jewries were protected by Simon's powerful castles but, if the figures can be trusted, Cambridge in 1159 was twice the size of Northampton, and almost that of Lincoln. By 1194 and for much of the thirteenth century both were important communities.[33]

The demand for money for warfare, castle-building and monastic foundation was very high but, with a central authority incapable of enforcing its rules of the game, the risks of lending were commensurate. The 1159 returns show many were prepared to accept the risks but, for Jewish settlement to succeed, there had to be a powerful patron, with castle, immediately to hand. For their defence the Jews looked not so much to the king as to the representative of his authority. In emergencies effective power lay locally, usually with the magnate as sheriff. At Norwich in 1144 it was Chesney who, with his armed guards, had delivered the Jews from their accusers. There was thus a strong, if not always apparent, financial nexus between the provincial Jewries and the local power brokers, even when the sheriff was not a magnate. As late as 1276 the mayor and bailiffs had to be given custody of the Oxford Jews 'to remove occasions of disturbance' between them and the sheriff, who was 'not to intermeddle in any way with the security of their estate'.[34]

Stephen's relaxed attitude to the English Jewry, as to his so-called 'election' by the Londoners, may well have been based as much on continental models as on necessity. As Count of Boulogne, he was well conversant with continental practice in relation to both. The Flemish burghers claimed rights of election; the French crown could not state, as did Henry I, that the Jews and all they had were the king's. The French king could only exercise such rights within his own domain. Elsewhere French Jewries were controlled by the local magnate with whom the community made its own terms.[35]

Given the fragmentation of political authority and the inadequacy of the documentary sources, it is difficult to establish who exercised effective authority in the towns with the new Jewries. 'Evidence for the extent of royal authority is

[31] K.T. Streit, 'The expansion of the English Jewish community in the reign of King Stephen', *Albion*, 25 (1993), 177–92, at 191.

[32] W.L. Warren, *The Governance of Norman and Angevin England, 1066–1272* (London, 1987), pp. 92–3.

[33] Anderson, *Early Sources*, pp. 150–5.

[34] *Thomas of Monmouth, Life and Miracles of St William*, pp. 46–9; *CPR 1272–81*, p. 157.

[35] *Gesta Stephani*, pp. 4–7; G.L. Langmuir, '"Judei nostri" and the beginning of Capetian legislation', *Traditio*, 16 (1960), 203–39, at 206–10; W.C. Jordan, *The French Monarchy and the Jews* (Philadelphia, 1989), p. 5; J.W. Baldwin, *The Government of Philip Augustus* (London, 1986), p. 51.

sporadic and imprecisely dated', as Blackburn says, 'apart from the coinage'. As some of the very few with access to cash in a society where land was wealth, relations between moneylenders, moneyers, goldsmiths and silversmiths had always been close. It was not merely castles that attracted Jews to the new centres. All but one of the nine mint towns in Table 1 had retained their mints during Henry I's reforms and even from Cambridge an independent baronial issue has now been found. Indeed, it has been suggested that some moneyers were Jewish.[36]

Distribution of mints of coin types 2 and 6 of the middle years of Stephen's reign shows England, for almost a decade, broadly divided in two: royal coinage, of uniform design and full weight, in the south-east; but the north and west, with most of the new and reopened mints, produced merely independent baronial issues of mixed character and variable, often light, weight. Here Stephen had lost control of monetary production.[37] Three of the 1159 Jewries lay in the north and west, but the Jews of Gloucester and Worcester, in the war-torn Severn valley, paying only 5 and 2 marks, were few and very late arrivals.[38] Lincoln castle, except for the years 1146–9, was the power centre of Ranulf, earl of Chester, who according to the *Gesta Stephani* controlled a third of England. Certainly his estates and those of his half-brother, William de Roumare, whom Stephen created earl of Lincoln, dominated Cheshire, the valley of the Trent and Lincolnshire. By 1159 Lincoln, with Norwich, was at the head of the ten provincial Jewries. How and when it became the heart of operations for Aaron of Lincoln, wealthiest of the provincial Jews, one can only speculate. The hostility between Ranulf and the townspeople may be the explanation.[39]

In the south-east support for Stephen was not assured. Norfolk and Suffolk were rent by the antagonism between Hugh Bigod, his 'most restless opponent', with castles at Framlingham and Walton, in Suffolk, and the earls of Warenne, William III and William of Blois, Stephen's second son who inherited the earldom by marriage in 1148. Hugh seized Norwich in 1136 but was soon reconciled to the king. In 1140 he sought to strengthen his position by taking Robert Beaumont, earl of Leicester's, castle and borough at Bungay, a position subsequently regularised by Hugh's marriage into that family. Bungay had no mint, but under the protection of the castle, Hugh established the Jewry recorded in 1159.[40]

Thetford Jewry was twice the value of Bungay. Settled by Danes in the late

[36] Blackburn, 'Coinage', p. 166 and Table 5.1; V. Lipman, 'Jews and castles in medieval England', *TJHSE*, 28 (1984), 1–19; W. Urry, *Canterbury under the Angevin Kings* (London, 1967), map 2b, large-scale sheet 5; G.C. Brooke, *A Catalogue of English Coins in the British Museum: the Norman Kings*, 2 vols (London, 1916), II, pp. 375 no. 222 and 381–2 nos 240–3; Nightingale, 'Some London moneyers', pp. 47–8.

[37] Blackburn, 'Coinage', pp. 154–6 and 159–60, Tables 5.1, 5.2 and 5.3.

[38] P. McGurk, ed. and tr., *The Chronicle of John of Worcester* (Oxford, 1998), III, pp. 271–85; Crouch, *Reign of King Stephen*, pp. 113–14, 116, 146–7, 255–8 and 289–90; J. Hillaby, 'Testimony from the margin: the Gloucester Jewry and its neighbours, c. 1159–1290', *JHS*, 37 (2002), 41–112.

[39] *Gesta Stephani*, pp. 184–5; P. Dalton, 'Ranulf II Earl of Chester and Lincolnshire in the reign of Stephen', in A. Thacker, ed., *The Earldom of Chester and its Charters* (= *Journal of the Chester Archaeological Society*, 71, 1991), 109–32; id., '*In neutro latere*: the armed neutrality of Ranulf II of Chester in king Stephen's reign', *ANS*, 14 (1992), 39–59.

[40] *Gesta Stephani*, pp. 174–5; Crouch, *Reign of King Stephen*, pp. 118–20; A. Wareham, 'The motives and politics of the Bigod family', *ANS*, 17 (1995), 233–42.

ninth century, a mint was established here about 960, becoming the second largest in the country. Astride a major route, the Icknield Way, and at fording points on the Little Ouse and Thet rivers, the town was large, with almost 1,000 burgesses and twelve churches in 1066, and the seat of the East Anglian bishops from 1072 to 1094. It is held, without evidence, that the first earl de Warenne founded both the borough and its formidable castle, with one of the highest mottes in Britain. Such evidence as there is underlines the Bigods' powerful interests in the town. Here Hugh's father had founded the Cluniac priory where all the Bigod earls of Norfolk were buried. In Stephen's reign Thetford's mint struck coins not only defaced but of a weight lower than the regular issue. Such defiance of royal authority, and the slighting of the castle in 1173 when the earl de Warenne was Henry II's half-brother, indicate that Thetford's Jewry grew up under Bigod's protection.[41]

The youthful William d'Aubigné II built the superb Castle Rising and its planned town to celebrate his marriage to the young dowager queen, Alice, in 1138. He was granted rights to a mint, but production ceased after Stephen's death. He also founded a Jewry as Jews with the toponym Rising are found in later pipe rolls: Benedict at Gloucester, and his son, Deulecresse, with Deulebene at Norwich; but the community evidently moved some five miles, to Lynn, in Henry II's reign for Deulebene de Rising died there in the massacre of 1190.[42] In Stephen's charters William is earl of Arundel on six occasions, Chichester four and Sussex twice. He had castles at both Arundel and Chichester, the latter with another short-lived mint. Chichester's Jewry was not listed in 1159 but paid £26 in 1194. Like Castle Rising, it was a d'Aubigné foundation but, on William's death in 1176, both Arundel and Chichester castles escheated to the Crown.[43]

Control and expansion of the provincial Jewries, 1154–1189

A year after Henry's designation as Stephen's heir and successor by the Westminster settlement of 1153, the king was dead. Henry II moved boldly but persuasively to restore royal authority and public order. Royal castles had to be returned, with Norwich the last in 1157. Against Bigod's castles of Thetford, Bungay and Framlingham he had to bide his time, destroying the first in 1173, the second in 1174. Next year 'Alnodus, the engineer, with carpenters and mason', was paid £14 15s 11d for demolishing Framlingham's defences.[44] The Thetford and Bungay communities were now defenceless. The 1194 tax lists show that many Bungay Jews sought protection at Norwich.

[41] Blackburn, 'Coinage', pp. 176–8, Tables 5.1 and 5.2; G.C. Dunning, 'The Saxon town of Thetford', *Archaeological Journal*, 106 (1951), 72–3; B.K. Davison, 'The late Saxon town of Thetford: an interim report on excavations 1964–66', *Medieval Archaeology*, 11 (1967), 189–208; T. Martin, *History of Thetford* (London, 1779), pp. 10–11; R. Allen Brown, *Castles from the Air* (Cambridge, 1989), pp. 213–14.

[42] Blackburn, 'Coinage', Table 5.1 and pp. 153–4, 159, 161; Brown, *Castles from the Air*, pp. 80–2 and n. 60; Rising toponyms: *PpR 34 Henry II*, pp. 58, 65, 108.

[43] Blackburn, 'Coinage', Tables 5.1 and 5.3 and pp. 176–7; H.M. Colvin, ed., *History of the King's Works: the Middle Ages*, II (London, 1963), p. 612.

[44] *PpR 19 Henry II*, p. 117; *PpR 21 Henry II*, p. 108; *Diceto* (see Abbreviations), I, pp. 384–5; *Benedict* (see Abbreviations), I, pp. 126–7.

Henry II embarked on a highly successful twenty-year policy to extend royal authority over the mints.[45] Having replaced almost all the old moneyers with his own men, he introduced a standard type coin, the cross and crosslets, in 1158. Solomon at Canterbury probably represented a new breed of financiers now farming the mints. By 1180 Henry had reduced the number of mints from about thirty to eleven and, by building royal exchanges, secured the considerable profits of coinage exchange. The Jews apart, the moneyers and goldsmiths, with their virtual monopoly in the trade in specie and precious metals, were the principal source of cash for loans. Thus both measures, by reducing the number of those able to offer credit in the mint towns, enhanced considerably the local Jewries' opportunities for growth for, recognising their value to the Crown, Henry II left untouched most of the provincial communities established in Stephen's reign.[46]

The first pipe roll of the reign at Michaelmas, 1156, marked the revival of the royal exchequer, which had almost collapsed under the strain of civil war. It refers to payment by three provincial Jewries: from Cambridge £40, Oxford a £5 *donum* and Norwich £2 6s 4d. In 1158 £13 6s 8d was paid by Norwich and 13s 4d by Cambridge. Next year came the general levy referred to above, the *Donum*, recording payments from ten provincial Jewries (Table 1). This was a firm statement of royal control over the provincial Jewries, including Bungay and Thetford. Subsequent pipe rolls are meagre in detail, except in relation to such giants of the London community as Abraham and Isaac, sons of the Rabbi.[47]

The London money market had been closed to Henry until 1153, but after Rouen fell to the Angevins in 1144 he could call on credit extended by William Cade of St Omer and William Trentegerons, vicomte of Rouen and, after 1159, his widow, Emma, who succeeded him as vicomtesse. In 1155 Cade and the Trentegerons were rewarded with the revenues of the two major cross-channel ports, Dover and Southampton, but Henry began to develop an extensive Jewish credit network to service the Crown's financial needs. Whether this was a revival or an extension of Henry I's arrangements may never be known. If it had weathered the vicissitudes of Stephen's reign then, in varying degrees, local power brokers would have diverted the facilities it offered to their own ends. His second pipe roll records a repayment, *in soltis*, of £47 6s 8d to the London Jews in 1157, but from 1159 to 1164 only Isaac and Abraham, sons of the Rabbi, received such repayments. A passage from the *Life of Becket* shows how the network would operate. While still royal chancellor, raising troops for the Toulouse expedition, Becket borrowed 500 marks from the Jewry.[48]

Some of the workings of the financial network, operated initially by Isaac, are found in the pipe rolls. Other aspects, hidden from view on the rolls of the royal chamber, are now lost. Furnishing such short-term credit to the king could be a dubious privilege. Profits were probably small, but risks of royal

[45] Allen, *Catalogue*, pp. lxxxii–xciv; Nightingale, 'Some London moneyers', pp. 45–50.

[46] Allen, *Catalogue*, pp. lxxxviii–xcv, cxxii, cxxxv and cxxi; Nightingale, 'Some London moneyers', pp. 48–50.

[47] *PpR 2, 3 and 4 Henry II* (reprinted PRO, 1931), pp. 8, 15, 36, 96 and 127.

[48] Richardson, *English Jewry*, pp. 50–6; Hillaby, 'London Jewry', p. 18, Table 2 and nn. 60–62; J.C. Robertson, ed., *William fitz Stephen: Life of St Thomas of Canterbury* (RS 67, London, 1878), III, pp. 33–4 and 53–4.

displeasure considerable. In 1163, Henry's loans from the vicomtesse ceased. When borrowings from Cade dropped from a peak of £882 in 1161 to £81 in 1165, Aaron of Lincoln joined Isaac in making loans to the Crown. In 1165 and 1166, Isaac was repaid almost £1,600 and Aaron £420. Isaac, whose only subsequent receipt was £21 6s 8d, withdrew from the market in 1168.

The next year Jurnet of Norwich, already providing the Crown with credit in that city, became Aaron's partner, both motivated no doubt by the false prospect of royal favour. Disaster struck in 1177, after a partnership was formed, with the Londoner le Brun and Jurnet as principals and Josce Quatrebouches of London and Jurnet's brother, Benedict, as juniors. A fine of £4,000 was imposed for an undisclosed offence. Le Brun, now the dominant member of the London Jewry, whose assessment in the 1186 tallage was to be almost £7,000, had to find half. It is a measure of Jurnet's wealth that by 1181 he had paid his one-third share of £1,333 6s 8d. The third and final partnership, in 1177–9, of four other Londoners avoided the reefs.[49]

Aaron and Jurnet were the first provincial leaders to rival the London magnates. Both had houses in London where Jurnet's son, Isaac, with keen development interests, spent considerable time. He paid 1,000 marks for his father's chattels in 1197, including a house at the south-western end of Lothbury, close to Old Jewry. Aaron's house was not far away, on the south of Lothbury, one plot west of the Walbrook. Both Aaron and Jurnet had direct access to the court and *magna scola*, behind the buildings of Lothbury and Old Jewry.[50]

Jurnet's life, work and family have been examined by Lipman. On Aaron, since 1899, there are only Richardson's comments.[51] His origins are unknown. Robert Chesney, bishop of Lincoln 1147–66, was probably the earliest of his clients. Rather than live in the tower above the east gate, Robert purchased, at no small cost, a site below the cathedral to the south where he started building an episcopal palace on a grand scale. In Holborn, for 100 marks, he bought the 'Old Temple' from the Templars for his London palace. He borrowed the necessary cash from Aaron on the security of the cathedral's sacred vessels and ornaments. The £300 outstanding had to be repaid by his successor, Geoffrey Plantagenet.[52] In 1165 Aaron joined Isaac, making money available to the Crown on a local basis, but his fortune was made through a highly developed network that not only enabled him to make loans across the nation but also facilitated the shrewd purchase, at discount, of bonds from other Jews. Eventually he extended his business links over some fifteen counties, from Northumberland in the north through Yorkshire to the Midlands, East Anglia and Dorset in the south-west.[53]

The Cistercians of York and Lincolnshire, anxious to expand their lucrative trade in wool, were probably Aaron's most important clients. His portfolio of

[49] Richardson, *English Jewry*, pp. 60–3.
[50] *Rot. Chart.*, I.i, p. 193; *CChR*, I, p. 168; Hillaby, 'London', pp. 97–100.
[51] Lipman, *Norwich* (see Abbreviations), pp. 95–113; Richardson, *English Jewry*, pp. 32–45 and 68–70; J. Jacobs, 'Aaron of Lincoln', *TJHSE*, 3 (1896–8), 157–79.
[52] J.S. Brewer, J.F. Dimock and G.F. Warner, eds, *Giraldus Cambrensis Opera*, 8 vols (RS 21, London, 1861–91), VII, pp. 34–6.
[53] For Aaron of Lincoln the only satisfactory assessment is Richardson, *English Jewry*, pp. 61–2, 74–6, 89–91, 115–17 and 247–53.

estates encumbered by debt was the means by which they satisfied their land hunger, even encumbering themselves with debt, which, they trusted, would be liquidated by future sales of wool. At his death in 1186 ten Cistercian houses, all but three in those two counties, owed Aaron more than £4,200. The rapid growth and great prosperity of York's Jewry no doubt owes much to this trade in land with the Cistercians. All Aaron's chattels, that is property and bonds, were retained by the exchequer on his death, probably because his sons could not raise the one-third of their value required as relief. Although a special department of the exchequer had been set up to realise Aaron's assets, Richard I, desperate to raise money for his crusade, came to terms in 1189 with ten Cistercian monasteries, accepting a settlement of 1,000 marks, less than one-sixth of their combined debt to Aaron. This was not Richard's only loss. The greater part of Aaron's treasure, in gold and silver one must assume, was lost at sea when the boat on which it was being carried from Shoreham to Dieppe foundered.[54]

At Lincoln Aaron acquired all the property on the west side of Steep Hill, now nos 23–34, within the south gate of Bail. This was opposite the castle gate and ditch. Valued at 60s on his death, it escheated to the Crown as did his own house within the Bail, which became the official residence of the constable of the castle.[55] When the mob attacked in 1190 the Lincoln Jews managed to escape from Steep Hill into the castle, unlike those at Norwich where the castle was equally close at hand. The Northampton *Donum* points up the contrast with Norwich, not only in amounts paid, £277 16s 3d as opposed to £71 11s 5d, but also in their respective population levels.[56]

According to Roger of Howden, it was in 1177 that Henry II granted provincial Jewries the right to establish cemeteries, outside town walls. Previously all their dead had to be taken to the London *bet 'olam* (house of eternity), outside Cripplegate. It was probably at this time that he extended to them the right to have their own communes, that is of self-government according to their own law in all matters 'except such as pertain to our crown and justice: homicide, unlawful injury, considered assault, burglary, theft, arson and treasure trove'. This right was confirmed to the provincial Jewries on 19 June 1218 by William Marshal, *rector regni*, and the Council of Regency, acting on behalf of the eleven-year-old Henry III.[57]

Richardson believed it was now that the king ceased borrowing from the Jews, instead taking what he needed by taxation. On the marriage of his eldest daughter to the emperor Henry V in 1168, the king had levied a feudal aid. Although not recorded on the pipe rolls, one would anticipate that this would also have been the occasion for a *donum* from the Jewry. Only Gervase of Canterbury reports such a *donum*, stating that it totalled 5,000 marks. There

[54] J.R. Walbran and J.T. Fowler, eds, *Memorials of the Abbey of St Marys of Fountains*, 3 vols (Durham, Surtees Society, 42, 1863; 67, 1878; 130, 1918), II, pp. 18–19, n. 4; J.S. Donnelly, *The Decline of the Medieval Cistercian Lay Brotherhood* (New York, 1949), pp. 38–52 has valuable comments on the economic practices of the order; *Gervase* (see Abbreviations), II, p. 5.

[55] C. Johnson and A. Vince, 'The south bail of Lincoln', *Lincolnshire History and Archaeology*, 27 (1992), 12–16, at 15 and fig. 3, quoting *Hundred Rolls*, I (London, 1812), p. 322b; PRO, E101/249/2, transcribed by I. Abrahams, 'The Northampton "Donum" of 1194', *MJHSE*, 1 (1925), lix–lxxiv.

[56] *Newburgh* (see Abbreviations), I, p. 312.

[57] *Howden* (see Abbreviations), II, p. 137; *Benedict*, I, p. 182; *Rot. Chart.*, I.i, pp. 1–93; *Patent Rolls 1218*, p. 157.

may well have been others that have gone unrecorded. What is clear is that the Crown's financial demands rose to a crescendo by the time of Henry's death in July 1189, not only *dona*, or tallages as they came more accurately to be called, but also the various fines to which the Jewry was liable. Thus in 1160 Gentil, a Jewess of Winchester, paid £15 not to marry a Jew and in 1169 Contessa of Cambridge, her son and the community were fined 7 gold marks, £42, because her son had married without royal licence; £24 was paid on the nail.[58]

In the late 1170s the exchequer began to target the wealthiest members of the Jewry. Jurnet of Norwich was fined £4,000 in 1184, which apparently led to his flight across the water and the placing of his bonds, and liability for his fine, with the community's leaders. Two years later he paid a further £1,333 for leave to return. His assessment for the 1186 Guildford tallage was £6,000, reduced to £1,221. In 1194 he was assessed at only some £400, but paid a mere £54 13s 4d. Abraham son of the Rabbi found himself in the royal mercy, to a total of £2,000. This probably related to the 1186 Guildford tallage, which may well have totalled £60,000, the figure mentioned by Gervase. Of this Richardson is sceptical. Le Brun's assessment was £6,666, Jurnet's £6,000 and, as Isaac son of the Rabbi would have been charged similarly, these three alone would account for a third of Gervase's £60,000. Such demands, whether tallage payments, or fines, were, as the pipe rolls show, quite unrealistic. Not only was Jurnet's reduced by 80 per cent but many of the larger Guildford assessments were just not met. The 1191–7 pipe rolls and the 1199–1200 memoranda roll show few reductions in the lists of arrears.[59]

The Jewry under attack, 1189–1190

By the last years of Henry II's reign, therefore, the financial pressure was intense, but the Jewry was in no way prepared for the horrors unleashed at Richard I's coronation on 3 September 1189, nor their transmission to many other parts of the realm early in 1190. For events at London William of Newburgh is the most reliable source. London and provincial Jews in the press about the western doors of Westminster abbey, finding themselves carried within, were attacked with sticks and stones. They fled to the Jewry and the Tower, pursued by retainers of the nobility, a mob and criminals who, granted an amnesty by Richard, were 'free to go forth to rob and plunder more boldly than ever'. Only next morning did 'satiety or weariness, rather than reverence for the king, allay the fury of the plunderers'. The number of fatalities is difficult to assess. For Newburgh 'much blood was shed', while Ephraim of Bonn refers to 'thirty men slain and others who slew themselves and their children'. Comparison of the Londoners listed as in arrears for the Guildford tallage with those named in the 1194 *Donum* suggests most prominent members survived. Other survivors included the magnates Josce and Benedict of York but, for the latter, only at the cost of apostasy.[60]

---

[58] Richardson, *English Jewry*, pp. 63 and 161; *Gervase* (see Abbreviations), II, p. 205; *PpR 6 Henry II*, p. 50; *PpR 15 Henry II*, p. 173.

[59] Richardson, *English Jewry*, pp. 40–2 and 162–3; *PpR 23 Henry II*, p. 201; *PpR 30 Henry II*, p. 9; *Gervase*, II, p. 205; Hillaby, 'London Jewry', pp. 21–4 and Table 3.

[60] *Newburgh*, I, p. 294; *Howden*, III, p. 14; Hillaby, 'London Jewry', pp. 26–30, Tables 3 and 4 and

The first attack on a provincial community was at Lynn in January 1190. Here Jews from Rising had settled close to the new, Tuesday, market. Lynn is of particular interest as an unusual range of evidence explains why, even without castle and mint, it attracted Jewish settlement. Its port, now doubled in size, was booming, offering opportunities that could not be resisted. Here Norwegians and Flemings came to buy corn brought down from Cambridge and Huntingdon by water to the new market place. In addition the Flemings were buying wool. Imports purchased by royal purveyors included spices, wines, hawks and falcons. Described in the Newelond survey of 1267–83 as 'on the north side of the town towards the east', Jews Lane entered the new market on the south-east. According to Newburgh the attack began when Jews pursued a convert into a church where he had sought refuge. Foreign traders from the port joined the crowd. The Jewry was plundered and burned to the ground, and its inhabitants, including Deulebene, its most prosperous member, were murdered or perished in the flames. The last victim of this madness was a Jewish doctor, an eminent physician, worthy man and friend of Christians. The assailants, laden with plunder, made for their boats moored at the wharves just across the Tuesday market and sailed away. Nevertheless at least one Jew, Isaac, had a house in the town in 1218. The name Jews Lane continued in use until c.1860 when it was changed to Surrey Street.[61]

News of the attack on the Lynn Jewry, and the authorities' failure to respond, spread throughout East Anglia and beyond as the season of Lent approached. On Shrove Tuesday, 6 February, all Norwich Jews who had not found security in the castle were slaughtered. In 1194 the Jewry was sadly depleted, only eight tax payers being listed, but survivors included Jurnet, his brother Benedict and his nephew, Josce. Jurnet, whose wealth had rivalled that not only Aaron of Lincoln but also of Isaac son of the Rabbi, with his family paid a mere £70 towards the 5,000-mark *Donum*. The other five Norwich Jews paid £3 13s 5d.[62]

The Norwich community was deeply divided in other ways. The Norwich Jews, with the Jewish court, synagogue and communal facilities behind, not far from the present Lamb Inn, lived on the east side of Haymarket. The Bungay Jews had their own quarter on the south side. They retained a strong sense of their identity well into the succeeding century for they had not been impoverished by their move from Bungay. Joseph of Bungay is mentioned in 1243 and Samuel in 1257. Abraham, Moses, Ursell and Isaac's contribution of £12 compares favourably with the £3 13s 5d of the five Norwich Jews not members of the Jurnet family. Other Bungay Jews were widely dispersed: Elias at Lincoln; Jacob at Northampton; and another Isaac as far away as Hereford.

references in nn. 84 and 87. Ephraim of Bonn cited in Dobson, *Jews of Medieval York*, pp. 21–2, n. 72. Eidelberg, *Jews and the Crusaders*, omits Ephraim's passage on the York massacre. *Newburgh*, I, pp. 308–10; D.M. Owen, ed., *The Making of King's Lynn* (Oxford, 1984), pp. 42, 84, 96 and 269; id., 'Bishop's Lynn: the first century of a new town?', *ANS*, 2 (1980), 141–53; H. Clarke and A. Carter, *Excavations in King's Lynn, 1963–1970* (London, 1977), pp. 424–31; E. and P. Rutledge, 'King's Lynn and Great Yarmouth: two thirteenth-century surveys', *Norfolk Archaeology*, 37 (1980), 92–114, at 94–5; *PpR 2 Richard I*, p. 95; *PpR 3 and 4 Richard I*, p. 182; *Rot. Litt. Claus.*, I, p. 367; H.J. Hillen, *History of the Borough of King's Lynn*, 2 vols (Norwich, 1907), I, p. 54.

[62] *Diceto* (see Abbreviations), II, p. 78; *PpR 2 Richard I*, p. 1; Lipman, *Norwich*, pp. 57–8.

By way of contrast, there is no reference in the pipe rolls or the 1194 *Donum* to any member of Thetford's Jewry. Given the number from Bungay, did Thetford's Jews move there before that Jewry was dispersed and thus come to be regarded as 'de Bungay'?[63]

Stamford did not figure as a Jewry in 1159, but there was a substantial community there by 1190, in which year Stamford's Jews were murdered by young crusaders at the Lenten fair on 7 March. At Bury abbot Hugh I had given Jewish women and children shelter in his pittancery during the rising of Bigod and the three earls in 1173, but the ritual child murder charge had been raised once again in 1181. Abbot Samson (1182–1211), who had to repay Hugh's debts to Jews and Christians, took a sterner line. Palm Sunday, 1190 witnessed the slaughter of fifty-seven more Jews, virtually within sight of the great abbey of St Edmund. The remainder Samson banished, writing to Henry II that within his liberty of Bury either they should be his Jews, not the king's, or be expelled. At Lincoln, when the mob attacked, most members of the community were able to find security at the castle. According to his biographer it was either here or at Stamford that Bishop Hugh of Lincoln, 'brandishing the sword of the Spirit . . . castigated with his tongue those who raised their swords to brain him' and at his funeral Lincoln's Jews paid their tribute, running beside his bier, weeping and wailing, fulfilling the divine word, 'the Lord gave unto him the blessing of all peoples'. The death of individual Jews in the early 1190s at Colchester and at Ospringe, on the pilgrimage route to Canterbury, as of Isaac of Bury at Thetford appear to be isolated incidents, recorded because profitable to the Crown.[64]

The greatest slaughter occurred at York where resort to the castle on 17 March proved of no avail. From the pipe rolls Barrie Dobson has confirmed Newburgh's judgement as to the motives of those who organised the attack. 'From beginning to end (it was) a conspiracy of indebted and pitiless land-lords.' Hence Benedict's house was the first to be attacked and, the onslaught on Clifford's Tower over, the leaders seized the Jewish bonds held at the cathedral for safety and burned them in the nave. Estimates of the dead vary, but Ephraim of Bonn is probably close, 'about 150 men, women and children slain by others, or by themselves for the sake of the Unity'.[65]

When Richard received the news, en route for the Holy Land, his indignation was for losses to the treasury and insult to the royal majesty. Preventative measures were introduced in 1194. The *Capitula Judeorum* became the basis for the Jewry's organisation for the next century. Places were to be appointed for the registration of loans, recorded on chirographs. One part, with the debtor's seal, was to be given to the Jew, the other to be kept in an offical chest or *archa*. Keys were to be held by Christian and Jewish chirographers who were to list all bonds in the chest. The Crown thus had remarkable insight into the wealth of the members of the various Jewries. The proposed six or seven centres proved quite inadequate, for the 1194 tax roll lists payments from twenty-one Jewries

---

[63] Lipman, *Norwich*, pp. 116–29, fig. 13.
[64] *Newburgh*, I, pp. 310–12; *Diceto*, II, pp. 75–6; D. Greenway and J. Sayers, tr., *Jocelin of Brakelond: Chronicle of the Abbey of Bury St Edmunds* (Oxford, 1989), pp. 10, 41 and 126; *PpR 2 Richard I*, pp. 1 and 16; D.L. Douie and H. Farmer, eds, *The Life of St Hugh of Lincoln*, 2 vols (Oxford, 1985), II, p. 228; *PpR 3 and 4 Richard I*, pp. 147, 203.
[65] *Newburgh*, I, pp. 312–22; Dobson, *Jews of Medieval York*; and see now Dobson in the present volume, below, pp. 145–56.

and the next extant roll, in 1221, records the revival of York and Stamford as well as fifteen that survived John's reign.[66]

The Northampton Donum, 1194

The *Donum* provides a conspectus of provincial Jewries at the end of the colonisation process. It lists not only the communities but all tax-paying members. Although the second, Michaelmas, roll is missing, the twenty-one communal entries on the Easter roll, which total slightly more than half the 5,000 marks to be levied, can be taken as just proportions of the sums due from each Jewry.[67] A comparison with the 1159 returns indicates the advances made during three and a half decades of Henry II's rule. By 1190 the number of provincial communities had grown from ten to twenty-four but, with the loss of York, Stamford, Bury and Lynn, only twenty are now listed (Table 2). London and Lincoln, as would be expected, dominate, providing 43 per cent of the total. Tallage totals for the boroughs during this reign indicate that the Lincoln and Norwich Jewries should have been in the same category but, as a consequence of the 1190 attack, the latter ranked eighth, with a 4 per cent contribution. Canterbury, a smaller town, was thus third. In part this reflects the Jewry's clientele in the country's principal ecclesiastical centre. About half the Jewries were at major ports. Overall, the expansion, in both numbers and wealth, had been remarkable.

The 1194 list furnishes details of all individual payments, thus enabling the establishment of hierarchies of wealth within as well as between communities. Provincial magnates can be identified, as can the degree to which they dominated their communities (Table 3). Jurnet's position at Norwich is distorted, by both the sequence of royal charges and the 1190 attack. Thirteen of the twenty-two magnates listed came from London or Lincoln. At London, where most of the affluent members survived the 1189 attack, eight contributed 75 percent, while at Lincoln five paid 56 per cent. Overall ratings are affected by the deaths of Aaron of Lincoln in 1185 and the York magnates, Josce and Benedict, in 1190. Nevertheless it is remarkable that, of the six major contributors, five were leaders of provincial communities: Jacob of Canterbury, Moses the Rich of Gloucester, Isaac le Gros of Canterbury, Jurnet of Norwich and Jacob son of Samuel of Northampton.

This raises interesting questions about their clientele. Jurnet's national role, like that of the Londoners, is easily identified, but could the considerable financial resources of the others have found adequate outlets at a merely local level?[68] Provincial magnates and their clientele have yet to be examined in detail. Some no doubt acted, in part, as agents for the great London financiers

---

[66] H.M. Chew, 'A Jewish aid to marry, AD 1221', *TJHSE*, 11 (1924–7), 92–111, transcribes PRO, E401/4; *Howden*, III, pp. 266–7; H. Rothwell, ed., *English Historical Documents*, III (London, 1975), pp. 305–6. For contributions of individual Jewries to the 1221, 1223 and 1226 tallages, J. Hillaby, 'The Worcester Jewry, 1158–1290: portrait of a lost community', *Transactions of the Worcestershire Archaeological Society*, 3rd series, 12 (1990), 73–122, Table 4.

[67] Abrahams, 'Northampton "Donum"', pp. lix–lxxiv.

[68] Hillaby, 'London Jewry', pp. 17–21 and Table 4; Richardson, *English Jewry*, pp. 61–2; Lipman, *Norwich*, pp. 95–8.

Table 2: The Northampton *Donum*, 1194. Contributions of Individual
Jewish Communities

(figures over 1 rounded to nearest 0.5%)

Community	£	s	d	%	Rank
London	471	6	3	27	1
Lincoln	277	16	3	16	2
Canterbury	242	14	4	14	3
Northampton	160	18	3	9	4
Gloucester	116	19	4	6.5	5
Cambridge	98	19	0	5.5	6
Winchester	84	15	7	5	7
Norwich	71	11	5	4	8
Warwick	62	7	10	3	9
Colchester	41	13	4	2	10
Oxford	35	13	6	2	11
Chichester	26	0	0	1.5	12
Bristol	22	14	2	1	13
Hereford	11	1	8	0.5	14
Nottingham	5	6	4	0.3	15
Worcester	4	8	4	0.25	16
Hertford	4	4	3	0.24	17
Bedford	1	14	0	0.09	18
Exeter	1	2	3	0.06	19
Wallingford	1	0	0	0.05	20
Coventry		11	9	0.03	21
Total	**1,742**	**9**	**2**		

Source: PRO, E101/249/2.

and for Aaron of Lincoln. In the late twelfth century much of the Jewry's
lending was to major ecclesiastical institutions. At Canterbury there were close
links between the Jewry and the monks of the cathedral. We know from Jocelin
of Brakelond's *Chronicle* that Jurnet and his brother, Benedict, lent money to
the abbey of St Edmund at Bury, as did Isaac, the son of the great rabbi, Josce;
and Isaac of Norwich made loans to monks of both Westminster and
Norwich.[69] At Gloucester Moses' clients included not only Prince John but
also the abbot and convent of the church of St Peter, as shown by an extant
deed of his son, Abraham.[70]

[69] *Gervase*, I, p. 405; *Thomas Elmham: History of St Augustine's Abbey, Canterbury* (RS 8, London, 1858), p. 431; H.E. Butler, ed. and tr., *Jocelin of Brakelond: Chronicle* (Edinburgh, 1949), pp. 3–4; Richardson, *English Jewry*, pp. 183–4; Hillaby, 'Ritual child murder', pp. 89–90; Lipman, 'Jews and castles', p. 4.

[70] Hereford Dean and Chapter Archives, no. 1323; text in R.B. Patterson, ed., *Original Acta of St Peter's Abbey, Gloucester, c. 1122–1263* (Bristol and Gloucs. Archaeological Society, Record Section, 1998), pp. 188–9; illustrated in Hillaby, 'Testimony'.

Table 3: Magnates contributing more than £20 to the Northampton
Donum, Easter Term, 1194

Magnate	Jewry	Contribution £ s d			% of community's payment (where known)
Jacob	Canterbury	115	6	8	47.5
Deulesault Episcopus	London	97	10	8	
Moses le Riche (heirs of)	Gloucester	58	6	8	50
Isaac le Gros	Canterbury	55	13	4	
Jurnet	Norwich	54	13	4	
Jacob son of Samuel	Northampton	53	17	6	33.5
Josce son of Isaac	London	53	0	0	
Benedict Parvus	London	51	0	0	
Abraham son of Bene	Winchester	44	19	0	53
Abigail	London	40	7	8	
Ursell	Lincoln	37	0	0	
Vives son of Aaron	Lincoln	36	6	8	
Benjamin	Cambridge	35	0	0	35.5
Benedict Quatrebouches	London	35	0	0	
Benedict Parnas	Lincoln	34	13	4	
Abraham son of Abigail	London	33	13	4	
Belassez and her sons	Oxford	26	15	0	75
Isaac	Colchester	25	0	0	60
Abraham son of Aaron	Lincoln	24	0	8	
Peitevin	Lincoln	23	9	4	
Abraham son of le Brun	London	21	11	8	
Muriel	London	21	3	4	
Total		**978**	**8**	**2**	

Source: PRO, E101/249/2.

Newburgh describes Benedict's and Josce's houses at York as 'built at very great expense and like royal palaces'. The site and nature of Jacob's house at Canterbury gives a more specific picture of a provincial magnate's house, c.1180. It was on a prime site in High Street, at the corner with Stour Street, then Hethenmanne Lane as at Bury, and opposite was the mint. Next door lived Isaac son of Benedict. It was built of stone across three holdings, on which the County Hotel now stands, preserving part of its very thick wall. Stone houses were not unique to Jews. Urry points to at least thirty others in the town, including those, close by, of Henry the Goldsmith, Terric, goldsmith and financier, and Wiulph and Luke, moneyers. Jacob's synagogue, like that of Josce the Rabbi in London, was in a court to the rear. Adjacent was Benedict's house. Jacob's house was sold c.1216 by his sons, Aaron and Samuel, for £17 15s 7d to the Christ Church monks. They let it to Cresse the Jew at a rent of 11s. Later, still in Jewish tenure, it was divided up.[71]

Any estimation of the total population of individual communities is highly problematic. Firstly, there is no means of establishing the tax-paying population as a percentage of the whole. Secondly, while a multiplier of five is often used for English Christian medieval households, and an average family size of 4.25, just over two children per family, has been established by Moore, it cannot be assumed that these figures apply to the medieval Anglo-Jewry for which as yet there is no estimate of the numbers of either children or living-in servants. Indeed, it has been argued strongly, both for Germany and for England, that the Jewish family was smaller than its Christian counterpart. However, the existence of very large families, at least among the upper echelons of the English medieval Jewry, throws doubt on such claims as far as this country is concerned. In fourteen families considered there were at least fifty-nine sons, an average of over four, for which the standard sex ratio suggests a total of about 118 children and an average of over eight. The most recent study of Jewish magnate families adds four further examples. Chera of Winchester had at least nine children, her granddaughter Belia at least six, while Licoricia of Winchester had at least five and her son Benedict at least seven by his first marriage. Demography has been described by Barrie Dobson as 'the single most frustrating problem facing the historian of medieval Anglo-Jewry'. This is another area where more work has to be done, based on studies of individual Jewries.[72]

The first years of John's reign augured well for the English Jewry. In April 1201, in return for a 4,000-mark tallage, John granted them all liberties and customs as in the time of Henry I. In 1204 he warned the mayor and bailiffs of London, 'we shall require their blood at your hands if by your fault any ill befalls them, which God forbid' but the loss of Normandy to Philip Augustus broke the links with the Rouen Jewry. In 1207 another tallage, of 4,000 marks, and a 10 per cent levy on Jewish bonds were imposed. In 1210 tragedy struck the English Jewry. John ordered a 'general captivity', in effect of all the wealthier Jews, and on his return from Ireland a further tallage, of £40,000. Many monastic chroniclers refer to the sufferings of the Jews: of the leaders listed in Table 3 Abraham son of Abigail was hanged; Isaac le Gros, the St Benet Hulme chronicler reports, had his eyes plucked out; Isaac of Norwich bought remission by promising a mark a day for 1,000 days. Comparison of the 1194 and 1221 tallage returns shows some smaller communities, Chichester, Hertford, Bedford and Wallingford, disappeared but Coventry found safety at Leicester. At Gloucester, of the ten Jews listed in the 1221 returns, four were women, three of them widows, and at Northampton of the five women listed at least four were widows. Elsewhere returns refer to those who 'died or crossed the seas'. York, however, staged a remarkable revival, as did Stamford.[73]

---

[71] *Newburgh*, I, p. 314; Urry, *Canterbury*, pp. 119–20, 150–2 and 193–4.

[72] J.S. Moore, 'The Anglo-Norman family', *ANS*, 14 (1992), 185–94, at Tables 5 and 6; K.R. Stow, 'The Jewish family in the Rhineland in the high middle ages: form and function', *AHR*, 92 (1987), 1085–92; Hillaby, 'Testimony'; S. Bartlet, 'Three Jewish businesswomen in thirteenth-century Winchester', *JCH*, 3 (2000), 31–54, at 36 and 43; R.B. Dobson, 'The role of Jewish women in medieval England', in D. Wood, ed., *Christianity and Judaism* (= *SCH* 29, Oxford, 1992), pp. 145–68, at pp. 150–4.

[73] *Rot. Chart.*, I.i, p. 93; *Rot. Litt. Pat.*, p. 33; *CPREJ*, I, p. 4; Richardson, *English Jewry*, pp. 167–72

The Jewish presence in Wales and Ireland

From our earliest record we find the London Jewry funding the campaign of the Anglo-Norman marcher lords in Wales. The 1130–1 pipe roll shows that Josce the Rabbi, Manasser and Jacob offered £36 for Henry I's support of their claim for repayment of a loan made to Richard fitz Gilbert, lord of Ceredigion. A considerable sum was at stake, for Gilbert's counter offer to the Crown was £133 6s 8d. In 1170 Richard's nephew, Richard de Clare, Strongbow, led an expedition of 200 Anglo-Norman knights and 1,000 men at arms against Leinster. After Aaron of Lincoln's death the records of those owing him money included Strongbow, while a Gloucester Jew, Josce, was fined in 1170 'for the moneys he lent to those who against the king's prohibition went to Ireland'. Although in both cases the amounts recorded are small, they are indicative.[74]

For the next half century the affairs of Wales and Ireland became increasingly interlocked. Fearing an independent Anglo-Norman state in Ireland ruled by Strongbow with his lords of the Welsh march, Henry II patched up his quarrels with the Welsh princes and in 1171 led his own expedition to Ireland. The result was compromise. Dublin and its pale, with Wexford and Waterford, came under royal control. Strongbow held the great lordship of Leinster and Hugh de Lacy that of Meath to the north, but on very different terms from those of the Welsh march. There was a feudal relationship between king and barons and the law of England became the law of Anglo-Norman Ireland.[75]

By his marriage in 1189 to Isabel de Clare, Strongbow's heiress, William Marshal became lord of Striguil, with its castles of Chepstow and Usk, and later lord of Leinster, with its caput at Kilkenny, and, in 1199, earl of Pembroke, with its great castle and port, the closest link to Ireland. Hugh de Lacy's son, Walter II, was the Marshal's close neighbour, in Ireland as lord of Meath and in Wales as marcher lord of Ewias. The caput of his English honour was the great castle overlooking the Teme at Ludlow. When the baronial opposition to John made open alliance with the Welsh in 1212 Marshal, de Lacy and the Norman baronage of Ireland and Wales publicly pledged their loyalty and military support for John. After John's death in 1216 the marcher lords, under William's leadership as *rector regni*, dominated the Council of Regency.[76]

and 291; H.R. Luard, ed., *Annales Monastici*, 5 vols (RS 36, London, 1864–9), I, p. 29, II, pp. 81 and 264, III, pp. 32 and 451, IV, p. 54; Chew, 'Jewish aid'.

[74] A.J. Otway-Ruthven, *A History of Medieval Ireland* (2nd edn, London, 1980), pp. 41–9; M. Dolley, *Anglo-Norman Ireland, c. 1100–1318* (Dublin, 1972), pp. 54–70; M.T. Flanagan, *Irish Society, Anglo-Norman Settlers, Angevin Kingship: Interactions in Ireland in the Late Twelfth Century* (Oxford, 1989), pp. 116–17, suggests that Strongbow 'wanted to get away from his creditors', but such an expedition would have been an expensive means of so doing; *PpR 16 Henry II*, p. 78; *PpR 3 and 4 Richard I*, p. 290.

[75] *Rot. Chart.*, pp. 176 and 178; H.F. Berry, ed., *Statute Rolls of the Parliament of Ireland, I: King John to Henry V* (Dublin, 1907), p. 20; P. Brand, 'Ireland and the literature of early common law', in P. Brand, *The Making of the Common Law* (London, 1992), pp. 445–50.

[76] D. Crouch, *William Marshal: Court, Career and Chivalry in the Angevin Empire, 1147–1219* (London, 1990); J. Hillaby, 'Colonisation, crisis management and debt: Walter de Lacy and the lordship of Meath', *Ríocht na Midhe*, 8 (1992/3), 1–50.

Having expelled the French, the Council, 'informed', as Tovey put it, 'what great profit might arise from the Jews if they were kindly dealt with', took immediate measures to revive the English Jewry. Sheriffs were 'to proclaim throughout your bailiwick that we have assured the Jews of our peace'. Civic leaders were held responsible for the safety of the persons and property of the provincial Jews from molestation by 'crusaders' or others. The privilege of local communes was confirmed and Jewish immigration encouraged. The Council's policy was in direct conflict with the last four decrees of the Fourth Lateran Council of 1215, which had sought to restrict not only Jewish lending at interest but also social contacts between Christians and Jews. The policy was all the more surprising since John had placed his kingdom in the pope's hands in 1213 and entrusted his heir to papal protection in 1216. The papal legate wrote, without effect, to the Marshal complaining that the Jews were unduly protected.[77]

The Council's actions revived England's Jewry for a further three-quarters of a century. The Marshal, de Lacy and the marchers had a sharp appreciation of the benefits of such a dramatic shift, not only on the royal exchequer but for themselves. William, portrayed as the flower of chivalry in the chanson *L'Histoire de Guillaume le Maréchal*, was in fact a very different man. For Crouch 'the Marshal and money' is, rightly, the interesting subject. 'His canniness' Crouch illustrates by citing the rapidity and ruthlessness with which he levied a relief from his new tenants on marrying the Striguil heiress, and his close relations with wealthy merchants such as Richard fitz Reiner of London and William fils Florent of St Omer. In 1200 King John granted the Marshal his personal Jew, Vives of Chambay, and commanded his ducal bailiffs to give Vives full assistance in collecting outstanding debts. As the Marshal managed to retain his Norman lands after 1204, this Jewish expertise continued to be at his disposal, there and in all probability either at Caerleon or Chepstow. Furthermore, this tradition of a personal Jew was maintained by the de Clare earls of Gloucester, the Marshal's successors at his last conquest, Caerleon. As late as 1278 the sheriff of Gloucester was to be sent there in person to 'receive from the bailiffs of Gilbert de Clare', the ninth earl, 'the goods late of David de Kaerleon, a Jew deceased', which the bailiffs had been ordered to 'to keep safely and deliver to the sheriff when required'.[78]

In Ireland the Marshal and Walter II de Lacy moved swiftly from conquest to transformation of the economy and landscape of their Irish lands by immigration, founding villages, towns, export facilities, and monasteries. De

---

[77] De Bloissiers Tovey, *Anglia Judaica* (Oxford, 1738), p. 77; *Patent Rolls 1216–1225*, pp. 157 and 180–1; P. Brand, 'Jews and law in England, 1275–90', *EHR*, 115 (2000), 1138–58, at 1138–9. *Rot. Litt. Claus. 1218*, pp. 354, 357 and 359; W.W. Shirley, ed., *Royal and other Letters of the Reign of Henry III*, 2 vols (RS 27, London, 1862–8), I, pp. 35–6.

[78] Crouch, *William Marshal*, pp. 61 and 168–70; *Rot. Chart. 1200*, p. 75; *Rot. Litt. Claus.*, II, p. 123; *Rot. Litt. Pat.*, p. 3. If Golb, *Jews in Medieval Normandy*, pp. 65–7, is correct in his assumption that Chambay is Chambois this may reflect an older relationship. At Chambois, Orne, are the remains of the magnificent keep built by William, earl of Essex, third son and heir of Richard de Mandeville. William bore the crown at the coronation of Richard I, who appointed him joint justiciar of the realm. The suggestion of Richardson, *English Jewry*, p. 298, of Chambes in Calvados appears more likely. David of Kaerleon: *CFR, 1272–1307*, p. 93.

Lacy was accustomed to raising money: to meet royal fines he had raised almost £2,000 between 1198 and 1209. In 1212 the half-yearly income from his Irish estates was more than £370 but he had to meet heavy charges for castle-building and garrisoning his 'lands of peace'. In 1214, during John's Poitevin campaign, Lacy went to Narbonne, which had the largest and culturally the most important Jewry north of the Alps. There he learned the benefits that could accrue to both Christian and Hebrew from a harmonious relationship. By 1222 his Irish demesne was intensively manorialised, producing huge surpluses of grain for export, handled in London by John Travers and Richard Renger, mayors in 1215–16 and 1222–7. Richard's uncle, Richard fitz Reiner, mayor 1187–9, had furnished the Marshal with the resources to celebrate his marriage to Isabel in 1189. Renger was close to court society during the Marshal's regency. He bought a three-year lease on the royal exchange, was its master 1226–33, and keeper of the royal treasure in 1238. To such men Marshal and Lacy would have looked for much of their credit, but both would have had to have another, more local, source in the marches of Wales and Ireland.[79]

Early in de Lacy's shrievalty of Herefordshire, 1216–23, Hamo, a magnate of great wealth, was persuaded to take up residence, with his family, at Hereford, to serve Walter's financial needs. His was the highest payment to the 1223 tallage, £70. For de Lacy Hamo was his private Jew, just as Ranulf III of Chester enjoyed his own seigneurial Jewry at Leicester. However, de Lacy's power base was Irish, not English like that of Ranulf. In 1223 he was removed from his shrievalty. At his death in 1240 his family owed £1,266 to the Crown, to which the assets of Hamo's family had escheated.[80]

Both Marshal and de Lacy would have looked to Jews such as Hamo as their source of credit in Ireland. Scraps of evidence, such as personal names, have been brought forward to confirm a Jewish presence in Ireland but the only firm evidence is in 1232. In June that year Peter des Rivaux was installed by Henry III as treasurer of his household. On 28 July he was granted the treasurer and chancellorship of the Irish exchequer. All Jews in Ireland were to be 'respondent to him in all things touching the king', and on 2 September a mandate to the Irish Jews commanded them to 'be intendant' to Peter in all such matters. What is apparently the only unambiguous reference to an Irish Jew occurs at Bristol in 1282. On 25 June Aaron of Ireland, son of Benjamin of Colchester, went to the shop of Robert of Arras, goldsmith, and before the eyes of many Christians, offered to sell him a silver plate. After weighing it Robert remonstrated that the plate was of fused coin clippings. Aaron, seizing the plate, ran to Avon Bridge and, before many Christians, threw it in the river. The concourse and clamour brought a constable on the scene who arrested him. On being charged with this

[79] Joe Hillaby, 'Hereford gold: Irish, Welsh and English land, part 2: the clients of the Jewish community at Hereford', *TWNFC*, 45 (1985), 193–270, at 197–217; A. Grabois, 'Les écoles de Narbonne au XIIIe siècle', in *Juifs et Judaisme de Languedoc* (Centre d'Études Historiques de Fanjeaux, Toulouse, 1977), pp. 141–57; for Richard fitz Reiner, see Brooke and Keir, *London 800–1216*, pp. 257, 376; for Richard Renger, G.A. Williams, *From Commune to Capital* (London, 1970); Crouch, *William Marshal*, p. 61; Hillaby, 'Colonisation', pp. 25–30.

[80] J. Hillaby, 'A magnate among the marchers: Hamo of Hereford, his family and clients, 1218–1253', *JHS*, 31 (1988–90), 23–82, at 41–52 and Table 8; id., 'Colonisation', pp. 24–35; *CPREJ*, I, pp. 65–8. For Ranulf III, see J. W. Alexander, *Ranulf of Chester* (Athens, GA, 1983), pp. 32–3 and n. 73, 97–8 and n. 36; *Rot. Litt. Claus.*, II, p. 123.

and 'other frauds and trespasses', Aaron refused to acquit himself before the customary jury of Christians and Jews. He was lodged in Hereford gaol until the following February when, promising to abjure the town of Bristol, he purchased release for three bezants or 6s.[81]

The charters of such Edwardian boroughs as Caernarfon, Conway, Criccieth, Flint and Rhuddlan of 1284, of Harlech in 1285 and even Bala in 1324 provide that 'Jews should not sojourn (there) at any time'. These have been cited as evidence of Jewish colonisation in north Wales, on the assumption that the clause was adopted from the 1234 Newcastle-upon-Tyne charter, but that was merely a regrant of the 1213 and earlier charters into which an expulsion clause was added: 'Henceforth no Jew shall remain . . . in the said town'. In north Wales, where castle, borough and wall construction began only after Llywelyn's death in December 1282, there were no resident Jews. These were foundation charters. Hence they included exclusion, not expulsion, clauses.[82]

Evidence of a Jewish presence in the marcher lands of south Wales, if more forthcoming, is fragmentary. The 1278 mandate to the sheriff of Gloucester, to go in person to Caerleon to collect David's chattels, cuts right across the basic concept of marcher lordship which, 'suffred to assume royal authoritie . . . which the kinges of England dyd for policie permit for a tyme'. Here the royal writ did not run and the king's only authority as suzerain was in the application of the laws of succession. Strangers or traders paid an annual fee to the local lord for residence and protection. Thus at Abergavenny Isaac the Jew paid 5 marks, £3 6s 8d, in 1256–7 for an annual licence but in 1277 Vives son of Vives paid a mere 4s. At Striguil, Chepstow, an advowry fine of one mark was paid by an unnamed Jew in 1270–1, while Peter the Jew paid only half a mark in 1283.[83]

The most extraordinary reference is to a Jew, almost a century after the Expulsion, at the commote court of Maenor Deilo, on the banks of the Tywi between Cardigan and Llandovery, in 1386–7. Edward I's act of expulsion of 1290 could well be ignored by the marcher lords but this was not marcher territory. Maenor Deilo was close to Dinefwr castle, the centre of the ancient kingdom of Deheubarth. By 1290, after the death of Llywelyn ap Gruffudd and the defeat of Rhys ap Maredudd, the lands of Cantref Mawr north of the Tywi became part of Cardigan lordship and thus the new, English, principality of

[81] L. Hühner, 'The Jews of Ireland', *TJHSE*, 5 (1902–5), 226–42, at 226–31; L. Hyman, *The Jews of Ireland* (Shannon, 1972), pp. 3–4; Shirley, *Royal and other Letters*, I, pp. 518–20; *CPR 1232–47*, pp. 493–4; Rigg, *Select Pleas*, pp. 120–1 and 127.

[82] M. Gilbert, ed., *Atlas of Jewish History* (5th edn, London, 1976), p. 41; H. Beinart, ed., *Atlas of Jewish History* (New York, 1992), map 48; Roth, *History*², pp. 82 and 92; A. Ballard, ed., *British Borough Charters 1042–1216* (Cambridge, 1913), p. cxliii; id. and J. Tait, eds, *British Borough Charters 1216–1307* (Cambridge, 1923), pp. 142 and 302; E.A. Lewis, *The Medieval Boroughs of Snowdonia* (London, 1912), pp. 33–4 and 279–87 provides text and sources; Colvin, *History of the King's Works*, II, pp. 318–24 and 371–7.

[83] 'A treatise of lordshipps marchers in Wales', in H. Owen, ed., *The Description of Pembrokeshire by G. Owen of Henllys* (London, 1892–1906), III, pp. 139–40; A.C. Reeves, *The Marcher Lords* (Llandybi, 1983), pp. 91–103; A.J. Roderick, 'Ministers' accounts for the lordship of Abergavenny, etc', *South Wales and Monmouth Record Society* (1950), ii, pp. 67–125, at p. 105, quoting PRO Ministers' Accounts 1094/11; *CPREJ*, II, p. 278; W. Rees, *South Wales and the March 1284–1415* (Oxford, 1924), p. 222, quoting PRO Ministers' Accounts 921/21, 921/24 and 1221/1.

Wales. The unnamed Jew was thus living under the jurisdiction of Richard II's constable at Dinefwr.[84]

Conclusion: A twelfth-century 'Golden Age'?

The fundamental topography of the provincial Jewry, in shire towns from York in the north to Exeter in the south-west, was established prior to Henry II's death in 1189. Much of its success is explained by the way the communities were linked, by informal framework of business and family relationships, as well as religious and cultural bonds. This overall pattern of settlement was modified in the thirteenth century, owing to the impoverishment of the Jewry. Even at Hereford, a relative success story after 1265, of 250 bonds recorded in the Old Chest in 1275 only twelve were valued at more than £10, of which the largest was for £45. Members of provincial communities sought trade in smaller centres. Thus Jews from Gloucestershire 'repair for three or four days a week' to Bridgnorth where they 'own a house'. Similarly the bonds of Hagin of Weobley of Hereford were kept in the Hereford chest, 1283–90, and his house there, in Malierestrete, was valued at 5s in 1290. The growing range of toponyms from lesser market towns such as 'Brug' (Bridgnorth), (Chipping) Camden, Dursley, Tewkesbury and Weobley confirms this trend.[85]

There had been an economic upturn after 1218 but it certainly ended with the Worcester 'parliament' of 1241. Yet other factors were at work. The 1189–90 massacres and the 1210 tallage and imprisonments transformed the world in which even the wealthiest members of the Jewry had to operate. That perceptive observer, William of Newburgh, who was over sixty years old when he wrote his *History of English Affairs* in 1196–8, already sensed the profound changes that were taking place. No longer were the Jews living in that 'England in which their fathers had been happy and respected'.[86]

---

[84] R.R. Davies, *The Age of Conquest: Wales 1063–1415* (Oxford, 1991), pp. 217–18, 362–4 and 380–1.

[85] Richardson, *English Jewry*, pp. 20–1; J. Hillaby, 'The Hereford Jewry, part 3: Aaron le Blund and the last decades of the Hereford Jewry, 1253–1290', *TWNFC*, 46 (1990), 432–87, Tables 6 and 9; *CPREJ*, III, pp. 289–90, 294 and 319; Z. Rokeah, 'Crime and the Jews in late thirteenth-century England', *HUCA*, 55 (1984), 95–157, at 151, quoting PRO, Just 1/274/14.

[86] *Newburgh*, I, p. 294.

2

The English Jews under Henry III

ROBERT C. STACEY

For the Jews of medieval England, the long reign of King Henry III (1216–72) began in chaos and ended in crisis. The reign was not, however, an unremitting tale of woe. During the eventful half-century between these disastrous 'book-ends', the Jewish communities of England experienced both heights of prosperity and achievement, and depths of degradation and despair unparalleled in their previous history in England.

The chaos with which the reign began originated with the extortions, imprisonments and assaults that arose from the Bristol tallage of 1210, and continued with the Magna Carta rebellion of 1215–17. Despite these blows, however, the English Jewish community recovered rapidly. By 1241, after two decades of economic and demographic growth, the five thousand men, women, and children who made up the English Jewish community controlled approximately 200,000 marks in liquidable assets, a sum equivalent to roughly one-third of the total circulating coin in the kingdom. Per capita, this made them almost certainly the wealthiest Jewish community in Europe.[1] A wide variety of Jewish communal institutions flourished in England during these prosperous years, including schools of Jewish learning in all the major towns. By 1258, however, this enormously wealthy Jewish community was financially ruined and spiritually demoralised. Twenty years of exorbitant royal taxation bankrupted its leaders and ignited destructive conflicts within it. In the resulting chaos, Jewish communal and charitable institutions collapsed and large numbers of Jews, including the archpresbyter (the royally appointed 'head' of the English Jewish community), converted to Christianity. Nor did the pressure ease thereafter. Between 1263 and 1267, Jewish communities throughout the country were looted and Jewish leaders murdered by the followers of Simon de Montfort. When the baronial wars ended, a series of statutory limitations on Jews and Jewish lending quickly followed, culminating in 1275 with a complete prohibition on lending at interest, hitherto the economic backbone of English Jewish life.

Jews would survive in England until 1290, and a few would even prosper. But by 1275, a turning point of sorts had been reached in the medieval history of the English Jews. The Statute of Jewry pronounced in that year did not make the Expulsion inevitable, but it did guarantee that an expulsion, if it came, would be economically inconsequential for England's Christian majority. When, in

---

[1] R.C. Stacey, 'Jewish lending and the medieval English economy', in R.H. Britnell and B.M.S. Campbell, eds, *A Commercialising Economy: England 1086 to c. 1300* (Manchester, 1994), pp. 78–101, at pp. 93–5. For estimates of Jewish population in thirteenth-century England, see V.D. Lipman, 'The anatomy of medieval Anglo-Jewry,' *TJHSE*, 21 (1968), 64–77.

1290, King Edward discovered that a Jewish expulsion would also be politically advantageous to himself, the fate of England's Jews was sealed.[2]

The Bristol tallage and its aftermath, 1207–1221

In 1207, King John levied a thirteenth from the moveable property of his Christian subjects. The tax raised approximately £60,000 from England and an unknown, but additional, amount from Ireland.[3] The money went partly to repay debts left over from his successful 1206 expedition to recapture Poitou, and partly to provide a war chest for the campaign he hoped to launch in future to recapture Normandy and Anjou. To accompany this tax, John also levied a 4,000-mark tallage on the English Jews. In addition, however, he also demanded that Jews hand over to the king, for direct collection by the Crown, one-tenth of the bonds owing to them. To enforce this latter requirement, each Jew was ordered to list all the debts he or she was owed, with a valuation assigned to each debt. These lists of debts were deposited in the king's treasury, with the king reserving the right to purchase any debt appearing on these lists at the valuation its Jewish owner had assigned to it, above and beyond the tenth of the bonds the king had already claimed.[4] This provision was an obvious way to deter Jews from assessing the debts owed to them at an unreasonably low valuation; but it also meant that King John now had, for the first time, a reasonably accurate inventory of the collectable debts owed to his Jewish subjects. Both innovations would prove disastrous, not only for the English Jews and their debtors, but also for the king.

For the Jews, the sums demanded in 1207 were onerous but not devastating.[5] For their debtors, however, the transfer of their debts to the Crown meant that the full weight of the king's administration now fell upon them to repay their loans. These were dangerous waters, as the Crown's experience with Aaron of Lincoln's resentful debtors during 1189–90 had already shown.[6] King Richard's government, however, had learned from its mistakes. After 1193, when Hubert Walter became Justiciar, pressure upon Aaron of Lincoln's debtors to repay their debts had been quite modest, and relatively few new debts owing to Jews had passed into the king's hands. In 1207, however, all this changed. Not only did John now bring into his hands the largest single cache of Jewish debts since 1186; he also ordered the exchequer to begin seizing the lands of debtors who had fallen behind in repaying the debts they had owed to Aaron of Lincoln.[7] As

---

[2] See Robin Mundill's chapter below, pp. 62–3. For the political context of the expulsion, see also R.C. Stacey, 'Parliamentary negotiation and the expulsion of the Jews from England', in R.H. Britnell, R. Frame, and M.C. Prestwich, eds, *Thirteenth Century England VI* (Woodbridge, 1997), pp. 77–101.

[3] Richardson, *English Jewry* (see Abbreviations), p. 168 and n. 1.

[4] *Rot. Litt. Pat.* (see Abbreviations), pp. 81b–82; *Rot. Litt. Claus.* (see Abbreviations), I, pp. 112b–113; T.D. Hardy, ed., *Rotuli de Oblatis et Finibus in Turri Londinensi asservati, temp. Regis Johannis* (London, 1835), pp. 391, 402–3, 418.

[5] This is Richardson's verdict also: *English Jewry*, p. 168.

[6] R.C. Stacey, 'Crusades, martyrdoms, and the Jews of Norman England, 1096–1190', in A. Haverkamp, ed., *Juden und Christen zur Zeit der Kreuzzüge* (Sigmaringen, 1999), pp. 233–51, at pp. 244–51. On Aaron of Lincoln, see Joe Hillaby's chapter, above, pp. 27–8.

[7] *Rot. Litt. Claus.*, I, pp. 98–98b.

J.C. Holt has rightly remarked, 'The King was aiming here not so much at the dispossession of the debtors as at tightening the screw, at using distraint on land or the threat of distraint as a method of compelling payment.'[8] To debtors short of ready cash, however, the king's intentions mattered little. Either way, they would lose their lands, whether to the king directly (by failing to repay the debt), or to another creditor from whom they would be forced to borrow yet more money in order to pay off debts they had initially contracted with a Jew, but which they now owed to the Crown.

The resentments resulting from this change in policy would explode against King John in the Magna Carta rebellion. The more immediate victims, however, were the Jews. Fuelled by his new knowledge of the scale of Christian indebtedness to Jews, and perhaps encouraged by the example of King Philip of France, John in 1210 embarked upon yet another new departure in extortionate fiscality.[9] Summoning the leaders of the English Jewish community to Bristol, John imprisoned and tortured them, perhaps claiming that they had fraudulently concealed many of their assets in 1207. Soon thereafter, all the Jews of England were seized and imprisoned, and their bonds confiscated. To redeem their bonds from forfeiture and themselves from prison, the Jewish community of England was forced to promise the king a tallage of 60,000 marks, with harsh penalties, including imprisonment, torture, or expulsion, for individual Jews who failed to pay their assessments on time.[10] The first term of the tallage was due to be paid on 1 November 1210; the final instalment was probably due in 1213, when a new round of imprisonments began of Jews who had failed to pay fully the tallage debts assigned to them in 1210.[11] Some of the wealthiest Jews, including Isaac of Norwich, may have been kept in prison continuously from 1210 to 1213 to guarantee the payment of the tallage.[12] Even the poorest Jews, however, were obliged to pay a minimum of 40s towards the tallage. Those who could not pay so large a sum were forced to flee the realm, along with many other Jews who either could not or would not meet their tallage obligations.[13]

The consequences of the Bristol tallage were devastating. Hundreds of Jews were imprisoned, and an unknown number were executed. Hundreds more fled abroad, many, it appears, to Brittany;[14] while in England, entire Jewish communities disappear from the records. A flood of new Jewish bonds fell into the king's hands for collection, exacerbating tensions already aroused among Christian debtors by the tallage of 1207; and a massive amount of

---

[8] J.C. Holt, *The Northerners: A Study in the Reign of King John* (Oxford, 1961), p. 164.

[9] For discussion of Philip Augustus's 1210 *captio* against the Jews of the French royal demesne, see W.C. Jordan, *The French Monarchy and the Jews: from Philip Augustus to the Last Capetians* (Philadelphia, 1989), pp. 64–72. The evidence is poor, but it appears that both seizures took place at some date between February and May 1210.

[10] Richardson, *English Jewry*, pp. 168–72, assembles most of the sources; to these add *CPREJ* (see Abbreviations), I, p. 4. An additional 6,000 marks was probably imposed as Queen's gold, leading to the total of 66,000 marks given by several chroniclers for the total amount of the Bristol tallage.

[11] For the 1 November 1210 date of the first instalment, see *PpR 13 John*, p. 105; for the confiscations and imprisonments of 1213, see *Rot. Litt. Pat.*, p. 102b and *Rot. Litt. Claus.*, I, p. 139, both dated 26 July.

[12] *Rot. Litt. Pat.*, p. 102b. Isaac later fined with King John to be released from prison in return for 10,000 marks, to be paid at a rate of one mark per day: *ibid.*, pp. 179, 180, 459.

[13] *Rot. Litt. Claus.*, I, p. 186b.

[14] Jordan, *French Monarchy*, p. 69.

Jewish urban property was confiscated, much of which the king gave away to his supporters.[15] As a result, when the Magna Carta rebellion erupted, Jews and Jewish property were among the principal targets of the rebels. In London, the rebels looted Jewish homes and destroyed synagogues, using the stones to fortify the city's walls against King John's army.[16] Similar attacks occurred in other Jewish communities around the country, while a number of individual Jews were seized and held for ransom by military leaders on both sides of the conflict.

As soon as John died, however, the men who ruled England in the name of the boy king Henry III began to take steps to restore some security to English Jewish life. Jews captured by baronial leaders were ordered released; royal safeguards for individual Jews were renewed or reissued; and bonds were returned to their Jewish owners for collection.[17] Officials guarding the ports were ordered to permit Jews entering England from overseas to do so without hindrance, provided the Jewish immigrants gave security to register themselves, as quickly as possible, with the newly appointed Justices of the Jewish Exchequer; but port officials were to prevent any English Jews from leaving the realm without the king's permission.[18] In Lincoln, where crusaders were known to be gathering, the sheriff was ordered to select twenty-four citizens of the town to protect its Jewish residents from harm. Similar orders were sent to protect the Jews of Oxford, Gloucester, and Bristol.[19]

Although a brief attempt was made to enforce the Fourth Lateran Council's requirement that all Jews wear a distinguishing badge on their clothing, this policy was quickly abandoned by the new king's government, which also reissued the customary rules exempting Jews from the jurisdiction of episcopal courts.[20] In 1222, another attempt to extend episcopal authority over Jews was similarly rebuffed.[21] Even more importantly, the new government began immediately to order its sheriffs to enforce debts owed by Christians to Jewish moneylenders, including interest payments at 2d or even 3d per pound per week.[22] In 1219,

---

[15] Most notably in Oxford and London; for London, see J. Hillaby, 'London: the thirteenth-century Jewry revisited', *JHS*, 32 (1990–2), 89–158, at 97–9. Dozens of references to such grants of Jewish houses can be found on the Close Rolls.

[16] Nicholas Vincent, 'Two papal letters on the wearing of the Jewish badge, 1221 and 1229', *JHS*, 34 (1997), 209–224, at 214 and n. 38; J. Hillaby, 'Beth miqdash me'at: the synagogues of medieval England', *JEH*, 44 (1993), 182–98, at 189–90.

[17] *Patent Rolls, 1216–1225* (see Abbreviations), pp. 59 (3), 95 (2), 98, 105, 179–80; *Rot. Litt. Claus.*, I, pp. 313, 317 (3), 342.

[18] *Patent Rolls, 1216–1225*, pp. 154, 180–1.

[19] *Rot. Litt. Claus.*, I, pp. 354b, 357, 359b.

[20] *Ibid.*, I, pp. 378b; *Patent Rolls, 1216–1225*, p. 157; Vincent, 'Two papal letters', p. 215.

[21] *Rot. Litt. Claus.*, I, p. 567, cited in Vincent, 'Two papal letters', p. 215 n. 43.

[22] WAM (see Abbreviations) 6719 is a draft of a writ dated 26 May (no year) at Westminster, from King Henry to the sheriff and chirographers of Nottingham, informing them that henceforth they are not to permit the deposit of any debt instruments in their *archa* that specify the payment of interest in excess of 2d per pound per week, 'because we do not wish that the assize previously held for 3d on the pound should any longer be maintained' (*quia nolumus quod assisa prius habita de iii denariis de libra ulterius teneatur*). This writ could be associated with the 1233 legislation limiting interest rates to 2d per pound per week published by Richardson, *English Jewry*, p. 294; but in neither 1233 nor 1234 was King Henry at Westminster on 26 May. Or it may reflect the similar legislation pronounced in November 1239, discussed at note 48 below. WAM 6719 does clearly establish, however, what previously we could only infer: that interest rates higher than 2d per pound per week were legally enforceable prior to 1233, and perhaps prior to 1239. I am grateful to Nick Vincent for advice on this writ.

efforts were made to determine and assess the arrears still owing on the Bristol tallage, but it appears that relatively little money was actually collected.[23] By 1221, however, Jewish life in England had recovered sufficiently to permit the assessment of a new tallage of 1,500 marks. In 1223, a 3,000-mark tallage was imposed; in 1225–6, a 6,000-mark tallage. Records of receipts from all three tallages are partial, but the levies appear to have been paid without difficulty, suggesting that the Jewish community was already recovering from the devastating blows of the previous decade.[24]

Recovery and expansion, 1221–1239

With the exception of Isaac of Norwich, the leaders of the English Jewish community during the 1220s and 1230s were new men, whose careers cannot be traced before 1210. So far as we can tell, all were born in England.[25] Some were the sons of families prominent in the years before 1210, who had somehow managed to preserve at least a portion of their familial wealth from destruction. This was particularly the case in London, where all the principal families of the 1220s and 1230s – the Blunds, the Crespins, the L'Eveskes, and the family of Abraham fil Abigail – were direct descendants of lenders prominent in the city between 1190 and 1210.[26] Outside London and Norwich, however, the greatest Jewish fortunes of the period were owned by men whose origins prior to 1221 we can trace but dimly if at all: Aaron, Leo and Benedict of York, David of Oxford, Hamo of Hereford, and David Lumbard of Nottingham. Aaron of York and David of Oxford both began their careers in Lincoln, but had left Lincoln by 1221, when they were already the wealthiest Jewish residents of their new cities.[27] Hamo's origins are unknown, but by 1221 he appears already as the wealthiest Jewish resident of Hereford.[28] Benedict and Leo L'Eveske were both well established at York by 1221, but cannot be traced before that date. David Lumbard is first recorded at Nottingham in 1221, but he too may have had earlier connections with Lincoln.[29]

---

[23] PRO, E101/249/13, portions of which have been transcribed and published by Richardson, *English Jewry*, pp. 288–91, and by Michael Adler, *Jews of Medieval England* (London, 1939), pp. 236–8.

[24] PRO, E401/4, E401/5 and E401/6 record some of the receipts from these tallages. The sums are conveniently tabulated in J. Hillaby, 'A magnate among the marchers: Hamo of Hereford, his family and clients, 1218–1253', *JHS*, 31 (1991), 28–82, at 28.

[25] David Lumbard of Nottingham and Hamo of Hereford are possible, but unlikely, exceptions. Although David's surname might associate him with Italy, he could equally well have been the son of Asher Lumbard, who is found residing in Lincoln in 1194. J. Hillaby, 'Hereford gold: Irish, Welsh and English land. The Jewish community at Hereford and its clients, 1179–1253, Part II', *TWNFC*, 45 (1985), 193–270, at 212, speculates that Hamo's unusual first name might suggest he was an immigrant from northern France, but there is no real evidence either way.

[26] Hillaby, 'London', pp. 107–34, assembles the evidence.

[27] PRO, E401/4 rot. 4, transcribed and published by H.M. Chew, 'A Jewish aid to marry, A.D. 1221', *TJHSE*, 11 (1924–7), 92–111, at 100, 106–7 and 109. Both David and Aaron are listed on this receipt roll for the 1221 tallage as being 'of Lincoln'; presumably each had moved from Lincoln only recently.

[28] Hillaby, 'Magnate', pp. 29–31. The fact that Hamo was often referred to as 'Hamo son-in-law of Elias' in financial records from the 1220s may suggest that Hamo acquired at least part of his wealth through marriage: see *CPREJ*, I, pp. 65–7.

[29] Chew, 'Jewish aid', pp. 103, 105; and see note 25 above. J.M.W. Hill's study of the Lincoln

Not only were the great Jewish magnates of the 1220s and the 1230s new men; they also earned their fortunes in provincial towns that had not previously been major centres for English Jewish life. Partly, no doubt, this was because ambitious new men tended to gravitate toward towns where they would not have to compete with the long-established and well-connected Jewish families of London, Norwich, Lincoln, and Canterbury. Partly too, this shift in Jewish wealth toward the north and west reflects the explosive economic growth of these regions, and the demand for capital that resulted from this growth. It is also, however, a reflection of the kind of lending in which the great Jewish magnates who dominated these provincial towns were involved. Most Jewish lending in thirteenth-century England involved relatively small-scale loans to townsmen, peasants, and the local gentry. During the 1220s and 1230s, however, men like Hamo of Hereford, Aaron and Leo of York, and David of Oxford made their greatest profits by lending large sums to very large clients: earls, barons, knights, and monasteries. Their willingness to engage in such loans on so large a scale is a testament both to the security they had come to feel in King Henry III's government and to the lucrative nature of the business in which they were engaged.[30]

The scale of the fortunes earned during these decades can best be appreciated by examining the payments made by these great Jewish magnates toward the 20,000-mark tallage of 1241, the first of a devastating series of huge royal taxes that would ultimately bankrupt the English Jewish community.[31] Because this tax was carefully assessed and collected in proportion to the total wealth of each Jewish community and each individual Jewish contributor, its returns provide us with an unrivalled picture of the distribution of wealth within the English Jewish community at the height of its thirteenth-century prosperity. What we find in 1241 is a concentration of wealth that is nothing short of astonishing. Aaron of York was assessed to pay 30 per cent of this 20,000-mark tax personally; David of Oxford and Leo L'Eveske of York were each to pay 12.5 per cent; David Lumbard of Nottingham was to pay 6 per cent; while in London, the Crespins were to pay 3.5 per cent, and Aaron Blund and Aaron fil Abraham were each to pay 3 per cent. Three-quarters of the tallage was levied upon thirteen men living in only five towns (York, London, Oxford, Nottingham, and Norwich). Communal wealth was even more concentrated. Three Jewish communities – York (47.6 per cent), London (21.8 per cent), and Oxford (12.3 per cent) – paid more than 80 per cent of the total receipts recorded toward this levy.[32]

Jewish community in *Medieval Lincoln* (Cambridge, 1948), pp. 217–38 is an admirable, pioneering effort, but it neither notes nor explains the rapidly declining significance of the Lincoln Jewish community after 1210. A new account of this community is badly needed.

[30] Stacey, 'Jewish lending', pp. 95–6. Hillaby has established this point particularly clearly with respect to Hamo of Hereford: 'Hereford gold: Irish, Welsh and English land. The Jewish community at Hereford and its clients, 1179–1253, Part I', *TWNFC*, 44 (1984), 358–419, at 400–9; 'Hereford Gold, Part II', pp. 258–60; and 'Magnate', pp. 37–43.

[31] For what follows in this paragraph, see R.C. Stacey, 'Royal taxation and the social structure of medieval Anglo-Jewry: the tallages of 1239–1242', *HUCA*, 56 (1986), 175–249.

[32] Hamo of Hereford had died in 1231, and his heirs had been exempted from all tallage payments until they had paid the enormous 6,000-mark relief the king had assessed upon Hamo's estate. Hamo's family was still struggling to pay off this relief in 1241, and so they were not assessed for the 1241 tallage. Had Hamo's heirs been assessed, Hereford's total contribution would probably have rivalled Oxford's. See Hillaby, 'Magnate', pp. 62–7.

The dominance of the great Jewish magnates over their communities was not only economic. It was also cultural and religious, and presumably social as well. Many of these magnates were themselves rabbis, including Isaac of Norwich and his son Samuel (both of whom were also physicians), David Lumbard, Leo L'Eveske of York, and, from the next generation, Peitevin of Lincoln, Peitevin the Great of Northampton, and Elijah Menachem of London.[33] Other magnates, such as Isaac and Samuel of Norwich, Aaron of York, and Benedict Crespin, were patrons of scholars, receiving in recognition of their generosity the honorific title *haNadib*.[34] Others possessed collections of Jewish books, including David of Oxford and Leo the son of Hamo of Hereford, both of whose collections may suggest that their owners had had rabbinical training.[35] Rabbis were numerous in thirteenth-century England, and Talmudic studies appear to have been a ubiquitous feature of English Jewish life until at least the 1260s. Every Jewish community in thirteenth-century England had at least one synagogue, and many had several. To build and maintain a synagogue was a traditional responsibility for Jewish magnates, and the evidence suggests that the English magnates took their obligations seriously.[36] Magnates were also generally responsible for supporting Jewish cemeteries and maintaining other institutions necessary to Jewish life, including *mikva'ot*, slaughterhouses, and communal ovens.

Recent work is also beginning to cast a more favourable light on the quality of Hebrew learning in thirteenth-century England.[37] Scholarly links between the continent and England may have become less regular after 1204 (when England lost most of its lands in France, including Normandy) than they had been in the later twelfth century, when luminaries such as Abraham ibn Ezra and Rabbi Yom Tov of Joigny are known to have resided in England. Hostilities between the French and English kings during the thirteenth century certainly made it more difficult for English scholars to maintain regular contacts with the Tosafists of northern France; while the declining significance of Rouen itself as a scholarly centre probably also contributed toward distancing English rabbis from their continental counterparts.[38] But we should not overestimate the extent of their isolation.[39] English Jews continued to maintain links with the Jews of France, and to look toward French rabbinical courts to appeal decisions rendered in England.[40]

---

[33] On Isaac and Samuel of Norwich as rabbis, see WAM 6794 and Lipman, *Norwich* (see Abbreviations), p. 150; for David Lumbard, WAM 6746.

[34] Cecil Roth, 'The intellectual activities of medieval English Jewry', *British Academy Supplemental Papers*, 8 (London, 1948), p. 15; Lipman, *Norwich*, p. 150.

[35] Roth, 'Intellectual activities', pp. 7–8; Hillaby, 'Magnate', pp. 35–6.

[36] Hillaby, 'Magnate', pp. 56–8; id., 'Beth miqdash me'at'.

[37] The most important recent contribution is Hans-Georg von Mutius, ed., *Rechtsentscheide Mittelalterlicher Englischer Rabbinen* (Frankfurt am Main, 1995). The classic work is Roth, 'Intellectual activities'.

[38] Norman Golb, *The Jews in Medieval Normandy: A Social and Intellectual History* (Cambridge, 1998).

[39] Compare Colin Richmond, 'Englishness and medieval Anglo-Jewry', in Tony Kushner, ed., *The Jewish Heritage in British History: Englishness and Jewishness* (London, 1992), pp. 42–59, at p. 53; and Roth, *History*[3] (see Abbreviations), p. 34.

[40] Most famously, of course, in the divorce case involving David of Oxford and his wife Muriel, on which see C. Roth, *The Jews of Medieval Oxford* (Oxford Historical Society, n.s. 9, 1945), pp. 51–

At the same time, the legal opinions of English rabbis were clearly known and respected elsewhere in the Ashkenazi world.[41] An appearance of increasing 'parochialism' among English rabbinical scholars during the thirteenth century may actually reflect a growing confidence among English Jews in their own independent capacities as interpreters of religious law. Much work remains to be done in the responsa literature before we will have a full picture of the stature of English rabbis in the intellectual world of thirteenth-century Europe. But the overall educational level of English Jewry appears to have been high. As Cecil Roth has observed, 'the surviving Anglo-Jewish legal deeds of the twelfth and thirteenth centuries are among the most interesting and elaborate of the medieval period from any country in Europe . . . and demonstrate both a mastery of the intricacies of Talmudic law and a good knowledge of Hebrew on the part of ordinary business men, even in remote places'.[42] Hebrew literary work is less well represented, but what survives is of high quality. In particular, the poems of Meir of Norwich are among the finest such works produced anywhere in thirteenth-century Europe.[43]

Expropriation and antisemitism, 1239–1258

The exceptional wealth the English Jewish community had attained by 1239 rested upon a combination of factors: a booming economy and a widespread demand for capital, especially among the aristocracy of northern and western England; an efficient secondary market in Jewish bonds that enabled larger Jewish lenders to buy up debts owed to their co-religionists, either in whole or in partnership; effective and relatively inexpensive mechanisms to collect debts through the Exchequer of the Jews; legally enforceable interest rates that varied between 43 per cent and 87 per cent per year; and moderate, predictable levels of royal taxation that since 1221 had averaged between 2,000 and 3,000 marks per year.[44] Although these arrangements had been briefly threatened in 1233–4 by the regime of Bishop Peter des Roches, the storm had passed, and no lasting damage had been done by the novel

---

4. The case is discussed with reference to David's subsequent wife, Licoricia, by Suzanne Bartlet, 'Three Jewish businesswomen in thirteenth-century Winchester', *JCH*, 3 (2000), 31–54.

[41] Cecil Roth, 'Why Anglo-Jewish history?', *TJHSE*, 22 (1968–9), 21–9, at 27–8 assembles some additional references. For earlier ones, see Israel Epstein, 'Pre-expulsion England in the responsa', *TJHSE*, 14 (1935–9), 187–205.

[42] Roth, 'Intellectual activities', p. 15; and see also L. Rabinowitz, 'The London *get* of 1287', *TJHSE*, 21 (1968), 314–22, at 319, who notes the invalidation of an English bill of divorce because the scribe who wrote it overran the line by a single letter. This, argues Rabinowitz, is clear evidence of the very strict halachic rigour of English rabbis.

[43] Roth, 'Intellectual activities', pp. 50–1; Lipman, *Norwich*, pp. 157–8 and Appendix. By far the best analysis of Meir's poetry is now Susan Einbinder, 'Meir b. Elijah of Norwich: persecution and poetry among medieval English Jews', *JMH*, 26 (2000), 145–62; and her book *Beautiful Death: Jewish Poetry and Martyrdom in Medieval France* (Princeton, 2002).

[44] Stacey, 'Jewish lending', pp. 95–7; id., '1240–1260: a watershed in Anglo-Jewish relations?', *Historical Research*, 61 (1988), 135–50, at 136–7. As stated in note 22 above, legislation in 1233 and 1239 fixed the maximum allowable rate of interest at 2d on the pound per week (43 per cent per year simple interest; compounding was illegal). On loans between Jews, however, some bonds continued to specify rates of interest as high as 4d per pound per week, a simple interest rate equivalent to 87 per cent per year (e.g., WAM 6869).

departures of those years.[45] After 1234, royal policy toward Jews and Jewish lending seems to have returned to normal.

Starting in 1239, however, the foundations of Jewish prosperity in England were systematically destroyed by the king's financial rapacity. The first blow came in June 1239, when King Henry, perhaps imitating similar measures taken by King Louis IX between 1227 and 1230, launched a sudden *captio* against the English Jewish community, imprisoning Jewish leaders and sealing the chests (*archae*) in which Jewish bonds were kept and registered.[46] To redeem themselves and their bonds, the Jews were then compelled to pay the king one-third of the value of their bonds and chattels.[47] In November 1239, the king's council followed up by dismissing all the keepers and clerks of the *archae* throughout the country and issuing a new statute of Jewry. This statute established new requirements for making and enrolling Jewish bonds; it limited the legal rate of interest on Jewish loans to 2d on the pound per week; and it declared a moratorium on all interest charges on Jewish debts from Midsummer 1239 (when the *archae* were closed by royal order) until Christmas, when presumably they were expected to reopen.[48]

Receipts from the Third were disappointing, however, and in June 1240 the king ordered the *archae* closed again in preparation for a much more thorough-going assessment of Jewish wealth. During the summer, teams of royal officials toured the countryside, inventorying the contents of the *archae*. The result was the imposition, in February 1241, of a 20,000-mark tallage to be paid within a year, accompanied by elaborate new procedures to guarantee that the tax would be assessed in strict proportion to the wealth of each individual Jewish taxpayer.[49] Further massive tallages followed swiftly thereafter: 60,000 marks between 1244 and 1250 (of which only about two-thirds was actually assessed); and a further 44,000 marks between 1250 and 1258. Although not all of these taxes were paid in full, it appears that King Henry nonetheless took something

---

[45] Nicholas Vincent, 'Jews, Poitevins, and the bishop of Winchester, 1231–1234', in D. Wood, ed., *Christianity and Judaism* (= *SCH* 29, Oxford, 1992), pp. 119–32.

[46] See Jordan, *French Monarchy*, pp. 129–32, for Capetian policy leading up to the 1230 Statute of Melun. For the 1239 English *captio,* see Matthew Paris, *Chronica Majora*, 7 vols (RS, London, 1872–84), III, p. 543, translated in Stacey, 'Royal taxation', p. 180.

[47] For analysis of the Third on Jewish Chattels (which somewhat underplays its importance), see Stacey, 'Royal taxation', *passim.*

[48] Four texts of this legislation are known. Three are witnessed by the king. Two are addressed to London and dated 10 December 1239 (*De Antiquis Legibus Liber: Cronica Maiorum et Vice-comitum Londoniarum*, ed. Thomas Stapleton, Camden Society, orig. ser. XXXIV (1846), pp. 237–8, and British Library Additional MS. 62534, ff. 257v–258r. I am grateful to Dr Paul Brand for this latter reference). Another text, dated 3 February 1240, is addressed to Colchester (WAM 9001). All three of these versions declare a six-month moratorium on interest charges on Jewish debts, and require all Jews to remain in their towns of residence for one year starting at Michaelmas 1239. A fourth text, addressed to Nottingham, is dated 16 May 1241 and witnessed by William of St Edmunds, one of the Justices of the Jews (WAM 9002). This text omits the requirement that Jews remain for one year at their customary places of residence, but declares a moratorium on all interest charges on Jewish loans from Midsummer 1239 until 'the day on which the *archa* was opened in the twenty-fifth year of the king's reign'. Henry's 25th year ran from 28 October 1240 until 27 October 1241; I have not been able to determine exactly when the *archae* were reopened, but unless the scribe wrote 'twenty-five' when he meant to write 'twenty-four', the *archae* must have been closed for a minimum of fifteen months, and perhaps for as long as two years.

[49] Stacey, 'Royal taxation', analyses the assessment and collection of this tax.

on the order of 100,000 marks in direct taxation from the Jews of England during these years, a sum amounting to about half of their total assets in 1241. Nor was this the full extent of the king's financial depradations against the Jews. Additional sums, of 7,000 marks and 5,000 marks respectively, were assessed in 1244 on the heirs of Leo of York and David of Oxford for permission to inherit their father's property. Even more grievously afflicted was Aaron of York, who was subjected to a host of arbitrary royal impositions above and beyond his enormous tallage payments. Aaron himself estimated that between 1243 and 1250 he had paid the king more than 30,000 marks in tallages and other exactions.[50] By 1255, Aaron was bankrupt, and had to be forgiven the tallage debts assigned to him in that year on grounds of poverty.[51]

The result was a spiral of collapse. To raise the enormous sums being demanded of them, Jews were forced to call in their loans to their Christian debtors. In the past, Jewish lenders had usually been content to resolve long-standing debts for considerably less than the total accrued interest on the loan.[52] As a result, there is little evidence of large-scale property losses by Christians indebted to Jews during the 1220s and 1230s. In the changed circumstances after 1241, however, Jewish lenders could no longer afford to offer such easy terms, even to their best customers. If a Christian could not pay his debt in full, Jews in desperate need of cash were often forced to turn the bond itself over to the king for credit against tallage debts, or else to sell the bond 'short' to another lender. In the past, the secondary purchasers of Jewish bonds had usually been other Jews. From the 1240s on, however, the purchasers were more often Christians. Henry's courtiers, including his Lusignan half-brothers, were particularly active in this traffic, which the king himself encouraged by granting Jewish bonds to courtiers in place of the cash fees and landed endowments he had promised them. Unlike Jewish lenders, however, Henry's relatives and courtiers were only too glad to use these debts to acquire permanent possession of the lands upon which they were secured.[53]

The escalating complaints of dispossessed Christian debtors are reflected in the grievances that brought down King Henry's government in 1258.[54] By then, however, irreversible damage had already been done. Two decades of merciless financial pressure between 1239 and 1258 destroyed the communal foundations of English Jewish life while poisoning the attitudes of Christians toward their Jewish neighbours. The resulting transformations in Jewish life and in Jewish–Christian relations are what make this period a watershed in Anglo-Jewish life.[55]

---

[50] Matthew Paris, *Chronica Majora*, V, p. 136.

[51] *Close Rolls, 1254–6* (see Abbreviations), p. 140.

[52] Jewish lenders were legally prohibited from acquiring permanent possession of freehold property pledged to them as collateral on a loan. They were permitted only to acquire possession for a term of years sufficient to pay off the principal of the loan plus accrued interest. This, however, could be a long and slow process, fraught with uncertainty. Jews usually preferred, therefore, to settle the debt for cash so that they could reinvest the money in new loans, even if that meant discounting the full value of the bond.

[53] This paragraph restates the argument of Stacey, '1240–1260', pp. 135–50.

[54] R.F. Treharne and I.J. Sanders, eds, *Documents of the Baronial Movement of Reform and Rebellion* (Oxford, 1973), pp. 86–7 (note that *minores* here means 'lesser men', not 'minors'), 108–9, 154–5; Stacey, '1240–1260', pp. 143–4.

[55] This is the argument of Stacey, '1240–1260', *passim*. Vincent, 'Jews, Poitevins, and the bishop of Winchester', argues for the 1230s, citing the parallels between the Jewish policies of 1232–4 and

Desperate to preserve their fortunes, some Jewish magnates sought and received favourable assessments for taxation, either by outright bribery of the assessors or by securing the special favour of the king. Such exemptions only increased the burden upon the rest of the Jewish community, however, which either lacked such connections or (in the case of Aaron of York) refused to take advantage of them. The resulting tensions between magnates, and between the magnates and the communities for whom they had traditionally assumed responsibility, undermined the solidarity of the English Jewish community. So hated did Elias L'Eveske become as a result of such machinations that when he finally fell from the king's favour in 1257 and was dismissed from his office as archpresbyter, the Jewish community offered King Henry three gold marks (the equivalent of thirty silver marks) for his promise never again to appoint Elias to any office. Soon thereafter, Elias and at least one of his sons converted to Christianity, apparently to avoid prosecution on charges that he had offered a Christian assassin 40s to murder Hagin of London, the brother of Rabbi Elijah Menachem and Elias's principal rival within the London Jewish community.[56]

By converting to Christianity, Elias L'Eveske joined a flood of other Jewish converts during these terrible years. King Henry had been attempting to encourage Jewish conversions since at least 1232, when he had founded, in London, a 'Domus Conversorum' to offer food and shelter to converts from Judaism to Christianity. Only during the 1240s and 1250s, however, did conversions reach significant levels. A list of approximately 150 such converts from 1255 reveals the social background to many of these conversions: single parents without spouses, siblings without parents, and single persons of both sexes predominate in the records. Ordinarily, such persons would have been supported either by the internal charitable mechanisms of their local Jewish communities or by their Jewish relatives. In the desperate situation during the 1240s and 1250s, however, the Jewish community's 'social safety net' had collapsed, leaving such persons with no alternative but to convert or starve. By the late 1250s, it appears that between 5 per cent and 10 per cent of the entire Jewish community in England had converted to Christianity.[57]

The difficulties converts faced in assimilating themselves into Christian society were considerable, however, and may have been growing during the 1240s and 1250s, as the number of converts increased. Some Christian theologians, most notably Thomas Cantilupe, openly doubted whether even baptism could alter the fundamental Jewish identity of a convert. At the same time, Christian notions of Jewish identity were also turning sharply more negative.[58] Lurid tales of Jewish perfidy appear in mid-century Christian

---

those of the period after 1239. The difference, however, lies in the relative impact of these policies upon the English Jews themselves. Royal policy was indeed similar, but Jewish communal institutions and solidarity did not collapse in the 1230s, as they clearly did during the 1240s.

[56] Stacey, '1240–1260', pp. 140–2; id., 'The conversion of Jews to Christianity in thirteenth-century England', *Speculum*, 67 (1992), 263–83, at 272.

[57] Stacey, 'Conversion', *passim*. On the 1255 lists of converts, see also Joan Greatrex, 'Monastic charity for Jewish converts: the requisition of corrodies by Henry III', in Wood, ed., *Christianity and Judaism*, pp. 133–43.

[58] For Cantilupe's remarks, see Stacey, 'Conversion', pp. 277–8, citing and translating *Acta Sanctorum, Octobris* (Paris, 1866), vol. I, pp. 547–8. On this passage, see also Paul Brand, 'Jews and the law in England, 1275–90', *EHR*, 115 (2000), 1138–58, at 1152–3.

literary sources, that associate Jews with magic, murder, and excrement; and a new round of ritual crucifixion stories emerges at London, Lincoln, Bristol, and Northampton, stories to which the Crown now began to add its official endorsement.[59] Henry III's 1253 Statute of Jewry imposed a series of long-sought (but hitherto unenforced, at least in England) ecclesiastical limitations on Jewish life, including, for the first time, a serious attempt to enforce the Jewish badge.[60] These measures, intended as they were to segregate and isolate Jews, rested on the fundamental presumption that Jews were a polluting and a dangerous presence in Christian society, and that Jewish 'malice' took many forms: ritual and malicious murder of Christian boys, the seduction of Christian women, and the destruction, through money-lending, of Christian fortunes.

In the eyes of his Christian subjects, King Henry III's response to these perceived Jewish 'threats' to English society was characteristically irresolute. Although he issued the restrictive 1253 legislation, it remains unclear how seriously these measures were enforced.[61] Although he initially endorsed the 1255 ritual murder accusation involving 'little St Hugh of Lincoln', Henry freed the majority of the accused Jews of Lincoln, turning them over to the protection of his brother, Earl Richard of Cornwall. And most significantly of all, the king did nothing either to protect Christian debtors from the consequences of his own rapacious policies with respect to Jewish taxation, or to restrain his relatives and courtiers from profiting from the resulting traffic in encumbered estates and Jewish bonds. By 1258, these grievances, together with those arising from the king's own indebtedness and his impending excommunication over the Sicilian debacle, combined to produce a baronial uprising that removed King Henry from control over his own government.

The end of the reign, 1258–1275

Despite its 1258 promises, by 1263 neither the baronially controlled royal council nor the king himself had done anything to respond to the grievances of knights in danger of losing their property as a result of Jewish debts. As a result, in 1263 and 1264 a great many of these indebted knights joined Simon de Montfort in outright rebellion against the king. De Montfort had already shown his support for such indebted knights in 1260, when he and the Lord Edward had led a short-lived rising in London, during which they had broken into the Jewish exchequer and stolen its records of debt.[62] In 1263 and 1264, however, the attacks by de Montfort's partisans on Jews and Jewish property were far more destructive. The first, and most devastating, of the attacks occurred in London, probably in April 1264, in which scores (the chroniclers say hundreds) of Jews were killed, including several of the greatest Jewish

[59] R.C. Stacey, 'Anti-Semitism and the medieval English state', in J.R. Maddicott and D.M. Palliser, eds, *The Medieval State: Essays Presented to James Campbell* (London, 2000), pp. 163–77; id., 'From ritual crucifixion to Host desecration: Jews and the body of Christ', *Jewish History*, 12 (1998), 11–28; id., '1240–60', pp. 147–50.

[60] J.A. Watt, 'The English episcopate, the state and the Jews: the evidence of the thirteenth-century conciliar decrees', in P.R. Coss and S.D. Lloyd, eds, *Thirteenth-Century England II* (Woodbridge, 1988), pp. 137–47, at pp. 143–4.

[61] Brand, 'Jews and the law', pp. 1143–4.

[62] PRO, E159/33 m. 10, cited in Richmond, 'Englishness', n. 18.

magnates of the city. Similar assaults quickly followed at Canterbury, Worcester, Lincoln, Bedford, Bristol, Northampton, Winchester, and Nottingham. In 1266, the remnants of de Montfort's supporters, holed-up in the Isle of Ely, ventured forth to attack the Jews of Cambridge; and in 1267, in a final blow, Earl Gilbert de Clare led yet another assault on the Jews of London.[63]

These attacks arose primarily out of the grievances of knights indebted to Jewish lenders. In every case, the attackers made a deliberate effort to capture or destroy the chests in which Jewish debt records were stored; de Montfort then followed up these attacks with a comprehensive cancellation of Jewish debts on behalf of his supporters.[64] It must be stressed, however, that it was not indebtedness itself that was the problem. Overall levels of Christian indebtedness to Jews in England were significantly higher in the 1230s than they were by the 1260s, and yet they did not promote the kind of violence we see in the 1260s. Rather, what made indebtedness to Jews so dangerous by the 1260s was the fear that it would lead to the permanent loss of the land on which these debts were secured. And this fear was specifically the product of the king's own extortionate policies toward Jewish taxation from 1239 on, coupled with his willingness to support his relatives' and courtiers' efforts to acquire such encumbered estates for themselves.

In 1265, when King Henry at last recovered control over his government after the Battle of Evesham, he annulled de Montfort's cancellations of Jewish debts.[65] But it soon became apparent that the political firestorm Henry's policies had aroused since 1239 would not be so easily quenched. Desperate to raise money to pay off his debts and to finance his long-delayed crusade, King Henry tried repeatedly between 1268 and 1271 to secure permission to levy a tax from his Christian subjects. He quickly discovered, however, that the knights of the shire would insist upon legislation to limit Jewish moneylending before they would consent to any such tax. In 1269, after much bargaining, the king finally agreed to annul perpetual fee-rents held by Jews; to prohibit the sale of such fee-rents to Christians; to prohibit the sale of all other types of Jewish debts to Christians without royal permission; and to allow the Christian purchasers of Jewish debts to collect only the principal owing on such debts. But it was not until 1270 that the king received permission to assess and collect his tax from his disaffected knights; and even then he had to agree to further legislation in 1271 banning Jews from holding freehold land and ordering, yet again, the complete enforcement of the 1269 legislation.

Even these measures, however, were inadequate responses to the grievances King Henry's policies toward Jewish taxation had created since 1239. This fact became immediately clear in 1274, when the new king, Edward I, adopted his father's policies and imposed yet another huge tallage on the Jews of England. All the old abuses and fears were immediately exacerbated, and a chorus of protest erupted. The new king, however, was a more astute politician than his father had been. Realising the dangerous opposition that was now developing,

---

[63] For these attacks, see Roth, *History*³, pp. 61–2; Hillaby, 'London', pp. 135–6.

[64] For Montfort's pardons, see *CPR, 1258–66*, p. 628; Rigg, *Select Pleas* (see Abbreviations), p. 44.

[65] The argument of this paragraph is drawn from Stacey, 'Parliamentary negotiation', pp. 94–101, where full references can be found. This argument owes much to J.R. Maddicott, 'The crusade taxation of 1268–1270 and the development of Parliament', in *Thirteenth-Century England II*, pp. 93–117.

Edward consented, in October 1275, to a complete ban on Jewish money-lending, together with a number of humiliating new restrictions on English Jewish life. In return, however, he secured from his grateful Christian subjects a grant of taxation on a scale unimagined by his impecunious father. This was a lesson Edward would remember. In 1290, when he expelled the entire Jewish community of England, he received, in return, the largest single grant of taxation in the history of medieval England. King Henry's policies had bankrupted the English Jewish community; but his ruthless son found a way to make even a bankrupted and despoiled Jewish community turn a final profit for the Crown.

3

Edward I and the Final Phase of Anglo-Jewry

ROBIN R. MUNDILL

For almost six centuries a body of documents relating to the Expulsion of the Jews from England lay relatively unnoticed, firstly in the Tower of London and then in the Public Record Office. The handful of contemporary commentators on the exile of the Jews in 1290 made little more than just passing reference to the event.[1] Some interest in sources connected with the medieval Jews of England was kindled in the years leading up to the readmission of the Jews in the seventeenth century.[2] However it was not until the eighteenth century that the founding father of Anglo-Jewish studies, De Bloissiers Tovey, tried to draw general attention to the fate of a lost community.[3] It was the Anglo-Jewish Historical Exhibition of 1887 which provided the catalyst that led to the flourishing of a greater study of the first Anglo-Jewish communities.[4] This exhibition helped to inspire the foundation of the Jewish Historical Society of England in 1894, the works of Myer D. Davis and Joseph Jacobs on the Hebrew sources and the work of B. Lionel Abrahams.[5] The latter provided the first systematic approach to the sources for the Expulsion of the Jews and one of the first explanations of the Expulsion.[6]

Later historians, such as Cecil Roth, tended to accept Abrahams' evidence for the Expulsion at face value and it was not until the 1960s that such evidence was revisited with any real enthusiasm. H.G. Richardson became interested in what he referred to as 'documents of Jewish interest or Jewish documents' in the Public Record Office. Although later bitterly criticised by Gavin Langmuir for 'anarchic empiricism', Richardson wrote a chapter in his study of *The English Jewry under the Angevin Kings* that reconsidered some

---

[1] A fuller examination of the references made by contemporary chroniclers and the types of sources that survive for the study of the medieval Anglo-Jewry can be found in Mundill, *Solution* (see Abbreviations), pp. 1–15. Reviews of the historiography in greater depth can be found in Robert C. Stacey, 'Recent work on medieval English Jewish history', *JH*, 2 (1987), 61–72; Robin R. Mundill, 'English medieval Ashkenazim – literature and progress', *Aschkenas*, 1 (1991), 203–10.

[2] Roth, *History*[3] (see Abbreviations), pp. 148–54; Prynne, *Demurrer* (see Abbreviations); David S. Katz, *Philo-Semitism and the Readmission of the Jews to England 1603–1655* (Oxford, 1982).

[3] De Bloissiers Tovey, *Anglia Judaica* (Oxford, 1738).

[4] Stacey refers to this as 'The Heroic Age' of Anglo-Jewish historical scholarship: Stacey, 'Recent work', p. 61; *Anglo Jewish Exhibition* (see Abbreviations).

[5] Davis, *Deeds* (see Abbreviations); Jacobs, *Jews* (see Abbreviations).

[6] B. Lionel Abrahams, 'The debts and houses of the Jews of Hereford in 1290', *TJHSE*, 1 (1893–4), 136–59; id., 'The expulsion of the Jews from England in 1290', *JQR*, 7 (1894), 75–100, 236–58, 428–58; id., 'Condition of the Jews of England at the time of their expulsion in 1290', *TJHSE*, 2 (1894–5), 76–105; id., 'The economic and financial position of the Jews in medieval England', *TJHSE*, 8 (1915–17), 171–89.

aspects of the Expulsion and rejected the prevailing idea that the Jews were expelled because they were no longer of financial significance to the Crown.[7] This was followed by a rekindling of interest in the Expulsion, which has opened debate and has led to the consideration of many other aspects of Anglo-Jewish history.

The Expulsion: Sources and records

The history of the medieval Anglo-Jewish community has always been over-shadowed and dominated by the Expulsion of that community in 1290. The Expulsion and Dissolution of the Jewries was an organised and well-orche-strated governmental operation, which has left a plethora of records for the historian. In the prelude to the final act of Expulsion such records include the laws and orders that affected the lives of the Jewish community. They include the issuing of safe conducts and the preparation for embarkation at ports as well as the details of the confiscation of Jewish-owned property, buildings, synagogues and burial grounds. They provide fine details of the appropriation, organisation and centralisation of Jewish credit notes from major towns in England in which Jewish communities had lived. The financial records also contain references to Jewish debts for several years after the final Expulsion.[8]

The Dissolution of the Jewries, which followed the Expulsion, involved the Exchequer clerks demanding details from the local sheriffs and officials regarding Jewish properties in several major towns. Once collated, these extents and valuations of Jewish property were given close consideration. The job of finding buyers for former Jewish properties was given to Hugh of Kendal. He was not slow in realising this 'windfall' as a source for royal finance.[9] Between 1291 and 1292 Edward I made eighty-five separate grants to new owners of the former properties of 113 Jews.[10] He also confiscated the debts which were owed to the Jews. *Archae* from twenty-one different towns were brought into Westminster in 1290. These were duly opened and the contents of them were enrolled.[11]

The grants of land and property only show the redistribution of Jewish lands after the Expulsion. It is clear that prior to 1290 many Jews had already lost their properties either by forfeit or by having been forced to sell. From 1272 until 1290, Edward granted many royal licences for Jews to sell their properties. The peak period for issues of these licences was 1280–1. The majority concerned properties that were in London.[12] What is inexplicable is that such

[7] Richardson, *English Jewry* (see Abbreviations). Gavin I. Langmuir, 'The Jews and archives of Angevin England: reflections on medieval anti-semitism', *Traditio*, 19 (1963), 183–244, at 183–7.

[8] For a wider perspective on the mechanics of the Expulsion, see Mundill, *Solution*, pp. 249–59.

[9] PRO, E101/250/1; British Library Additional Manuscripts 24511, fols 48–9. By December 1290 Hugh of Kendal had realised just over £1,835 from former Jewish properties: Zefira Entin Rokeah, ed., *Medieval English Jews and Royal Officials: Entries of Jewish Interest in the English Memoranda Rolls, 1266–1293* (Jerusalem, 2000), entries 1239–43.

[10] British Library Lansdowne MSS 826, 4, fols 28–64; see also Mundill, *Solution*, pp. 257–60.

[11] Only details for eleven towns have survived: PRO, E101/249/29 and E101/250/2–12.

[12] See Robin R. Mundill, 'The Jewish entries from the Patent Rolls 1272–1292', *JHS*, 32 (1990–2), 25–88.

sources only reveal the properties that had been owned by about forty Jews. Not all Jews were property owners, and this number together with those property holders identified during the period 1291–2 might account for as many as 600 Jews. It thus poses an, as yet, unanswered question as to where the rest of the Jewish community lived.[13] Whatever the answer it is clear that the Jewish community under the rule of Edward I was unsettled.

Jewish settlement in Edwardian England

Even before Edward's return to England from crusade in 1274 his government seems to have been preoccupied and concerned with exactly where Jews had settled. In the early 1270s, Prior Joseph de Chauncy issued orders to seventeen sheriffs to the effect that all Jews should come in to the main towns from the 'vills outside'.[14] This preoccupation with where Jews lived led to local expulsions and to tighter control on Jewish residence. On 18 June 1273 the royal council issued instructions to the barons and bailiffs of the port of Winchelsea in Kent. They were to remove those Jews who had, 'recently entered the town . . . . without delay, without any damage to their bodies or goods – as according to the custom of the king's Jewry, Jews ought not to dwell in any cities or boroughs or towns except those wherein they were wont to dwell of old time'.[15] A similar royal order was issued in October 1274 to the sheriff of Shropshire instructing him to remove the Jews who had entered and were dwelling in the town of Bridgnorth.[16]

The polarisation of Jewish residence was to become even more pronounced. After his arrival in England, Edward I visited his mother, Eleanor of Provence, in early 1275.[17] Edward gave her permission to make her will and to enter the convent of Amesbury in Wiltshire (8 miles north of Salisbury).[18] Eleanor demanded the removal of the Jews from her lands, which she held as 'dower towns' – towns or lands that gave her an income. On 12 January 1275 Edward granted that, 'no Jew shall dwell or stay in any towns which the queen mother holds in dower'.[19] The Jewish community of Marlborough was expelled on 16 January 1275 and was moved to Devizes. The communities of Jews at Gloucester were moved to Bristol, those of Worcester to Hereford and those of Cambridge to Norwich. The dowager queen held several other towns such as Andover in Hampshire, Bath in Gloucestershire and Guildford in Surrey.[20] Although it was

---

[13] Mundill, *Solution*, p. 26, for a recent estimate of the Jewish population.
[14] Zefira Entin Rokeah, 'A Hospitaller and the Jews: Brother Joseph de Chauncy and English Jewry in the 1270s', *JHS*, 34 (1994–6), 189–207, at 189.
[15] *CCR 1272–1279*, p. 50.
[16] *CCR 1242–1247*, p. 130.
[17] L.F. Salzman, *Edward I* (London, 1968), p. 47.
[18] M. Biles, 'The indomitable Belle: Eleanor of Provence', in Richard H. Bowers, ed., *Seven Studies in Medieval English History and other Essays presented to Harold S. Snellgrove* (Mississippi, 1983), pp. 113–31, at p. 129.
[19] Mundill, 'Jewish entries', p. 48.
[20] Rigg, *Select Pleas* (see Abbreviations), p. 95; it is possible that these expulsions in 1275 also affected Guildford: Mary Alexander, 'A possible synagogue in Guildford', in G. de Boe and F. Verhaeghe, eds, *Religion and Belief in Medieval Europe: papers of the Medieval Europe 1997 Conference, Brugge*, IV (Bruges, 1997).

not mentioned directly in the grant there is clear evidence that the Jews were also removed from Andover. In January 1275 Jacob Cok, a Jew, brought a charge of felony against Guy de Tanton who had forcibly removed him from Andover on Eleanor's orders.[21] In the same year the Statute of the Jewry ruled that all Jews must only live in towns with *archae*. Such restrictions must have led to turmoil for many Jewish families and again the records attest to the subsequent disposal of many former Jewish-held domiciles. Six years after they had been forcibly removed from Marlborough the former Jewish domiciles were granted to a close-knit group of Queen Eleanor's household.[22] Perhaps such actions were, as Barrie Dobson has hinted, dry runs for total expulsion.[23]

Tallage and taxation

Another area concerning the Edwardian Jewry that has received some attention in recent years is the tallages or the taxes that were levied from the Jewish community. Originally these were taken piecemeal by historians to show that the community had become impoverished and thus provided a motive for their expulsion. It cannot be denied that many Jews became impoverished and several entries, such as the payment made by 'two poor Jews of Northampton', testify to this.[24] However, a close examination reveals that the situation had not changed much from that before Magna Carta and that taxation on the Jews also became a tax on their debtors.[25]

Although much has been achieved in studying this aspect of the Anglo-Jew there is still a large amount of work to be done to make complete sense of the Edwardian tallages. Sir Hilary Jenkinson once referred to the evidence for these as 'dull . . . and repetitious at times but plentiful and detailed'.[26] Peter Elman was the first to try to tackle this gargantuan task, and his preliminary examinations showed a general pattern in the tallage assessments:

> The imposition of tallage became severer and more frequent towards the forties of the century; it fell off during the Baronial wars to rise to its apex around the year 1275. There appears to have been a more or less close synchronization between the rise and fall of the Jewish tallages and the general history of the thirteenth century.[27]

There are, however, specific difficulties in Elman's approach to the tallages of Edward's reign. There is a danger that in placing the apex at around 1275 he undervalued the importance of the last tallage of 1287. There are also problems posed by the opposite poles of 'tallage assessed' and 'tallage collected'. Indeed, according to Elman's figures of tallage assessed during Edward I's reign, just over £35,664 was demanded from the Jewish community. However, the tallage

---

[21] *Seventh Report of the Deputy Keeper of the Public Records* (London, 1846), p. 240.

[22] Mundill, 'Jewish entries', p. 71.

[23] R.B. Dobson, 'The Jews of medieval Cambridge', *JHS*, 32 (1990–2), 1–24, at 17–18.

[24] PRO, E401/1567.

[25] Ralph V. Turner, *King John* (London and New York, 1984), pp. 107, 218–19, 226–7, 241.

[26] Sir Hilary Jenkinson, 'The records of Exchequer Receipts from the English Jewry', *TJHSE*, 8 (1915–17), 19–54, at 20.

[27] Peter Elman, 'Jewish finance in thirteenth century England with special reference to royal taxation', *BIHR*, 15 (1938), 112–13, at 112.

receipts only show payments for the same period as £9,272.[28] This apparent discrepancy is further complicated by the fact that payments for tallage do not necessarily appear on one special roll. Neither were tallage payments all in cash. Payments for tallage could be hidden in payments made by officials and labelled by the Exchequer scribes as simply *de debitis pluribus Judeis*. Finally, there are a whole range of intricate dealings, mystery and unanswered questions where demands for a single tallage become blurred into new tallages and the collection of arrears.[29]

No better example of such difficulties can be provided than by the evidence of the Great Tallage of 1274, which has left behind it the largest amount of documentary evidence for any thirteenth-century tallage imposed upon the Jews. It provides a serious challenge in trying to reconstruct accurate estimates of the final amount that was collected. Thus far the available evidence does not seem to indicate that the Great Tallage realised as much as the assessors had hoped.[30]

Further tallages followed, and these have left evidence of a different type. It is evident that a general scrutiny of the Jewish *archae* preceded a tallage. Such a scrutiny was ordered sometime between December 1275 and February 1276.[31] Richardson claimed that the tallage of 1276 was nominally £1,000, which he asserted was paid in cash by the Jews and with 'remarkable promptitude'.[32] The receipt roll for this particular tallage has survived. By 13 December 1276, £954 8s 3d had been collected, and a further £22 6s 8d as well as the Hereford fine was collected by 14 February 1277. For once a target assessed by the Crown had been almost realised.[33]

The Jews were tallaged again in 1277, but the evidence for this tallage is extremely thin.[34] The Exchequer of the Jews was certainly kept busy that year. In April 1277, now preoccupied by the Welsh wars, Edward ordered the governmental departments of state to move to Shrewsbury where, by September, they took up residence in the abbey.[35] In May 1277 the king empowered Hugh de Digneuton to make an enquiry throughout the land as to where the Jews were living and also to enforce the wearing of the *tabula*.[36] Later in the same month the king ordered John de Cobham, Philip de Willoughby and William de Middleton to assess a tallage on the Jews.[37] In June the king sent Roger of Northwood to Canterbury to reopen the *archa*, which had presumably been sealed since the last scrutiny. Roger was empowered to transcribe all the charters in it and to deliver those that were quit to the Christian debtors. On

---

[28] W.M. Ormrod, 'Royal finance in thirteenth-century England', in P.R. Coss and S.D. Lloyd, eds, *Thirteenth Century England V* (Woodbridge, 1995), pp. 141–64, at pp. 149 and 162.

[29] In any such investigation, it is also important to differentiate between tallage and non-tallage Receipt Rolls: see Jenkinson, 'Records', pp. 31–7; Rokeah *Medieval English Jews*, pp. 363–4; Mundill, *Solution*, pp. 74–5 and 79.

[30] Mundill, *Solution*, pp. 81–6.

[31] Some of these scrutinies remain extant: *ibid.*, p. 151, Table 8.

[32] Richardson, *English Jewry*, pp. 215–16.

[33] PRO, E401/1572.

[34] Richardson, *English Jewry*, p. 216. A single roll survives, which records payments totalling £10 5s 7d made between September 1276 and February 1277: PRO, E401/1573.

[35] G.O. Sayles, ed., *Select Cases in King's Bench: Edward 1st*, II (London, 1936–9), p. lxiii.

[36] *CPR 1272–81*, p. 240.

[37] *Ibid.*, p. 211.

the evidence of governmental activity alone it does seem that preparations for another tallage were being made.[38]

Recent research has helped to clarify some of the controversy surrounding the last tallage collection of Edward's reign. Elman referred to the tallage assessment of 1287 for 20,000 marks (£13,333 6s 8d) as the final turn of the screw but claimed that there was little evidence that it was collected.[39] Roth claimed that on 2 May 1287 there was a sudden reversion to the harsh methods of past reigns, in that all the leading Jews were arrested and imprisoned as a preliminary to exacting a fresh tallage.[40] Richardson compromised in claiming that the tallage of 1287 and 1288 yielded £4,023 8s 9d, but remained sceptical about the imprisonment. But it seems there is no reason, in fact, to doubt that these well-used methods to extract money from the Jews were tried again, and new evidence has recently emerged for the last Jewish tallage in the reign of Edward I.[41]

Imprisonment or protection?

Imprisonment for non-payment of tallage and for other reasons was something that was common among the lives of the Jewish community. Thus many of the Edwardian Anglo-Jews knew the Tower of London fairly intimately. The Tower was of course a repository, a prison and an administrative centre. At the end of Henry's reign the sheriff of Oxford expended 13s 4d on conveying Lumbard and Boneveye of Cricklade from Oxford to the Tower.[42] It was also a safe haven in uncertain times, as on 25 November 1272 when Ben' fil Cok', a London Jew, was 'in hiding in the tower of London because of the king's death'.[43] Further evidence remains that throws some light on the relationship between the Jews of London and the authorities at the Tower.

During the period 20 January 1275–8 June 1277 many Jews were imprisoned inside the liberty of the Tower. A surviving record hints as to the conditions of their imprisonment there.[44] Jews paid for celebrating festivals. Four pious Jews paid £2 13s 4d to keep New Year and Yom Kippur. Jews were lodged in the tiled stable, a Jewess in the Elephant house, and others in the tower beyond the Elephant house, Hagin's Tower, Brother John's stable and the tower of Benedict of Winchester. While under arrest within the Tower they clearly still had money, and there are also references to coinage offences outside the Tower liberty for passing light half-pennies in the fishmarket and for exchanging coin. Details of everyday life in the running of the London Jewry are also revealed, including

[38] *CPR 1272–81*, p. 215.
[39] Peter Elman, 'The economic causes of the expulsion of the Jews in 1290', *Economic History Review*, 7 (1936–7), 145–54, at 146.
[40] *CCR 1279–88*, p. 456. Roth, *History*³, p. 79.
[41] Richardson, *English Jewry*, p. 227; Roth, *History*³, p. 275. F.C. Hungeston, ed., *Johannis Capgrave Liber de Illustribus Henricis* (RS, London, 1858), p. 167; *Annales Londonienses*, in W. Stubbs, ed., *Chronicles of the Reigns of Edward I and Edward II*, I (RS, London, 1882), p. 96; Rokeah, *Medieval English Jews*, pp. 363–4, where she corrects my initial findings.
[42] Rokeah, *Medieval English Jews*, entry 449.
[43] *Ibid.*, entry 430.
[44] A roll kept by William of Graveley, Serjeant of the Tower, exists of receipts and perquisites from the Jews of London from 20 January 1275 to 8 June 1277. The monies were handed over to Stephen de Pencestre, Walter de Heliun and John de Cobham. PRO, E101/249/22.

episodes of Christians fighting there. Nicholas the Convert, goldsmith of London, was fined £5 for his servants fighting in the Jewry. Further conflicts and strains between the two communities are also revealed when Josce of Bedford was fined £5 for spitting and a further £2 for spitting back at a certain Christian. Christians were fined for being in the Jewry by night. Capyun was fined for striking and beating a Christian. Mendaunt le Bocher and Jaew were fined for fighting on Easter day. Jews were also imprisoned elsewhere in London, and the community of the Jews of London paid £13 17s for the gates of the Guildhall. Two York Jews remained imprisoned in the Guildhall. The Jews of Stamford paid £1 10s 0d to be by themselves. During their imprisonments Abraham of Dorking, Mendant of Fulham and Capion were fined for dicing.[45]

It is now some twenty years since Vivian Lipman highlighted the conditions of the Jews who were imprisoned in the Tower. He also established the connection between Jewries and castles.[46] Imprisonment was obviously a constant threat to the Jewish community, which was to grow under Edward I's rule. In Hereford, in the 1250s, the Jews' prison, which was below the ring wall of the castle keep and was in disrepair, was rebuilt.[47] Encapsulated in a piece of graffito in Winchester castle was further evidence for the imprisonments that accompanied the collection of the 1287 tallage: 'On Friday, Eve of the Sabbath in which the pericope *Emor* is read, all the Jews of the Land of the Isle were imprisoned. I, Asher, wrote this. 2 May 1287.'[48] For many Jews the last decade of Edward's reign meant confinement or worse.

Increasing pressure: Coinage offences

Probably the worst imprisonments were during the coin-clipping allegations of 1278–9. Many years ago I was first drawn to references of 'suspensi' and 'damnati'.[49] I was also affected by a reference to the Lincoln Jewess, Belasset of Wallingford, who had once owned the fine house, now known as Jews House, on Steep Hill in Lincoln.[50] I was stunned by a reference made to a mass hanging of over 280 Jews in London.[51] Such references also drew the attention of Dr Zefira Rokeah, who had already begun to work on the inventories of goods of Jews who had been condemned during these years, which in themselves form a major contribution to the social life of Edwardian Anglo-Jewry.[52] However, she

---

[45] PRO, E101/249/22, printed in *CPREJ*, IV, pp. 148–94.

[46] Vivian D. Lipman, 'Jews and castles in medieval England', *TJHSE*, 28 (1984), 1–19.

[47] Ron Shoesmith, *A Short History of Castle Green and Hereford Castle* (Hereford, 1980), p. 19.

[48] Roth, *History³*, p. 275.

[49] Lipman, *Norwich* (see Abbreviations), pp. 168–71; PRO, C/47/9/50.

[50] John Ross, *Annales Lincolniae* (unpublished, handwritten, Lincoln Public Library), 3, pp. 219, 252. This of course was not the only time there were mass arrests in Lincoln: in 1255 over one hundred Lincoln Jews were transported to the Tower for their alleged part in the death of Little St Hugh of Lincoln. Roth also confirms the hangings of over 293 Jews as a result of the 1278 coin-clipping allegations: Cecil Roth, *Medieval Lincoln and its Jewry* (London, 1934), pp. 17 and 19.

[51] Ross, *Annales Lincolniae*, 3, p. 219, citing Mathew of Westminster.

[52] Zefira Entin Rokeah,'Some accounts of condemned Jews' property in the Pipe and Chancellor's Rolls: part 1', *Bulletin of the Institute of Jewish Studies*, 1 (1973) 19–42; part 2, *ibid.*, 2 (1974), 59–82; part 3, *ibid.*, 3 (1975), 41–66; Michael Adler, 'Inventory of the property of the condemned Jews, 1285', *MJHSE*, 2 (1935), 56–71.

was to take her research much further. Despite the rather pithy references by chroniclers and historians alike, her work has thrown more light on the coin-clipping arrests of 1278–9, which can only be seen as a watershed in the lives of the Edwardian Jewry.[53]

Rokeah has put the matter of the scale of these persecutions beyond any further doubt. Her lists of condemned Jews read like a register of leading Edwardian Jews and show that many different Jewish settlements were affected. She proves that for every Christian executed for coinage offences over ten Jews were also executed. Her work can be taken to show the sufferings and miseries of nothing more than a general pogrom in 1278–9.[54] She has also shown how those accused were rounded up. In 1280, the sheriff of Oxford expended £2 16s 0d 'spent on carrying various Jews arrested for clipping the king's money from Oxford to London'.[55] The sheriff of Northampton was given £3 6s 8d for conveying various Jews from Northampton at different times.[56] In 1281 the sheriff of Oxford received £1 13s 4d for carrying some prisoners from Oxford to Newgate and 'for baptizing some Jewish children'.[57] The late 1270s and the early 1280s were extremely dark days for the Jewish community, but there was worse to come.

The 'Edwardian Experiment' and the Expulsion

For most of last century the explanation behind the Expulsion of the Jews from England remained a purely economic one.[58] In recent years historians have stepped out of this model, and it is now widely acknowledged that there are many factors behind the final solution of the medieval Anglo-Jewry. Gain is of course still a favourite, and this line of argument, which takes its roots from Holinshed, has more recently been argued by Robert Stacey.[59] Sociological aspects have been argued by Sophia Menache.[60] A new investigation of the Expulsion from Gascony in 1287, originally identified as crucial by Salzman and Richardson, has also done much to help put the English Expulsion into a wider context. It does seem possible, that as Wade Labarge pointed out, Gascony was a testing ground for Edward's policies in England. It is frighteningly obvious that some of those who administered the Gascon

[53] Zefira Entin Rokeah, 'Money and the hangman in late thirteenth-century England: Jews, Christians and coinage offences alleged and real: part 1', *JHS*, 31 (1988–90), 83–109; part 2, *ibid.*, 32 (1990–2), 159–218.
[54] Rokeah, 'Money and the hangman, part 1', p. 108, n. 71, surveys the various chroniclers' accounts of the hanging of over 280 Jews. Her lists for coinage offences show that the communities at London, York, Northampton, Lincoln, Norwich, Oxford and Bristol suffered over 58 per cent of the charges: 'Money and the hangman, part 2'.
[55] Rokeah, *Medieval English Jews*, entry 873.
[56] *Ibid.*, entry 876.
[57] *Ibid.*, entry 904.
[58] For a recent review and new consideration of the causes of the expulsion, see Mundill, *Solution*, pp. 249–85.
[59] Robert Stacey, 'Parliamentary negotiation and the expulsion of the Jews from England', in R.H. Britnell, R. Frame and M. Prestwich, eds, *Thirteenth-Century England VI* (Woodbridge, 1997), pp. 77–101.
[60] Sophia Menache, 'The king, the Church and the Jews: some considerations on the expulsions from England and France', *JMH*, 13 (1987), 223–36.

Expulsion were the same governmental *curiales* who held sway over the English Expulsion.[61]

Yet much of the explanation for the Expulsion of 1290 still lies in the 'Edwardian Experiment' of 1275.[62] It is in the workings and implications of the Statute of the Jewry of 1275 that historians still have more to glean of medieval society in general. When Edward passed the statute it was immediately copied and sent to the Justices of the Jews and sealed with the Exchequer seal.[63] It was widely promulgated and the Jewish community were well aware of it.[64] Some of the major effects of this have been discussed elsewhere, but it is clear that this was the death knell of the medieval Jewish community. It put impossible restrictions on the community as a whole, confining them as it did to live in the *archae* towns, enforcing the wearing of the *tabula* and strengthening a poll tax for the upkeep of the *Domus Conversorum*.[65]

However, the last two clauses of the statute addressed the new role of the Jew within society as defined by Edward I. The first encouraged the Jews to 'gain their living by lawful merchandise and their labour . . . by selling and buying'. This permission to become legal merchants has caused much debate. As Roth commented: 'For the first time in English history they were empowered to become merchants and artisans.'[66] The wider evidence shows that many Jews did conform and become merchants living by buying and selling commodities.[67] The second clause allowed the Jews to buy houses where they lived and gave them a special fifteen-year licence to take and buy farms or land 'that they may be able to gain their living in the World'.[68]

Case history: Abraham and Isaac fil Deulecresse

A case history of the effects of the statute and the realities of what happened to some of the Jewish population after it had been passed is provided by the plight of two Norwich Jews. With grim irony, in eighteenth-century Norwich on the corner of a plot, known even then as Abraham's Hall, an inn sign bore a depiction of Abraham offering up Isaac for sacrifice.[69] The fate of two Norwich Jewish brothers, Abraham and Isaac fil Deulecresse, amply exemplifies some of the changes that confronted the Anglo-Jewish communities during the final years before the Expulsion.

[61] Mundill, *Solution*, pp. 281–2; M. Wade Labarge, *Gascony: England's First Colony, 1204–1453* (London, 1980), pp. 41–4.

[62] Mundill, *Solution*, p. 14, and for actual document, pp. 291–3.

[63] Rokeah, *Medieval English Jews*, entry 701.

[64] Mundill, *Solution*, p. 121; Paul R. Brand, 'Jews and the law in England, 1275–1290', *EHR*, 115 (2000), 1138–58, at 1140–4.

[65] The *Domus Conversorum* or House of Converted Jews in London on the site of the old Public Record Office, Chancery Lane: Mundill, *Solution*, pp. 119–21; Brand, 'Jews and the law', pp. 1140–2.

[66] Roth, *History*[3], pp. 70–1.

[67] Robin R. Mundill, 'Anglo-Jewry under Edward I: credit agents and their clients', *JHS*, 31 (1988–90), 1–21; id., *Solution*, pp. 146–208; id., 'Edwardian Jewry: usurers or legal merchants?' *JCH*, 3 (2000), 73–97.

[68] Mundill, *Solution*, p. 293.

[69] Vivian D. Lipman, 'The Roth "Hake" manuscript', in John M. Shaftesley, ed., *Remember the Days: Essays in Honour of Cecil Roth* (London, 1966), pp. 49–71, at p. 53; Lipman, *Norwich*, pp. 125–9.

By the 1250s Abraham fil Deulecresse was clearly an important member of the local community. In August 1251 the sheriff of Norfolk and the chirographers of the Norwich *archa* were ordered 'to lay no hand on Abraham fil Deulecresse or on his chattels and if any of them have been seized to restore them forthwith . . .' as he had paid his tallage.[70] By 1258 Abraham was already involved with buying properties in Norwich itself. His subsequent dealings were to secure him a whole block of messuages, which became known as Abraham's Hall. By the time of his death he even owned seven shops that fronted on to the Sheepmarket and the Haymarket while at the same time backing on to the Horsemarket.[71] Operating within the city he continued to build his business. More of his dealings and successful settlements were duly recorded by the Norwich chirographers.[72]

His dealings took him further afield from Norwich in search of business.[73] In 1259, two bonds made between Abraham and John Oilly 'which came from the Chirographers' chest at Lincoln among the chattels of the condemned Jews of Lincoln . . .' were delivered to Norwich and Abraham was granted free administration of them.[74] Abraham even sold a property to Peter, the parson of Newgate, in 1265. Interestingly, over this transaction he had to have the consent of his wife, Abigail, who resigned her claims on the property on account of her marriage settlement.[75] He continued to buy up properties in St Stephen's parish.[76] He even appears to have become a landlord when he received a quitclaim from Semann Wruiel of a yearly rent of 2s that Simon Wriuel was accustomed to receive from Benedict fil Avegaye.[77] In order to raise money for Prince Edward in 1266 several of his larger debts totalling £60 were taken from the *archa*. At the same time the Crown fined the chirographers of Norwich a further £10 because they had continued to place and extract charters in the chest even though Symon Le Paumer who had the key had been captured by outlaws.[78] In 1269, Robert son of Eustace the Baker had granted Abraham a stall in the draper's quarter in the market place at Norwich.[79]

Early in Edward's reign, Abraham became one of the two Jewish chirographers in Norwich as the Justices of the Jews requested that Samuel of Norwich and Abraham fil Deulecresse have their portion of one penny for each charter extracted from the Norwich *archa*.[80] In July 1274, he even had to extract all of his own charters in response to a demand for arrears of tallages.[81] Thirty-seven of his charters were taken out of the *archa* and were not replaced until his tallage payments were settled.[82] Some of his tallage at least was paid by one of his Christian debtors, William Cumin, tenant of the land once held by John son

---

[70] WAM (see Abbreviations) 6951.
[71] Lipman, *Norwich*, p. 128.
[72] WAM 6926, 6948, 6981.
[73] *CPREJ*, I, p. 180.
[74] WAM 6906.
[75] WAM 6792.
[76] WAM 6713, 6712, 6716.
[77] WAM 6079.
[78] WAM 6921.
[79] WAM 6709.
[80] WAM 9067.
[81] WAM 6980.
[82] WAM 6725 and 9010.

of William de Wikham. This payment was ordered by brother Luke de Hemmington. A charter for £26 13s 4d in the names of John and Abraham was taken from the Sudbury *archa* delivered and acquitted – these monies were only a partial payment.[83]

Abraham's dealings were not just confined to Norwich but involved him in land transactions in the surrounding countryside. In 1275, in the presence of the two Justices of the Jews, he made a *starr* at Norwich that was later enrolled on the Plea Roll. In it Abraham acknowledged and waived his rights 'from the creation to the end of the world' to the lands, rents, liberties, pastures and marshes in the villages of Marham (Marsham) and Heuingham (Hevingham) and other vills that had belonged to Isabel Malerbe.[84]

But of greater interest, for the light it throws on the effects of the statute, is a case brought before the Justices of the Jews in 1276 by John de Gurnay. John asked for Abraham fil Deulecresse to come to account for the debts that he owed him. Abraham came with three bonds worth £120.[85] John claimed that for a debt of £40 he had paid £24 on 1 November 1275 and had also paid £15 on 13 April 1276 for a debt of £30. A third debt for £50 had been negotiated with Abraham by John and two other Christians. For this last debt Abraham did not demand any payment from John but asked for his right of recovery against the two other Christians. John invoked the Statute of the Jewry, claiming 'that the King granted of his grace to Christians indebted in Jewry that all penalties and usuries should cease from the feast of 13 October 1275 retrospectively'. The other two Christians, Hervey and William, simply stated that the claim for £50 was unlawful as they had a *starr* made by Abraham that set down payments amounting to £15 16s 6d and one coomb (half a quarter) of wheat payable on 18 November 1275. They claimed they had made payment of 16s 6d and the cereal on 11 November 1275 and they still owed only £15. Abraham said that he had received nothing. Subsequently a valuation was made of John's lands, which came to £17 3s 1d, and the whole case was handed over to the judgment of Edward I himself.[86]

It was perhaps no surprise that John de Gurnay received such personal attention. He was clearly in favour with the king and a royal knight who was described as 'having provided long, faithful and praiseworthy service in the Holy land and elsewhere'.[87] The king delivered his judgment 'in keeping with the recent provision and grant made graciously to Christians indebted in the Jewry'. He instructed the barons to allow John to have his chief residence and half of his lands and to allow him reasonable terms to pay the debts.[88] Both John and Abraham were again summoned in front of the Justices. They stated that John owed Abraham a clear debt of £54 16s 6d (without penalties and usuries). They admitted that the total amount of John's property was £17 3s 1d,

[83] Rokeah, *Medieval English Jews*, entry 629.
[84] *CPREJ*, III, pp. 71–2.
[85] *Ibid.*, III, pp. 167–8. The other two Christian debtors were Hervey son of John of Surlyngham (Surlingham) and William son of John of Redlond of Corston.
[86] *Ibid.*
[87] Rokeah, *Medieval English Jews*, entry 720; Simon Lloyd, *English Society and the Crusade 1216–1272* (Oxford, 1988), Appendix 4, p. 266, shows a John de Gurnay with connections in Norfolk and Suffolk; Sir John de Gurney who went on crusade had lands in Harpole, Wootton and Hardingham in Norfolk: C. Moor, *Knights of Edward 1st* (Harleian Society, 81, 1929), p. 163.
[88] Rokeah, *Medieval English Jews*, entry 718.

and they finally ruled that Abraham was to have half the lands valued at £8 11s 6½d per year and John was to pay Abraham by instalments of £4 5s 9¼d, the first of which was payable on 13 October 1276, the second on 11 April 1277 and so on annually until the debt was paid off. They stressed that the money must be paid to the Jew in his house.[89]

John de Gurnay died in 1281. His son, William, inherited his debts and Edward allowed him the same terms.[90] However, there was further confusion at the Exchequer and a claim was made against William for £120. As a result of this William Gurnay was summoned to appear in front of the Justices of the Jews on 18 April 1282.[91] It was clarified that John de Gurnay's debts to Abraham had been only £54 16s 6d. However, in the pogroms of 1278–9, Abraham fil Deulecresse of Norwich had been hanged 'for a money trespass and some other trespasses . . .' As in all such cases the property had reverted to the king. Sometime in 1284 William came to London and brought with him four *starrs* concerning payments his father had made – £4 5s 9½d on 11 April 1277, a similar sum on 29 September 1277 and at the following Easter (17 April 1278), and a similar amount on 29 September 1278. However, William also brought a further *starr* in which Abraham acknowledged that if John were to pay £5, a quarter of wheat and two quarters of oats on 2 February 1279 then Abraham would cancel all debts between him and John in the Norwich *archa*. If John failed to pay then a pardon would not happen and the debts would continue.

William claimed that his father had gone to the chirographers of the Norwich *archa* on 2 February 1279 with the money and the grain but the chirographers would not accept the payment as by that time Abraham had been accused of coin-clipping and taken and imprisoned at the Tower of London. To try and verify William's story the barons called for a subsequent inquisition in the presence of the Jewish and Christian chirographers of the Norwich *archa* along with six Christians and six Jews. The case was heard at Norwich on 14 March 1285 in the presence of the Christian and the Jewish chirographers, Simon Le Paumer, Hubert de Merle, Isaac fil Deulecresse and Isaac le Chapelyn as well as other influential Christians and Jews. They all verified the legality of all of the *starrs* and the fact that John did attend at the *archa* with the payment in front of all of the chirographers in February 1279.[92]

This case illustrates the workings of the Exchequer of the Jews on a local level and shows that the statute was fairly strictly adhered to for the collection of debts. It also shows that by the late 1270s Abraham was prepared to have quantities of wheat and oats as part payment of a debt. It would seem that Abraham had started to diversify his interests. This switch to commodity repayments was being mirrored all over the Jewish communities of England.[93] There is further evidence of this change in Abraham's repayments. In 1277

---

[89] Rokeah, *Medieval English Jews*, entry 721. There were also provisions about the three parts of the bond.

[90] *Ibid.*, entry 893.

[91] *Ibid.*, entry 941.

[92] *Ibid.*, entry 975. They also stated that in that year a quarter of wheat was worth 5s and a quarter of oats was worth 2s.

[93] Mundill, *Solution*, pp. 146–208; Robin R. Mundill, 'Lumbard and son: the businesses and debtors of two Jewish moneylenders in late thirteenth century England', *JQR*, 82 (1991), 137–70.

Abraham fil Deulecresse acknowledged by his *starr* that he had quitted and pardoned Nigel Payn and his heirs of a debt for twelve quarters of wheat.[94] In 1278, Abraham was promised a hundred soams (quarters) of good dry wheat by Jacob fil Gilbert. The wheat was to be repaid 'according to worldly measure or for each sum a half a mark of silver' to Abraham or his attorney at his house in Norwich. Against this legal recognisance he pledged all his lands.[95]

The Statute of the Jewry had other impacts on the businesses of the Jews. In what Vivian Lipman dubbed the Kelling transaction, there are traces of references to land holding that were embodied in the Statute of 1275. In order to liquidate and clear up another debt, Abraham fil Deulecresse made a different form of agreement. Abraham had taken over a debt of £80 between Sir James fil Gilbert of Ilketshalle (Ilketshall in Suffolk) and Isaac fil Benedict of London. In 1277 a covenant was made in the Jewish Exchequer between James fil Gilbert, knight, and Abraham. James demised and handed over to Abraham all his land in Kelling (24 miles north-north-west of Norwich near the coast). This included all rights to meadows, pastures, roads, paths, reliefs, heriots, service of both free men and villeins, preserves, fisheries, ponds, rents and woods. The agreement was made 'according to the statutes of the King touching his Jewry'. James also granted Abraham his capital messuage with buildings and appurtenances for a period from 16 May 1277 to 29 September 1287.[96] It was also agreed that if Abraham wished to sell his rights in Kelling, first refusal would be given to James's family. A clause that stated that James would not be allowed to sell the land while it was under Abraham's control was included. The agreement was extremely detailed and even stated that if any houses fell into disrepair, then James would find timber and would meet all other expenses to repair them. Abraham subsequently deposited a signed digest of the agreement in the Norwich *archa* and took possession of the manor of Kelling.[97] Abraham was not to hold the land for long. As observed above, in 1279, he was 'drawn and burned for blasphemy'.[98] Subsequently the lease on the manor of Kelling was sold for £33 6s 8d to Thomas de Weylaund in June 1280.[99]

Abraham's brother, Isaac fil Deulecresse, also had influence outside the city of Norwich and encountered similar problems in pressing for his debts. In 1277 Isaac brought a case against William de Blouill' for a debt of £50. William's lands and chattels had already been valued and a moiety of them had been granted to Isaac. Isaac's attorney attended in London and claimed on his behalf that he had a moiety of de Blouill's cattle but that he was also due a moiety of his crops.[100] Evidently even after the Statute of 1275 Isaac still went on making cash loans. In a further judgment the barons and justices ruled that Robert le Estormy who owed Isaac fil Deulecresse £24 13s 4d should have respite of the debt penalties and usuries until 3 May 1287. They also ordered the distraint that had been imposed for the debt to be lifted.[101] Soon after this

[94] *CPREJ*, III, p. 303.
[95] *CPREJ*, V, entry 264, p. 42. This bond was technically worth 100 quarters at 6s 8d each, or £33 6s 8d, the price of the manor of Kelling (see below, note 99).
[96] *CPREJ*, III, p. 297; the Kelling transaction also in WAM 6811.
[97] WAM 6811
[98] *CChR*, II, p. 213.
[99] Mundill, *Solution,* p. 275; id., 'Jewish entries', p. 377.
[100] *CPREJ*, III, pp. 308–9.
[101] Rokeah, *Medieval English Jews*, entry 1081.

Table 1: Isaac fil Deulecresse's bonds in the
Norwich *archa* in 1290

Year	Number of bonds
1281	1
1282	0
1283	1
1284	6
1285	3
1286	1
1287	2
1288	3
1289	7
1290	0

Edward I seems to have intervened personally in a further debt that involved Isaac fil Deulecresse and Robert when he 'relaxed and pardoned such penalties and usuries' and ordered Robert to make a payment by 1 November 1287.[102] Despite the problems he encountered in pressing for his debts, Isaac was singled out by the officials preparing for the 1287 tallage as being one of the more important 'among the richer and more prudent Jews' of the Norwich community.[103]

The extant bonds in the Norwich *archa* confirm that Isaac was probably the richest lender in late Edwardian Norwich. Certainly the details of his twenty-four transactions confirm this. They were worth a face value of £338 13s 4d. They also show how Isaac was able to continue acting as a creditor between 1281 and 1290 (Table 1).[104] Isaac, like his brother before him, seems to have diversified and to now favour bonds that demanded return in cereal. Of his twenty-four bonds, fifteen demanded repayment of 470 quarters of cereal, seven demanded twenty-six sacks of wool and two demanded £8 13 4d in cash.[105] The bonds that demanded repayment in specie were dated 1288 and 1289 and show that making agreements for monetary repayments were either not totally outlawed in 1275 or made a return in the 1280s.[106] What is revealing is the fact that one of these bonds for repayment in specie was made with a client with whom Isaac had previous dealings in a transaction made in January 1285, which offered a cereal repayment.[107] Isaac's transactions clearly reflect the effects of the Statute of 1275 upon local dealings. They also show that there was

---

[102] Rokeah, *Medieval English Jews*, entry 1083.
[103] *Ibid.*, entries 1116 ff.
[104] PRO, E101/250/7.
[105] Lipman, *Norwich*, pp. 164–7.
[106] For fuller discussion of this point, see Mundill, *Solution*, pp. 128–9.
[107] In 1285 Warin de Hereford, knight, fil Thomas of Hereford and William fil John Palefrey of Coston owed Isaac forty quarters of cereal. In 1288 William fil John Palfrey of Coston and John fil Roger of Barnham owed £2: PRO, E101/250/7. Sir Warin de Hereford was in debt for over £800 to Edmund Earl of Cornwall in 1275. In 1282 he held a knight's fee at Hareham in Norfolk: Moor, *Knights*, p. 220.

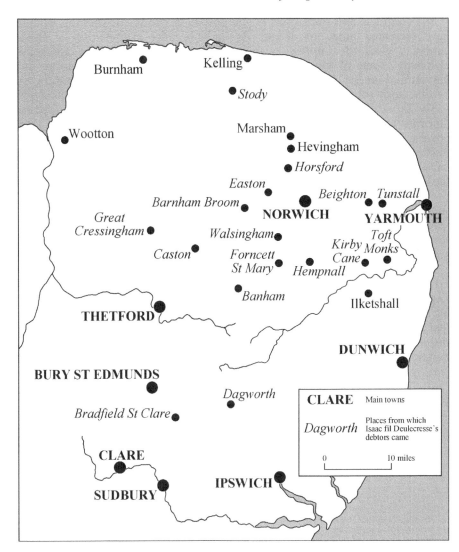

Map 2. Distribution of the debtors of Isaac fil Deulecresse of Norwich, 1281–90

no need to camouflage transactions as it was still possible to demand monetary repayments.[108] Isaac, who had after all had close dealings with the Justices of the Jews, who had lost his brother in the coin-clipping allegations and who was a chirographer, was unlikely to make fraudulent transactions. His bonds clearly reflect a major shift towards a preference for commodity repayments in the closing decade of Jewish presence.

[108] Mundill, *Solution*, pp. 146–208.

The contracts and operations of the post-1275 bonds elsewhere in Britain have presented much to debate. A much broader examination of these contracts gives the impression that, despite the dominance of Christian merchants, some of the wealthier Jews were able to make advances on the harvest and on the clip and in some cases, within the spirit of the statute, to become fairly successful legal merchants who thus avoided the taint of usury.[109]

The extant bonds of 1290 have another side to them. They can be used to illustrate how Christians obtained credit on a local level. It is in this, the obverse side of Jewish lending, that there is still much work to be done. The tracking down of Christian debtors, like looking for the proverbial needle in the haystack, helps to build up networks of borrowers.[110] Such networks illuminate the lower levels of local credit and show how consortia as well as fairly ordinary people sought credit and arranged repayments with Jewish financiers that suited them.[111] Such transactions can reveal a microcosm of medieval life. To take just one example, Isaac's debtors included a chaplain, a knight and four sons of knights or lords plus other locals from a fairly wide catchment area around Norwich that extended into Suffolk (see Map 2 above).

It is clear from his dealings that Isaac fil Deulecresse of Norwich survived the Edwardian Experiment. It is not, however, clear that he survived the final Expulsion. It can only be hoped that he did not embark, in 1290, with some of his fellow Jews from the Norfolk port of Burnham on Crouch. Their fate, like that of others, was not only to be sent into exile but to be condemned to being shipwrecked, murdered and robbed.[112] Edward I had achieved his final Jewish Solution.

---

[109] Mundill, *Solution*, pp. 131–145; Brand, 'Jews and the law', p. 1153; Mundill, 'Edwardian Jewry'.
[110] Mundill, *Solution*, pp. 209–48.
[111] *Ibid.*, pp. 246–8; Robin R. Mundill, 'Christian and Jewish lending partners and financial dealings', in P.R. Schofield and N.J. Mayhew, eds, *Credit and Debt in Medieval England, c.1180–c.1350* (Oxford, 2002), pp. 42–67.
[112] Rokeah, *Medieval English Jews*, entries 1236–7.

PART II

Case Studies and New Evidence

4

The Jewish Community of England in the Records of English Royal Government

PAUL BRAND

The Exchequer of the Jews

The obvious starting-point for the historian looking for evidence relating to the Jewish community of thirteenth-century England is the records of the Exchequer of the Jews. This institution was created in the final years of the twelfth century,[1] and abolished around the time of the Expulsion of England's Jewish community in the autumn of 1290.[2] Throughout its existence it possessed a special responsibility for the oversight and control of England's Jewish community.

The Exchequer of the Jews exercised a number of specific administrative responsibilities. Probably from the time of its inception it bore an overall responsibility for the proper functioning of the network of chests or *archae* set up under the arrangements first devised in 1194 in all the main centres of Jewish settlement in England. Each chest was run by two Christian chirographers and two Jewish chirographers plus one or two clerks.[3] The clerks wrote the bipartite (later tripartite) chirographs or bonds recording acknowledgements of debt to Jewish creditors; the chirographers were responsible for admitting one part of each chirograph into the chest, its safe custody, and its withdrawal when the debt was paid. The Exchequer of the Jews controlled the appointment and dismissal of these local officials, although the choice of an official was some-times delegated to a local jury.[4] It also sometimes gave orders for the admission and withdrawal of bonds from local chirograph chests.

---

[1] For the creation of the Exchequer of the Jews during the 1190s and its possible links with the special branch within the Exchequer established on a temporary basis in 1186 to deal with the bonds of Aaron of Lincoln, see Richardson, *English Jewry* (see Abbreviations), pp. 114–20.

[2] A royal writ addressed to the Barons of the Exchequer, dated 7 November 1290, ordered them to consult with the former Justices of the Jews (*justiciarii nuper ad custodiam judeorum assignati*) on a particular matter relating to a Jewish debt: PRO, E159/64, m. 7d. The last Justices of the Jews, William of Carleton and Peter of Leicester, were paid not only the half-yearly instalments of their fees that fell due at Michaelmas 1289 and Easter 1290 (PRO, C62/66, m. 2), but also a final instalment for Michaelmas 1290 (PRO, C62/67, m. 3).

[3] The original scheme of 1194 had envisaged the employment of two clerks for each chest: W. Stubbs, ed., *Roger de Howden: Chronicle* (RS 51, London, 1868–71), III, pp. 266–7. Later evidence, though not conclusive, suggests that there was only a single clerk except at London and York (for the latter, see *CPREJ*, II, p. 181 and *CPREJ*, I, p. 303).

[4] For the direct appointment of new chirographers, see *CPREJ*, I, p. 153; *CPREJ*, II, pp. 43, 49, 108, 114, 183, 240. For the election of new chirographers, see Rigg, *Select Pleas* (see Abbreviations), p. 11; *CPREJ*, I, p. 69.

By the mid-1260s, and probably for some time before that, the Exchequer of the Jews also administered the system controlling where members of the Jewish community could live. No Jew could change his or her residence without official permission. An application had to be made to the Exchequer of the Jews;[5] a small sum was paid; and local sheriffs were notified of the permission by writ.[6] Unlicensed residence in a town could lead to an order for the seizure of the body and movable possessions of the Jew concerned, and might lead to the forfeiture of the latter.[7] There is little evidence for a continuation of these functions after 1276,[8] though in 1277 and in 1284 the Exchequer of Jews was instructed to enforce that part of the 1275 Statute of Jewry which had prohibited the residence of Jews in towns that did not possess chirograph chests.[9]

The Exchequer of the Jews also oversaw the collection of chevage, an annual tax of three pence payable by all Jews aged twelve or over. The payment is first mentioned in the 1275 Statute of Jewry,[10] though it may predate the statute.[11] Although collection of the tax was entrusted to commissioners appointed by chancery writ,[12] and the proceeds went (from 1278 onwards) to the *Domus Conversorum*,[13] the whole arrangement was under the supervision of the Exchequer of the Jews, where the collectors were required to present their accounts.[14]

At the death of a Jew, the king was entitled to a sum equal to one-third of the value of his or her movable goods, of outstanding debts, and of the value (for one year only) of any houses or other immovable property in his or her possession.[15] The Exchequer of the Jews also had administrative responsibilities for enforcing this. By 1268 a standard form of writ was sent by the Exchequer

[5] But for temporary residence permits issued by Chancery in 1275, see *CCR 1279–88*, pp. 259, 260.

[6] For examples, see *CPREJ*, I, pp. 134, 150; *CPREJ*, II, pp. 13, 48, 50, 51, 52, 103, 104, 145, 151, 163, 173, 242, 243, 278; *CPREJ*, III, pp. 109, 127.

[7] Rigg, *Select Pleas*, pp. 61, 82; *CPREJ*, III, pp. 59–60. But for orders from Chancery for the removal of Jews from particular towns, *CCR 1272–9*, pp. 50, 130; *CCR 1279–88*, p. 241; and for the issuing by Chancery of an order for a proclamation to be made that Jews were not to live outside towns in the counties of Oxfordshire and Berkshire, *Close Rolls 1268–72*, p. 116.

[8] For evidence of Chancery issuing temporary residence permits in 1277, see *CCR 1279–88*, pp. 370, 376, 382, 385.

[9] *CPREJ*, III, pp. 317, 319; *CCR 1279–88*, p. 256.

[10] *Stat. Realm* (see Abbreviations), I, p. 221a.

[11] In 1240 Jeremy of Caxton and William of Hardel were commissioned to make a scrutiny of the chests in eight English counties, and to make inquiries on various matters. The local sheriff was ordered to let them know the names, and produce the bodies, of all Jews aged over twelve (the age at which chevage was later payable): *Close Rolls 1237–42*, pp. 238–9. Some system of regular checking-up on all adult Jews (with possibly a payment made on each occasion) is implied by the regulation of 1239 requiring each Jew to stay for a year at his place of residence at Michaelmas: Thomas Stapleton, ed., *De Antiquis Legibus Liber: Cronica Maiorum et Vicecomitum Londoniarum* (Camden Society, orig. ser. 34, 1846), p. 237.

[12] *CPR 1272–81*, p. 240; PRO, E9/35, m. 8; *CPR 1281–92*, p. 398.

[13] PRO, E9/35, m. 8; *CPR 1272–81*, p. 372.

[14] PRO, E9/35, m. 8 (6 Edward I). But the account of the keeper of the *Domus Conversorum* for 8–13 Edward I appears to have been rendered in the main Exchequer: PRO, E101/249/24. This has been edited by M. Adler in the Appendix of documents attached to his article 'History of the "Domus Conversorum"', *TJHSE*, 4 (1899–1901), 16–75, at 59–63.

[15] The king's third is mentioned as early as 1220 (*CPREJ*, I, p. 37) but is probably older. That the king's entitlement was only to a third of the annual value, not the full value, of immovable property is shown by PRO, E9/34, m. 7 and E9/35, m. 7.

of the Jews to the appropriate local sheriff(s) ordering a full inquiry to be held as to the goods and chattels (especially gold, silver and other valuables), bonds in chirograph chests and immovable property that a deceased Jew had held on the day s/he had fallen sick or (in the case of sudden, violent death) on the day of his or her death. The inquiry was a kind of Jewish analogue to the inquisition *post mortem* into the lands held by a deceased Christian tenant-in-chief.[16] These inventories and their valuations formed the basis for calculating the king's share, and the widow or heirs of the deceased normally granted him 'clear' debts belonging to the deceased to the appropriate value. A similar inquisition was held when a Jew converted to Christianity.[17] However, only relatively small numbers of these inquisitions are recorded on the surviving rolls. It is possible that the system largely depended on the initiative of relatives of the deceased who could only obtain clear title to the debts and chattels of the deceased after such an inquiry.

The Exchequer of the Jews also functioned as a court. It heard all cases concerning title to real property (primarily houses and rents in towns) in which either of the litigants was Jewish.[18] It also exercised a jurisdiction over cases where the king claimed real property should have escheated to him when a Jew converted to Christianity[19] or on conviction for felony.[20] A second significant area of jurisdiction was over title to movables where either of the litigants was Jewish. Such cases mainly arose from two specific types of situation: where Jews had confided movables to Christian neighbours during civil disturbances;[21] and where Jewish creditors were holding movables as security for a loan.[22] The Exchequer of the Jews did not have exclusive jurisdiction over this kind of case. Certain local courts are also known to have heard such cases.[23] It is unfortunate that the almost total loss of their records means that the surviving records may well give a misleading impression of the scale and mechanics of Jewish moneylending in thirteenth-century England. Small-scale

---

[16] The earliest surviving example seems to be *CPREJ*, I, p. 201.

[17] For an example, see PRO, E9/36, mm. 7, 9.

[18] For litigation where the demandant was Jewish, see *CPREJ*, I, pp. 118–19, 192; *CPREJ*, II, pp. 35, 93–4; *CPREJ*, III, p. 242. For litigation where the tenant was Jewish, see *CPREJ*, I, pp. 2, 7, 16, 36, 129, 147; *CPREJ*, II, pp. 124, 197, 210, 215–16.

[19] E.g., *CPREJ*, II, pp. 288, 295; *CPREJ*, III, pp. 22, 34–5, 177; Rigg, *Select Pleas*, pp. 99–100.

[20] E.g., *CPREJ*, I, p. 167; *CPREJ*, II, pp. 210, 257.

[21] E.g., Rigg, *Select Pleas*, pp. 31–3; *CPREJ*, I, pp. 131, 132–3; Rigg, *Select Pleas*, pp. 37–8; *CPREJ*, I, pp. 142, 143–4, 145, 169. For goods entrusted to a neighbour when Jews were expelled from a village by royal order, see PRO, E9/36, m. 2, and for goods allegedly pledged to Christians, see Rigg, *Select Pleas*, pp. 17–18 and 63–4.

[22] For examples, see *CPREJ*, I, pp. 22, 139–40; PRO, E9/64, m. 3; E9/35, mm. 2d, 3; E9/35, m. 5; E9/38, m. 4.

[23] The constable of the Tower of London is known to have exercised a jurisdiction in cases concerning the pledging of chattels where the chattels were worth less than forty shillings: *Close Rolls 1259–61*, p. 385 and cf. *CPREJ*, II, p. 211. A similar jurisdiction may have been exercised by other local constables and sheriffs. For evidence that some other kind of jurisdiction was exercised by the constable of Exeter in cases involving Jews in 1220, see *CPREJ*, I, p. 18; and by the constable of Winchester in cases involving Jews in 1270, see *CPR 1266–72*, p. 417. For the wider significance in other types of local court of a forty-shillings limitation, see J.S. Beckerman, 'The forty-shilling jurisdictional limit in medieval English personal actions', in Dafydd Jenkins, ed., *Legal History Studies* (Cardiff, 1975), pp. 110–17. The chancellor of the university of Oxford also exercised a jurisdiction over certain types of litigation involving Jews and students of the university: *Close Rolls 1259–61*, pp. 360–1; *CCR 1272–9*, pp. 232–3; *CPR 1281–92*, p. 236.

moneylending on the security of pawned movables and to a wide variety of customers may have been much more common as a form of Jewish money-lending than the surviving evidence indicates. The forfeiture of a Jew's movable goods to the Crown for whatever reason also led to actions brought by the king in the Exchequer of the Jews to recover such of their goods as were in the possession of third parties.[24]

The Exchequer of the Jews possessed a trespass jurisdiction, where either of the parties was Jewish or the trespass was closely connected with a Jewish debt. It possessed a criminal jurisdiction over private appeals of felony, too, where either of the parties was Jewish[25] and where Jews were indicted of felony.[26] It may also have exercised an *ex officio* jurisdiction to inquire into the death of any Jew who appeared to have been murdered.[27]

By far the greatest amount of business conducted by the Exchequer of the Jews was, however, generated, either directly or indirectly, by the practice of Jews lending money to Christians on the security of their lands, and the subsequent efforts of the creditors or their assigns to secure repayment of the moneys loaned plus (where appropriate) interest.[28] For reasons discussed later, there is little evidence in the court's own records relating to the enforcement of payments from living debtors (see below, p. 79). Much more common are entries in which third parties are sued for their share of a debt owed by someone who has since died. The general rule seems to have been that anyone in possession of lands that the debtor held at the time of contracting the debt or subsequently acquired was liable for a share proportionate to their share of the debtor's lands.[29] The creditor had normally to secure their appearance at the Exchequer of the Jews and obtain a judgment before s/he could obtain execution.[30] Debts also passed on a considerable scale into the hands of the king for a variety of reasons, and much of the time, and effort, of the Exchequer of the Jews went into levying these sums for the king.

Debtors themselves initiated two types of related litigation. In actions of unlawful distraint debtors sued their creditors for having them distrained for debts that they denied owing. The defendant might deny having taken any such

---

[24] E.g., PRO, E9/34, m. 3d; E9/36, mm. 5, 8d, 9; E9/38, mm. 2, 3, 8, 8d; E9/53, m. 1; E9/66, mm. 8, 8d, 11.

[25] For appeals by Christians against Jews, see Rigg, *Select Pleas*, pp. 4–5; *CPREJ*, I, pp. 296–7; *CPREJ*, II, pp. 56, 110; *CPREJ*, III, pp. 157–8, 162–3, 185–6, 189, 288; PRO, E9/35, m. 9 and cf. E9/36, m. 6. For an appeal removed to the Exchequer of the Jews because the vouchee of the appellee was Jewish, see Rigg, *Select Pleas*, p. 78. For appeals by Jews against Christians, see *CPREJ*, I, pp. 31, 46, 130–1. For appeals by Jews against Jews, see *CPREJ*, I, pp. 33, 39, 42–3, 45, 50–1, 69, 76; Rigg, *Select Pleas*, pp. 11–12. For an appeal by a Christian against a Christian, heard in the Exchequer of the Jews because it involved a Jewish debt, see *CPREJ*, I, pp. 250–1.

[26] *CPREJ*, I, pp. 107, 280; *CPREJ*, II, p. 149.

[27] *CPREJ*, I, p. 31; *CPREJ*, II, pp. 44–5, 186, 249. These entries suggest that the *presbiter Judeorum* exercised some function in such matters. For an indictment of Christians for the death of a Jew removed into the Exchequer of the Jews for trial, see *CPREJ*, III, pp. 248, 292–3.

[28] After the enactment of the Statute of Jewry of 1275 it became illegal for Jews to make new loans of money at interest, and interest ceased to accumulate on loans already made and not repaid: *Stat. Realm*, I, pp. 221–221a. There are comparatively few cases where a Christian creditor can be found suing a Jewish debtor, but for an example, see *CPREJ*, III, p. 31.

[29] *CPREJ*, I, p. 215; PRO, E9/64, m. 2d.

[30] This rule was restated in the Statute of Jewry of 1275 (*Stat. Realm*, I, p. 221). It is alluded to in 1268, though in a way that suggests that it was then possible, as of grace, for the king to waive it: *CPREJ*, I, p. 197.

action.[31] More commonly, the issue would be whether the debt had already been levied,[32] or whether the bond was genuine.[33] In a special form of action of account (quite different in its purpose from the action of account of the common law courts) debtors sought to make creditors state in court how much they owed, and to produce the chirographs that proved their entitlement.[34] Since a debtor was entitled to a suspension, for up to a year, of the measures the creditor was employing to secure payment,[35] some may have brought the action simply to secure some temporary respite.[36] Others, however, had more legitimate purposes. When money was owed to several creditors, for example, it was necessary that the precise total owed to each be ascertained before the process of attermination (an arrangement under which a debt, notionally payable immediately as a single lump sum, was made payable instead by instalments over time) could be completed.[37] A common preliminary to the action of account was the procedure in use by 1244,[38] under which a local sheriff or constable was ordered to ensure that proclamation was made in the synagogue on two or three sabbaths, requiring any Jew with claims against a particular individual to appear at the Exchequer of the Jews on a future (specified) date to account with him.[39] This may sometimes have been a preliminary to a sale of part or all of an individual's lands, disclosing to a potential purchaser the extent of the indebtedness attaching to the lands. Where a debt had passed to the king, the actions of unjust distraint and account were not available to debtors, but in practice they were able to challenge the amounts demanded,[40] and to purchase royal writs to the Exchequer of the Jews ordering an investigation of their cases.

The primary record of the various activities of the Exchequer of the Jews during this period was the so-called 'plea-rolls'. They are misnamed because most of the surviving rolls observe a clear division of their material into separate sections of 'pleas', 'memoranda' and 'starrs'.[41] For at least half its

---

[31] E.g., *CPREJ*, I, pp. 283–4; *CPREJ*, II, pp. 134–5, 253–4; *CPREJ*, III, pp. 169–70.

[32] E.g., *CPREJ*, I, p. 185.

[33] E.g., *CPREJ*, I, pp. 185, 229–30; *CPREJ*, II, pp. 210–11.

[34] The writs initiating such litigation seem normally to have been issued by the Exchequer of the Jews itself: see, e.g., Rigg, *Select Pleas*, p. 42; *CPREJ*, II, p. 12. They might, however, also be issued by Chancery: *CPREJ*, III, pp. 9–10. If the original creditor had sold the debt, then both he and his grantee would have to put in an appearance in court to answer: e.g., *CPREJ*, I, pp. 161, 162, 179.

[35] *CPREJ*, I, pp. 223, 273; Rigg, *Select Pleas*, p. 42; PRO, E9/35, m. 1.

[36] E.g., *CPREJ*, I, p. 174; *CPREJ*, II, p. 231.

[37] E.g., *CPREJ*, I, pp. 177, 182 (and *Close Rolls 1264–8*, p. 279); *CPREJ*, II, pp. 221, 224, 260, 261, 292; *CPREJ*, III, pp. 36, 55 (and *CCR 1272–9*, pp. 97, 103).

[38] *PpR 10 Richard I*, p. 210; Rigg, *Select Pleas*, pp. 9, 12–13. For possible forerunners, see *Close Rolls 1234–7*, pp. 87, 462.

[39] E.g., *CPREJ*, I, pp. 75–6, 106, 193, 194, 197, 198, 199.

[40] E.g., PRO, E9/34, m. 4d; E9/66, m. 8d; E9/35, m. 7d; E9/66, m. 8d.

[41] The 'memoranda' section includes all entries of an administrative nature plus a record of all litigation of direct or indirect interest to the king. Such material appears in a separate section in 1244 (see PRO, E9/2, mm. 4–4d; E9/3, m. 3; E9/4, m. 2d); the first membrane with such a heading comes from 1253: E9/5, mm. 7, 7d. The 'starr' section contains only copies of *starrs*. There is a separate section of them in a roll for 1244 (E9/2, m. 3), and there may have been separate membranes now lost for them in 1219–20 for the surviving roll (E9/1) includes no enrolled *starrs*. There were also often separate sections of attorney appointments, adjournments made at the request of the parties and *essoins* (those submitting an excuse for non-appearance in court), but these were closely related to the plea section.

existence, four plea-rolls were compiled for the justices of the court each year;[42] and from at least 1259 onwards, if not from the beginning, a separate set of rolls was made for each of the justices.[43] If the court held sessions each term (as it probably did except for brief periods of political upheaval) there must originally have been more than four hundred plea-rolls. Only seventy-two now survive.[44] It is unfortunate that a significant number (around nineteen) of the surviving rolls are partial duplicates of rolls covering the same terms made for different justices, and that their survival is so patchy. The earliest surviving roll covers the period from Michaelmas term 1219 to Trinity term 1220.[45] There is then a gap of over twenty years before the next three surviving rolls for three terms in 1244 and a further gap before the single roll for Easter term 1253.[46] The rolls survive in a reasonably continuous sequence (though still with some gaps) for the two decades after 1266,[47] but no rolls at all survive for the final years of the medieval community. Many of the surviving rolls are damaged and a significant number are clearly incomplete.[48] An even sadder loss for the cultural and linguistic historian are what seem to have been a related series of Hebrew records. There are references in 1236 and again in 1243 to a 'counter-roll' of proceedings in the Exchequer of the Jews made for the *presbyter judeorum*. This seems to be the same as the Hebrew plea-roll of the Exchequer of the Jews mentioned in other references of 1252 and 1259.[49] Such a roll may have been compiled from the beginning of the existence of the Exchequer of the Jews. The total absence of references after 1259 suggest that it was discontinued around that date. It is impossible to know how full a record it was, but we can reasonably assume that it was a Hebrew version of what the other rolls contained.

Even if more rolls had survived we would not have a full picture of the activities of the Exchequer of the Jews. Much of its more routine administrative activity was not recorded. It is, for example, at first surprising that the surviving plea-rolls contain so few entries relating to the attempts of Jewish creditors to

---

[42] The earliest surviving roll (PRO, E9/1) from 1219–20 appears to be a single annual roll and not a composite of four originally separate rolls, though the membranes do not seem to be in their original order. The next surviving roll (E9/2) is for a single term, Easter term 1244, and termly rolls were clearly the pattern thereafter.

[43] The earliest surviving duplicate rolls are for Trinity term 1273 (PRO, E9/14 and E9/62), but for evidence that a separate roll was being made for each justice as early as 1259, see Lindsay Fleming, ed., *Chartulary of the Priory of Boxgrove* (Sussex Record Society, 59, 1960), p. 44.

[44] Seventy of these are in the PRO Class of Exchequer of Jews Plea Rolls (E9). Two are strays now in the British Library (Additional Rolls 7218 and 19299). PRO, E9/58 and 60 are probably parts of the same roll as are E9/57 and E9/63; but three membranes of E9/38 may belong to a different roll, and E9/40A has membranes from two distinct rolls. Membrane 3 of E9/51 also probably comes from a distinct roll, as may parts of E9/44.

[45] PRO, E9/1.

[46] PRO, E9/2–4; E9/5.

[47] There are no surviving rolls for 1269, 1271 or 1285. A full sequence of four rolls survives only for the period 1275–80 and for 1283.

[48] Only a single membrane survives of the only rolls to cover Michaelmas term 1267, Easter term 1268, Trinity term 1270 and Easter term 1272: PRO, E9/8, 10, 61; BL Additional Roll 19299. Only a single misplaced membrane included in a roll of another term survives for Michaelmas term 1272 and Hilary term 1277: PRO, E9/12, m. 1; E9/23, m. 12.

[49] For references to the counter-roll, see *Close Rolls 1234–7*, p. 408; *Close Rolls 1242–7*, p. 51. For references to the Hebrew roll, see *Close Rolls 1251–3*, pp. 164, 271; *Chartulary of Boxgrove Priory*, p. 44.

secure repayment of loans from their original debtors. Almost all the recorded debt cases relate to claims against the tenants of lands belonging to dead debtors. The reason seems clear. Creditors had to obtain a writ to the local sheriff to give them possession of chattels of the debtor to the value of the sum owed and, if these did not suffice, to put them in possession of the debtor's lands until they had received what was owed. However, such a writ was issued without the debtor being summoned to appear at the Exchequer of Jews, and the issuing of the writ and the action subsequently taken on it normally left no trace on the plea-roll or in the writ-files of the court.[50] The Statute of Jewry of 1275 brought about significant changes. The creditor was now allowed only to take possession of half the debtor's chattels, and only given seisin of half the debtor's tenements (excluding his or her house).[51] A case of 1277 suggests that the creditor's writ of execution was also now made returnable to the Exchequer of the Jews, where the extent of the chattels and tenements of the debtor was filed with the writs returned into the court, though not normally transcribed onto the plea-rolls.[52] However, none of the writ-files of the Exchequer of the Jews now survive.

Even the writs sent to local sheriffs ordering or authorising them to levy Jewish debts in the king's hands were not normally transcribed in full onto the plea-rolls,[53] though they do intermittently record the despatching of sum-monses to particular sheriffs.[54] Nor was the action taken by the sheriffs in response necessarily recorded on the plea-rolls. If the sheriff levied part or all of the sum owed, this was not recorded, though he would be required to account for the sum raised when, periodically, he was summoned to render his account at the Exchequer of the Jews.[55] These accounts were recorded on separate rolls. Only a fragment of one such roll now survives.[56]

Other records: King's Chancery

Despite the existence of a specialist bureau for Jewish affairs, much of the more important business relating to the Jewish community was dealt with not by the Exchequer of the Jews but on an *ad hoc* basis by specially appointed

---

[50] The rule that the sheriff or local bailiff needed a royal warrant to place a creditor in seisin (rightful, or apparently rightful, possession) of the debtor's lands is apparent in the earliest rolls: *CPREJ*, I, pp. 41, 48. The form of the writ, requiring primarily distraint on chattels, and seizure of lands only if the chattels did not suffice for the debt, can be deduced from *CPREJ*, II, pp. 255–6, and from the post-1275 version of the same writ.

[51] *Stat. Realm*, I, pp. 221–221a.

[52] *CPREJ*, III, pp. 308–9. But for entries relating to such returns, see PRO, E9/34, m. 5d; E9/53, m. 1.

[53] But, for examples, see *CPREJ*, I, pp. 205–6.

[54] E.g., *CPREJ*, II, pp. 162, 184; *CPREJ*, III, p. 190 (estreats of pleas: lists of the financial dues and penalties adjudged as due to the Crown in the course of a legal session, extracted from the fuller written record of the session); PRO, E9/36, m. 9d.

[55] For the summoning of sheriffs to render account for Jewish debts in the Exchequer of the Jews, see *CPREJ*, I, pp. 135, 150, 151, 154, 250, 256; *CPREJ*, II, pp. 64–5, 107, 163, 174, 272; *CPREJ*, III, pp. 49, 51, 92, 93, 203–4, 294, 317.

[56] A single membrane from such a roll for the counties of Bedfordshire and Buckinghamshire, which shared a single sheriff, covering the period 50 Henry III to 2 Edward I, is now PRO, E101/249/17. In the inventory of the treasury of the Exchequer of the Jews made in December 1272 two such rolls are mentioned (*duo magni rotuli de diversis compotis vicecomitum*) as well as two rolls of fines: E101/249/15. For further references to these rolls, see *CPREJ*, II, p. 272; III, pp. 51–2.

commissioners, and it is to the records of the King's Chancery that we must turn for information about them. Chancery was responsible for authorising the periodic closing of chests (*archae*) and enrolment and *appuramentum* ('cleansing') of the bonds they contained, identifying those bonds paid in full, those bonds paid only in part, and the 'clear' bonds, where the whole debt was still owed.[57] The justices of the Jews were among those commissioned for this purpose, but only on an individual basis and not *ex officio*.[58]

A tallage of the Jews of England, and the closely related fines paid in lieu or for a respite from tallage for a limited period, were forms of extraordinary taxation that were probably always discussed and approved in advance by the King's Council. The original assessment of tallage and the apportionment of fines (the assessment of particular sums as due from individuals) and the subsequent collection of tallages or fines from the individuals concerned, were not the concern *ex officio* of the Exchequer of the Jews or its officials. Particular individuals were commissioned for these tasks, and the Exchequer of the Jews was, at most, called in after the process of collection had begun, to enforce the payment of arrears.

Chancery also issued other documents of considerable significance for our knowledge of the Jewish community. Under the terms of the Statute of Jewry of 1275, it became necessary for Jews to obtain a royal licence to dispose of their real property.[59] The licences were issued by Chancery, although both these and the charters recording transactions were also normally recorded on the plea-rolls of the Exchequer of the Jews.[60] Even before 1275, it was not uncommon for vendors and purchasers to obtain royal confirmation or ratification of such transactions. These were also obtained from Chancery.[61] The sale of a debt by a Jewish creditor to a Christian also required a licence after the 1269 Statute of Jewry, and the licences regularly recited its terms.[62] Again, the licences were issued by Chancery, though it seems to have been normal for the Exchequer of

---

[57] For a commission to make an *appuramentum*, with detailed instructions, see *CPR 1272–81*, p. 158 (cf. *ibid.*, p. 184). A writ, issued under the attestation of Hamo Hauteyn, for the transfer of certain bonds from the Hereford chest after its *appuramentum* in 1273 mentions that both the scrutiny of the chest (the enrolment of its contents) and the subsequent *appuramentum* had been authorised by the King's Council: PRO, E143/1/3, no. 4.

[58] There were scrutinies of the chests at London and Colchester (and perhaps elsewhere) in 1269 by John of Weston, Walter de la Croce and William of Middleton: *Close Rolls 1268–72*, pp. 50, 54; PRO, E159/47, m. 3d; E159/45, m. 8A. In 1272/3 there was a scrutiny of the chest at Norwich by William of Middleton, and one of the chest at Canterbury by Ellis of Hertford: *CPR 1266–72*, p. 708; PRO, E159/47, m. 4. In February 1273 four commissioners (including the two Justices of the Jews) were ordered to make a scrutiny of between four and six chests each: *CPR 1272–81*, p. 6. A total of twenty-two commissioners, working in groups of two, were ordered to make scrutinies of between one and four chests each in November 1275: *CPR 1272–81*, pp. 126–7. (For the resulting records, see PRO, C47/9/48 (Colchester), C47/9/49 (York), E101/249/31 (Exeter) and E9/22, m. 18 (Hereford).) Three commissions were issued during 1276 for work on the scrutiny of the London chest: *CPR 1272–81*, pp. 148, 158, 184. Further scrutinies appear to have been made in 1277 (*CCR 1272–9*, p. 432, cf. *ibid.*, p. 215), 1281 (*CPR 1272–81*, pp. 458, 459) and 1286 (*CPR 1281–92*, p. 227; PRO, E159/59, mm. 23d, 27d).

[59] *Stat. Realm*, I, p. 221a.

[60] For examples, see *CPR 1272–81*, p. 332 and PRO, E9/34, m. 4.

[61] For examples, see *CPR 1258–66*, pp. 544, 565; *CPR 1266–72*, pp. 82, 255, 572, 606, 621, 664–5. For confirmations in the form of licences, see *CPR 1272–81*, pp. 42, 43, 88. For one licence to sell given by the Exchequer of the Jews in 1274, see *CPREJ*, II, pp. 173, 191.

[62] *CPR 1266–72*, p. 376. The first licence under the statute was issued in July 1269: *ibid.*, pp. 359–60.

Jews to enrol the terms of the licence and the *starr* recording the terms of the sale.[63] Even before the statute it was not uncommon to obtain a royal confirmation of such transactions.[64]

Individual debtors might be able to secure a pardon of their debts from the King. Pardons were issued not just for debts that had passed into the king's hands,[65] but also for debts still in the hands of creditors.[66] Such pardons were issued by Chancery, and the only role played by the Exchequer of the Jews was to ensure that the 'official' copies of the relevant bonds were withdrawn from the treasury of the Exchequer of the Jews or from the local chest. More limited forms of pardon released the debtor from liability to pay interest,[67] or allowed him or her to repay only what s/he had borrowed, rather than the sum recorded in the bond.[68] Again, such pardons were issued by Chancery, and the role of the Exchequer of the Jews was normally limited to ensuring the withdrawal of the relevant bond when the sum owed was paid.[69] Lesser acts of royal grace also issued by Chancery included the temporary suspension of the accumulation of interest,[70] or the temporary prohibition of measures to enforce repayment.[71] The king could also show favour to a debtor (even where money was owed to a third party) by ordering that s/he be allowed to pay off the debt in fixed (and easy) instalments. Sometimes, all that was ordered was the attermination of a debt, that it should be paid off at the rate of so much a year.[72] More common was an order for the Justices of the Jews to have the debtor's lands valued, as a preliminary to (and basis for) the assignment to the debtor of 'reasonable terms' for the repayment of the debt.[73] Also obtainable only from Chancery,

---

[63] E.g., *CPREJ*, II, p. 276 (and *CPR 1272–81*, p. 83); *CPREJ*, III, p. 115 (and *CPR 1272–81*, p. 115); PRO, E9/66, mm. 4d, 7 (and *CPR 1272–81*, p. 425).

[64] For examples, see *CPR 1258–66*, pp. 614, 628; *CPR 1266–72*, pp. 29, 67, 177 (and Rigg, *Select Pleas*, p. 177), 184, 185 (and *CPREJ*, I, p. 195 and Rigg, *Select Pleas*, p. 46), 235, 261.

[65] For pardons of specific debts which had come into the king's hands, see, e.g., *Close Rolls 1264–8*, pp. 403, 404; *CPR 1266–72*, pp. 430, 441; *Close Rolls 1268–72*, pp. 175–176; *CCR 1272–9*, pp. 458, 472–3; *CCR 1279–88*, pp. 258, 259, 329–30. For pardons covering all the Jewish debts of a particular debtor in the king's hands, see *CPR 1272–81*, pp. 334, 335–6; *CCR 1279–88*, p. 387.

[66] For pardons of specific debts to specific creditors, see, e.g., *Close Rolls 1264–68*, pp. 78, 214–15, 309–10, 343, 350–1, 431; *Close Rolls 1268–72*, p. 187; *CPR 1281–92*, pp. 228, 234. For pardons of all debts to specific debtors, see *Close Rolls 1264–68*, pp. 201–2, 203; *Close Rolls 1268–72*, p. 153; *CPR 1266–72*, pp. 502, 503. For pardons of all debts to all Jewish creditors, see *CPR 1258–66*, pp. 648, 661 and *Close Rolls 1264–68*, pp. 199, 200.

[67] E.g., *Close Rolls 1264–8*, pp. 266, 333–4; *Close Rolls 1268–72*, pp. 56, 202, 583–4; *CCR 1272–9*, p. 177.

[68] E.g., *Close Rolls 1268–72*, pp. 222, 479.

[69] Both the Justice of the Jews and the Barons of the Exchequer co-operated in the proceedings required to establish what was the original sum or sums borrowed by the abbey of Stratford of Master Elias son of Master Mosse in 1275–6. For related material, see *Close Rolls 1268–72*, pp. 583–4; *CCR 1272–9*, pp. 8, 140, 172–3, 271, 320; PRO, E159/49, m. 7d; E13/3, mm. 9d, 17; *CPREJ*, III, pp. 223–4, 285–6 and *CPREJ*, IV, p. 128.

[70] E.g., *Close Rolls 1264–8*, pp. 160, 180, 265–6, 305, 306; *Close Rolls 1268–72*, pp. 370, 486.

[71] In the case of these prohibitions, it is not always easy to know whether or not the debt in question is one that has already come to the king's hands. For examples, see *Close Rolls 1264–8*, pp. 339, 466; *CCR 1272–9*, pp. 8, 30, 65, 96, 137, 150, 154–5, 157, 194, 222, 465.

[72] For examples of the attermination of debts in the king's hands, see *CCR 1272–9*, pp. 105, 152, 362–3; *CCR 1279–88*, pp. 5, 166, 275. For examples of the attermination of debts owed to Jewish creditors, see *Close Rolls 1264–8*, pp. 194, 274, 351; *Close Rolls 1268–72*, pp. 219, 314; *CPR 1266–72*, p. 505; *CCR 1272–9*, pp. 184–5.

[73] For examples of such orders issued between 1265 and 1272, see *Close Rolls 1264–8*, pp. 78, 145, 152–3, 202, 265, 278, 279, 294, 423–4, 444–5. There was then a halt to the issuing of such orders

though it was the Exchequer of the Jews that enforced its observance, was a grant to the alienee of land once held by a debtor, exempting him/her from liability for a share of the debt.[74] This was of value principally where debtors or their heirs were unable to fulfil the obligation they would normally have assumed of acquitting the alienee of all claims for Jewish debts.

The main Exchequer

The third major institution whose records show it playing a significant role in Jewish business was the Exchequer. Jewish debts that had come into the king's hands were often collected through the main Exchequer rather than the Exchequer of the Jews.[75] In the early thirteenth century revenues arising out of the work of the Exchequer of the Jews or collected under its supervision were paid into, and retained in, a separate treasury.[76] By mid-century these moneys seem to have been paid into the ordinary Exchequer of Receipt along with other royal revenues.[77] When Henry III granted the Jewry of England for a three-year period to his son Edward in June 1262,[78] these moneys were paid to receivers acting on Edward's behalf instead. After 1265 some Jewish revenue was received by the Justices of the Jews and paid over to the king's wardrobe.[79] Early in 1269 the Justices of the Jews received an instruction to return to payment of all money received from fines, amercements and other issues of the Exchequer of the Jews to the main Exchequer, with the money being earmarked for the works at Westminster. However, the supposition was still that they would be the initial receivers of the money.[80] After the appointment of Hamo Hauteyn (on whom see Dobson's comments, below, p. 151) and Ludham as Justices of the Jews in 1273 almost all the revenues collected through the

until Edward I's return from the crusade, when some kind of general guidelines were agreed as to their issue. They were in the future only made available to those who without such an attermination would be unable to support themselves and their families. For examples, see *CCR 1272–9*, pp. 97, 100, 101, 102, 104, 105, 106, 137, 149, 176, 180–1. For orders for extent and attermination issued after the Statute of 1275, see *CCR 1272–9*, pp. 321, 335, 357, 409; *CCR 1279–88*, p. 466. For variants still more favourable to debtors, see *Close Rolls 1264–8*, pp. 479–80; *CCR 1272–9*, pp. 214–15, 359, 395.

[74] For examples, see *CPR 1266–72*, pp. 34, 210 (during a lease), 255 (a debt owed by a Jew), 398, 401, 449, 522–3, 577; *CCR 1272–9*, p. 181; *CPR 1272–81*, p. 249.

[75] In 1260, for example, the Exchequer of the Jews was ordered to transfer all royal debts over twenty marks to the Exchequer for them to be levied through it: *Close Rolls 1259–61*, p. 38. Entries on the Memoranda Rolls in the 1270s and 1280s appear to indicate that Jewish debts continued to be levied through the Exchequer during this period as well. See now the entries in Zefira Entin Rokeah, ed., *Medieval English Jews and Royal Officials: Entries of Jewish Interest in the English Memoranda Rolls, 1266–1293* (Jerusalem, 2000).

[76] Richardson, *English Jewry*, pp. 136–7.

[77] The evidence for this is mainly negative and is a deduction from the absence of any authorisations for outpayments from a separate Jewish treasury. In 1250 the king clearly expected that the Treasurer and Chamberlains would be in receipt of income from the Exchequer of the Jews: *Close Rolls 1247–51*, pp. 255–6.

[78] *CPR 1258–66*, p. 233.

[79] *CPR 1266–72*, p. 191. See also *CPREJ*, I, p. 149 (order for money to be paid directly into the wardrobe).

[80] *CPR 1266–72*, p. 317. For orders for money to be levied and paid over to the Justices issued after 1269, see *CPREJ*, I, pp. 265, 268, 269, 311, 312.

Exchequer of the Jews were once more paid directly into the Exchequer of Receipt.[81]

It was also at the Exchequer that the Justices of the Jews were liable to be tried for any alleged misconduct while in office. Both trials of master William of Watford for misconduct in 1272 were conducted by the Treasurer and Barons of the Exchequer and in the Exchequer, though for one trial they were reinforced by a number of justices from other royal courts.[82] The trial of Hauteyn and Ludham in 1286 was also conducted in the Exchequer by the Treasurer and Barons, though again they were 'reinforced', this time by the king's regent as well as various members of the judiciary.[83]

The main Exchequer also supervised the Exchequer of the Jews through the rehearing of individual cases previously heard there. This practice appears to have begun only in 1267.[84] Over twenty cases were reheard by the Exchequer between 1268 and 1286. The Justices of the Jews were summoned into the Exchequer to appear in person, bringing with them the 'record and process' of the case being reviewed, probably the the original rolls containing the relevant entries plus related writs.[85]

This is only part of a much broader picture of subordination of the Exchequer of the Jews to the main Exchequer. Another clear indication is provided by the Statute of Jewry of 1275. Despite its overwhelming importance for the Exchequer of the Jews no text of the Statute was sent directly to it by Chancery. A copy was sent to the Exchequer, which was later instructed (almost as an afterthought) to make and send on a copy to the Exchequer of the Jews.[86]

We are fortunate that so much information about the Jewish community of thirteenth-century England survives in the records of the English royal government and particularly fortunate, in light of the poor survival rate of the records of the Jewish Exchequer, that so much of governmental interaction with the affairs of that community took place in other institutions and is reflected in their records, whose survival rate is so much better. The surviving governmental records cannot tell us all we would like to know about the community but they are certainly one significant source that no historian can afford to ignore.

---

[81] During 1273 and 1274 some small payments for writs and other payments in the nature of *oblata* were still being made to the Justices and other officials of the Exchequer of the Jews: *CPREJ*, II, pp. 11–13, 48–52, 102–5, 144–5, 173–4. For still later evidence of small sums being paid directly to the Justices and other officials, see PRO, E9/36, mm. 6d, 9; E9/66, mm. 8d, 9. For receipt rolls of the main Exchequer of Receipt specifically devoted to income from the Exchequer of the Jews for this period, see PRO, E401/1574–82.

[82] PRO, E159/46, mm. 9, 9d.

[83] G.O. Sayles, ed., *Select Cases in the Court of King's Bench under Edward I*, I (London, 1936), pp. clix–clx.

[84] The earliest reference to the procedure seems to be in Michaelmas 1267 when Isaac of Warwick is recording as paying ten bezants for a case between himself and William 'de Dunesle' in the Exchequer of the Jews to be heard and determined before the Treasurer and Barons of the Exchequer: PRO, E159/42, m. 5; *CPREJ*, I, pp. 146–7, 151.

[85] For an entry that appears to envisage them bringing the original records relating to a case, see PRO, E159/42, m. 21d. Two entries appear to envisage them sending and not bringing the relevant records: E159/46, m. 1 and E13/2, m. 9d.

[86] PRO, E159/50, m. 3d.

5

The Church and the Jews in Medieval England

JOHN EDWARDS

Introduction

> I was completely unprepared for the discovery that it was the Christian Church,
> and the Christian Church alone, which turned a normal xenophobia and normal
> good and bad communal relations between two human societies into the unique
> evil of anti-Semitism.[1]

Thus wrote James Parkes, in his 1969 autobiography, *Voyage of Discoveries*. As
is well known, Parkes, an Anglican Guernsey man, had, after serving in the
British army in the First World War and reading history at Oxford, joined the
Student Christian Movement (SCM) in 1923, and had served, between 1928
and 1935, as Secretary of Cultural Co-operation in the International Student
Service, based in Geneva. From that vantage point, he observed the coming to
power of the Nazis in Germany, and was among the first to identify the
resulting threat to the Jewish population of the new Third Reich.[2] In 1930,
Parkes published his first book, *The Jew and his Neighbour: a Study of the
Causes of Antisemitism*.[3] Four years later, his doctoral thesis appeared in book
form, as *The Conflict of the Church and the Synagogue: a Study in the Origins of
Antisemitism*.[4] Although it originated as an Oxford D.Phil. thesis, Oxford
University Press refused to publish this learned, trenchant and still valuable
study of the origins and effects of anti-Jewish ideology in the Church. Instead,
it appeared under the imprint of the Soncino Press, in London.[5] In 1938, a year
so ill-fated for the world in general and for Jews in particular, Parkes published,
again with the Soncino Press, a pioneering study, by a non-Jew, under the title
*The Jew in the Medieval Community: a Study of his Political and Economic
Situation*.[6] Although this substantial study, produced in stressful personal and
general circumstances, has been superseded in academic terms, it began the
slow and painful process, which is still under way, whereby the history of the
Jews in Europe has moved out of the specialised area of 'Jewish Studies' and on

---

[1] James Parkes, *Voyage of Discoveries* (London, 1969), p. 123.
[2] Nicholas de Lange, 'James Parkes: a centenary lecture', in Siân Jones, Tony Kushner and Sarah
Pearce, eds, *Cultures of Ambivalence and Contempt: Studies in Jewish/non-Jewish Relations*
(London and Portland, 1998), pp. 31–49, at pp. 31–2.
[3] James Parkes, *The Jew and his Neighbour: a Study of the Causes of Antisemitism* (London, 1930).
[4] Id., *The Conflict of the Church and the Synagogue: a Study in the Origins of Antisemitism* (London,
1934).
[5] De Lange, 'James Parkes', p. 32; Gavin I. Langmuir, 'The faith of Christians and hostility to
Jews', in D. Wood, ed., *Christianity and Judaism* (= *SCH* 29, Oxford, 1992), pp. 77–92, at p. 91.
[6] James Parkes, *The Jew in the Medieval Community: a Study of his Political and Economic Situation*
(London, 1938).

to general historical and Christian theological syllabuses. The main focus of this essay, though, is on Britain, and in particular on England, since the vast majority of medieval Jews in the British Isles lived there, and not in Wales, Scotland and Ireland. Between the Norman conquest and the expulsion in 1290, Jews subject to the English Crown were repeatedly subject to policies developed on the Continent of Europe, not least in matters of religion.

Medieval England

In 1939, just a year after the appearance of *The Jew in the Medieval Community*, F. Ashe Lincoln, less perspicacious, perhaps, than Parkes, wrote the following in his history of the Hebrew *starrs* (legal and administrative documents) in England:

> A word must be said about the relationship between the Jews and the Church. From the religious point of view, of course, some degree of antagonism was natural [*sic*], and occasionally individual churchmen were seized with the desire to proselytize which resulted in a certain amount of discomfort [*sic*] and possibly even massacre [*sic*]. . . . Apart, however, from antagonism on the religious side, which was in the circumstances natural and only to be anticipated, the relations between the Jews and the Church, especially in commercial transactions, were on the whole friendly and harmonious.[7]

To discover why Lincoln should have regarded 'religious antagonism' between the Church and the Jews as 'natural' will be the main purpose of what follows, but, first, here is a contrary statement, in the post-1800 tradition of Jewish historiography. It comes from Albert Hyamson's *A History of the Jews in England*, first published in 1908, and issued in a second edition in 1928, the year in which Parkes began his work with the International Student Service. In his 1908 preface, Hyamson (who was a Fellow of the Royal Historical Society) wrote:

> The history of the Jews in England is the history in miniature of the Diaspora. Since the opening of the Christian era the story of the Jews has everywhere been the same – continual alternations of prosperity and persecution. With nations as with individuals the wheel of fortune ever revolves, but with the Jews its progress seems to have been more rapid, for the alterations have been more numerous than with any other race [*sic*].[8]

Clearly some effort has to be made to reconcile Hyamson's statement with Lincoln's, but the two authors evidently share a fundamental conviction that conflict between Jews and non-Jews is, if not 'natural', in any case endemic, and that the relationship between Jews and Christians in medieval England, between 1066 and 1290, is a case in point.

The relevant pattern of events is only too familiar and may be briefly outlined. It is well known that the locations of Jewish settlement in Anglo-Norman, Angevin and Plantagenet England included ecclesiastical centres, as well as the two universities where the elite of the Christian clergy was trained:

---

[7] F. Ashe Lincoln, *The Starrs: their Effect on Early English Law and Administration* (London, 1939), p. 25.
[8] Albert M. Hyamson, *A History of the Jews in England* (London [1908], repr. 1928), p. vii.

London, York, Norwich, Lincoln, Oxford and Cambridge (see Hillaby's chapter in this volume, above, pp. 15–40). The wide range of financial services provided by Jews to the majority Christian population notoriously included the loan of money to individual churchmen, whether secular priests or religious, as well as ecclesiastical corporations, including cathedrals and abbeys. Economic interaction between Jews and the Church, both individually and institutionally, also included the storing of the records of financial transactions. Often, the pledged goods involved were kept in churches, which by the solid nature of their construction rendered themselves natural strong-rooms. Thus despite the overwhelming importance of the Crown in the administration of the affairs of England's Jews in this period, the Church, too, was a factor with which English communities had constantly to contend, in economic terms.[9] Nevertheless, Ashe Lincoln, whatever the faults of his analysis, was right to focus on the specifically religious animosity that existed in medieval England between at least some Christians and some Jews. Even if abstractions such as '*the* Church' and '*the* Jews', against which both this writer and Gavin Langmuir have warned in various studies, are avoided, it cannot be doubted that something in the defining scriptural texts and traditions of what came to be described as 'Christianity' and/or 'the Church' has led to officially supported or sponsored hostility towards Jews.[10] Thus the aim of what follows is to examine relations between Jews and Christians in twelfth- and thirteenth-century England, in the context of this tortured and centuries-old relationship between the ancient Chosen People of God and the followers of Jesus of Nazareth.

Scripture

When selecting, editing, and in most cases translating, the book of sources entitled *The Jews in Western Europe*, this writer began the collection with some much earlier texts, from the Christian New Testament. These were the Epistle of St Paul to the Romans, chapter 11, verses 1–2 and 11–24, Matthew's Gospel, chapter 27, verses 22–26, and John's Gospel, chapter 8, verses 42–45.[11] Between them, these significant passages of New Testament Scripture demonstrate clearly the ambiguity of Jewish–Christian relations. In chapter 11 of Romans, Paul (who may be regarded as the patron saint of converts from Judaism to Christianity) offers a positive view of the relationship between Jews and Gentiles. He uses the famous image of the wild and the cultivated olive, the latter representing the Jews and the former non-Jewish Christians, an image much beloved of those who engage in Jewish–Christian dialogue in the present day. Paul sums up his approach in verse 23: 'The Jews, if they give up their unbelief, [will be] grafted back in your place', a statement that appears to suggest not only that God will never abandon his first Chosen People, but also that, if they come to Christ, Jews may have priority over Gentile believers. As

---

[9] John Edwards, 'The Church and the Jews in English medieval towns', in T.R. Slater and Gervase Rosser, eds, *The Church in the Medieval Town* (Aldershot, 1998), pp. 43–54, at pp. 43–4.

[10] John Edwards, 'Religious faith and doubt in late medieval Spain: Soria, *circa* 1450–1500', *Past and Present*, 120 (1988), 3–25, at 24 (reprinted in id., *Religion and Society in Spain, c. 1492* (Aldershot, 1996), essay no. III); Langmuir, 'Faith of Christians', pp. 77–9.

[11] John Edwards, *The Jews in Western Europe, 1400–1600* (Manchester, 1994), pp. 25–30.

'the Apostle' (to employ medieval usage) puts it in the following verse, 'After all, if you were cut off from your natural wild olive to be grafted unnaturally on to a cultivated olive, it will be much easier for them, the natural branches, to be grafted back on to the tree they came from'. The passage from Matthew's Gospel, on the other hand, gives an apparently very different view of the status and fate of Jews in the Christian era. In the twelfth and thirteenth centuries, as since, these verses would have been sung, often in a dramatised form, on Palm Sunday, during the liturgical commemoration of the final entry of Jesus into Jerusalem, before his arrest and trial. By placing in the mouths of the Jewish crowd at Jesus's trial before Pilate the notorious words, 'His blood be on us and on our children', Matthew appears to ascribe corporate guilt for Jesus's subsequent crucifixion to the entire Jewish people. The Gospel of John goes even further, in a manner that was to have a sinister effect on late-medieval Jews, in England as elsewhere. The 'beloved disciple' has Jesus himself say, to a group that is indiscriminately labelled '*the* Jews', 'The devil is your father, and you prefer to do what your father wants'.

As religious disputations between Christian and Jewish representatives, in England and, increasingly, on the continent between the 1090s and the fifteenth century were to demonstrate, the now divided faiths had very different ways of reading the Hebrew Bible, which they held in common. To Jews, what Christians regarded as the 'Old Testament' was not only the Word of God, but also provided, in Anna Abulafia's words, 'an understanding of their past, guidelines for their present situation, and hopes for future redemption'. To Christians, on the other hand, Jews committed the fatal error of reading their common Scriptures 'carnally', that is according to physical and earthly, rather than spiritual and heavenly, criteria. In particular, Jews were accused of ignoring, or else rejecting, the entire basis of Biblical study in the medieval Church, which was the belief that the 'Old Testament', in its entirety, foretold Christ's birth, ministry, suffering, death and resurrection, and could only be accurately read as a prelude to the 'New' Testament.[12] The doctrinal differences that lurked behind these conflicting interpretations of what were, in effect, the same Scriptural texts were to emerge, during the period of Jewish life in medieval England, in various forms, many of them damaging to the prospects of security for Jews in this and other kingdoms. The aspects of the subject that will be considered here are education and learning among both Christians and Jews, movements for reform in the Western Church, between 1050 and 1300, the experience, in this period, of conversion from Judaism to Christianity, and the role of doubt, as opposed to faith, in the Catholicism of the time. These general questions will be applied more particularly to three notable areas of doctrinal contention between Jews and Christians – the Incarnation, or birth, of Jesus of Nazareth, his Crucifixion, and the Eucharist, or Mass, as a service of commemoration, and/or re-enaction, of his saving acts. First to be considered, then, is the question of education and learning, which are, of course, not necessarily the same thing.

---

[12] Anna Sapir Abulafia, 'Jewish carnality in twelfth-century Renaissance thought', in Wood, ed., *Christianity and Judaism*, pp. 59–75, at pp. 59–60.

Education and learning

Disputes about the interpretation of the Hebrew Bible inevitably concerned the most educated members of both communities. As Anna Abulafia has rightly remarked, 'no Christian theologian coming face to face with the Jewish non-Christological reading of the Scriptures could remain indifferent to it. For that too much was at stake.'[13] The resulting conflict went beyond intellectual and doctrinal matters, spilling into society at large. R.I. Moore has identified, as a cause of conflict between Christians and Jews, the growth of bureaucracy in twelfth-century Europe, particularly in the Papal Curia at Rome and in the leading monarchies, of which England was a notable example. One reason for the growing pressure on Western European Jewish communities, including the English one, in the late twelfth and thirteenth centuries was the increase in written communication between royal governments and the papacy. Thus, apart from the areas of religious and theological conflict that will be considered shortly, papal guidelines for Jewish–Christian relations, dating from both before and after the decrees of the Fourth Lateran Council in 1215, were increasingly brought to the attention of rulers. As a result, kings came under pressure to dispense with their Jewish officials and counsellors, and Jews became increasingly vulnerable to the, now ecclesiastically sanctioned, jealousy of their Christian rivals. Ruthlessness, and at least overtly unquestioning obedience of the powerful, were notorious features of late twelfth- and thirteenth-century courts, a fact that makes the case of Thomas Becket all the more remarkable, though in reality he simply chose to change masters from king to pope. Many of the Christian servants of English monarchs in this period were the legendary 'new men', who rose from nothing, at the royal whim, to form a new literate elite that would lord it over their own families and former neighbours. In addition, these men were 'clerks', members of the Catholic clergy who at least possessed minor orders. Thus they were in the vanguard of the papally sponsored reform movement in the Church, which will be discussed below.

These royal clerks, many of whom went on from direct government service to superior Church posts such as bishoprics, faced competition, though, from Jews who were legally under royal protection and in some cases ensconced in the service of the Crown. Despite their 'servile' status, the Jewish rivals of the newly promoted Christian bureaucrats, whether they were working directly for the Crown or for other lords or ecclesiastical corporations, were very far from being the contemptible and degenerate individuals who were increasingly imagined in the verbal and visual teaching of the Church. On the contrary, as Moore has pointed out, 'Except in the matter of their faith, the Jews were in fact what the clerks represented themselves as being.' At least up to about 1200, they were culturally superior to virtually all their Christian contemporaries. Whereas cathedral schools might educate a small minority of (male) clerics, European Jews, in England as elsewhere, inherited and continued a much more universal instruction in literacy, numeracy, and the handling of legal texts, which often involved women as well as men. Only after 1215, under the combined pressures of papal injunctions and royal bureaucratic

---

[13] *Ibid.*, p. 73.

development, did Jews begin to lose their superiority and their special role in government.[14]

Church reform

The decline in the conditions of Jewish life in Western Europe in the late Middle Ages is generally held to have begun with the attacks on communities in northern France and the Rhineland, which coincided with the beginning of the First Crusade to Jerusalem in 1096. Yet the very calling of the crusade by Pope Urban II, in Clermont towards the end of the previous year, had been part of a general reform movement in the Church, which had been inspired partly by Cluniac monasticism and partly by the popes themselves, notably Gregory VII (reigned 1073–85). Overtly, the 'Gregorian' or 'Hildebrandine' reform (the latter term originating in the pope's prior name) was an affair entirely internal to the Catholic Church. Its primary concerns were to stress the distinction between the clergy and the laity, and to elevate the quality and standing of the former. Thus the rule of celibacy, which already applied to monks, was to be extended to parish priests and other so-called 'secular' clergy, and the practice of simony, or the purchase of clerical benefices, was to be ended. However, Gregory VII's policies, which were continued by his successors, also had an effect on the Jews. The reform was based on the notion that an appeal in all matters should be made not only to Scripture but also to the laws, practices and theological writings of the early centuries of the Christian Church.

It was inevitable that, in this process, increased attention would be paid to the thoughts of the Church Fathers on the character of Jews, and their status in Christian society. The conclusion that resulted was that, while Jews were to remain among the Christian majority, they should be kept in a subservient condition, to increase devotion to Jesus by reminding the faithful of his sufferings and death. In accordance with this theological view, the late Roman Civil Law code, the *Codex Juris Civilis*, was to be revived so as to prevent a Jew from ever having authority over a Christian.[15] Thus when Pope Innocent III and his thirteenth-century successors, especially Gregory IX, made a serious effort to legislate on the subject of the Jews in Christian Europe, they either repeated or developed much earlier conciliar canons. It was inevitable that the decrees of the Fourth Lateran Council, issued in 1215, would sooner or later be brought to England. Basic principles of this legislation were that, while Jews were to retain basic religious freedom, in the forms of dedicated buildings and rabbinical leadership, their synagogues were never to be more ostentatious than neighbouring churches, and no new synagogues were to be built. The principle of Jewish subservience was also reasserted in canon 69 of the Lateran IV decree *Etsi Judaeos*: 'It is too absurd for a blasphemer of Christ to exercise the force of power over Christians.' The other concern of the Lateran fathers, as it had been of so many of their predecessors, was to minimise, and if possible to end, all social contact between Christians and Jews.

---

[14] R.I. Moore 'Antisemitism and the birth of Europe', in Wood, ed., *Christianity and Judaism*, pp. 33–57, at pp. 51–7.
[15] *Ibid.*, p. 37.

Henry III and Edward I, like their contemporaries in other kingdoms, were in principle required to implement the Lateran decree at once, by incorporating it into English law, as well as supporting its ratification by the two provinces of the English Church. As with papal legislation in general in the Middle Ages, English Church, or canon, law concerning the Jews formed only a small part of the total output in this period. Between 1208 and the expulsion year of 1290, only eleven of the thirty-six sets of canons enacted by councils of the English Church touched on Jewish matters, and many of these were simply reissues of earlier material. However, the council, or synod, called by Archbishop Stephen Langton of Canterbury, at Oxford in 1222, did indeed apply the relevant Lateran IV decree to the English communities. English Jews had already been affected by the measures passed by the Third Lateran Council, in 1179. As a result of these decrees, the bishop of Worcester had already issued statutes forbidding Jews to hold liturgical books, vestments and ornaments as pledges for loans, as well as banning them from storing goods in churches. He had also forbidden Christian wetnurses to look after Jewish children, and instructed female Christian servants not to sleep in the houses of their Jewish employers. These latter provisions, which were to be enacted throughout Catholic Europe, more than appeared to make a link between religion and genetic origin, and would have huge implications, particularly in Spain. The 1222 Oxford decrees went further: Jews were not to build synagogues in places in England where they had not previously settled; they were not to remain in the kingdom at all unless they had adequate financial means and guarantors; they were not to make excessive noise while worshipping, and they were not to employ Christian women as servants. Jews were not to buy, or even eat, meat during the Christian penitential season of Lent, they were not to disparage Christianity as a religion or, surprisingly in view of both previous and subsequent developments, to engage in religious disputation with Christians. Sexual relations between Jews and Christians were forbidden, and in order to prevent transgressions of this piece of canon law, Jews were henceforth to wear badges, two fingers wide and four fingers long, and of a different colour from the garment onto which they were sewn. In practice, the badges generally took the form of discs or rings of material, coloured white, yellow or red. Jews were not to enter churches, or to work to persuade other Jews not to convert to Christianity. In order to prevent the spread of the perceived threat that Jews posed to Christian society, they were not to move to new places of settlement in England without a royal licence.

The Oxford provisions of 1222 seem draconian, to say the least, and were followed by a series of more locally applicable enactments and reissues between then and the Expulsion in 1290. Nevertheless, despite the policies of successive popes, it was not until over thirty years later, in 1253, that the decrees of the Council of Oxford were incorporated into secular law by means of a statute of Henry III. Zefira Entin Rokeah has blamed this measure partly on the king's lack of understanding of Christianity, and partly on the influence of his queen, Eleanor of Provence, who later, in 1275, was to expel Jews from the English towns that she held. It is evident, though, that Henry was simply attempting to apply, in common with his contemporaries, Louis IX of France and Alfonso X of Castile, the developing papal policy. What is clear is that the provisions of the Council of Oxford were to influence the whole of medieval Jewish life in

England, until it legally ended, for some centuries, in 1290.[16] Before then, though, a new development was to take place, in which the Church attempted to undermine Jewish life in another way, by converting Jews to Christianity.

Conversion

Ever since Jeremy Cohen published his book *The Friars and the Jews* in 1982, debate has raged over the effect on Jewish communities in Western Europe of the new kind of 'active monasticism', which was given papal approval, in the early thirteenth century, in the form of the Franciscan and Dominican orders, as well as a number of others.[17] Cohen's well-known and stimulating thesis is that the period after the Third Lateran Council of 1179 saw a transformation in Catholic teaching on Judaism and the Jews. In brief, the traditional notion of a defeated and subservient Jewish people, with the function of advertising simultaneously the failure of Judaism and the rightness and attractiveness of Christianity, was, according to this interpretation, transformed into an urgent missionary impulse. In thirteenth-century England, as later on the continent of Europe, movements, whether official or unofficial, to assist God in the bringing forward of the 'Last Days', foretold in the Book of Daniel and the Revelation of St John the Divine, commonly involved active missionary efforts to convert Jews to Christianity.[18]

During the thirteenth century, attempts were made by royal authorities, and in particular by the Dominican order of friars, to separate converted Jews from their former communities. This was often done by means of the establishment of 'Houses of Converts' (*Domus Conversorum*), which had the twofold aim of protecting the converts from efforts by Jews to win them back to their former faith, and of shielding them from attack by hostile and suspicious members of the Christian community. In addition, baptism commonly caused Jews to lose their former wealth and employment, so that the Houses of Converts were also intended to supply economic aid. In England, the first such institution seems to have been set up in Southwark in 1213, while, eight years later, the Dominicans established a similar house in Oxford. The most famous House of Converts, though, was the one founded by King Henry III, in 1233, in Chancery Lane, London. Despite Edward I's expulsion of the Jews from England, in 1290, the institution survived into the sixteenth century, Henry VIII's Secretary, Thomas Cromwell, being its warden in 1534.[19] Financial provision for converts from Judaism, who resided in specialised houses or else with normal monastic communities, was modelled on 'corrodies'. These were annual payments, made by monasteries to individuals in kind, such as food, drink, clothing and accommodation.[20] Overt and specific campaigns to convert Jews were rare

---

[16] Zefira Entin Rokeah, 'The State, the Church and the Jews in medieval England', in Shmuel Almog, ed., *Antisemitism through the Ages* (Oxford, 1988), pp. 99–125, at pp. 112–14; Edwards, 'The Church and the Jews', pp. 49–51.

[17] Jeremy Cohen, *The Friars and the Jews: the Evolution of Medieval Anti-Judaism* (Ithaca, NY and London, 1982).

[18] *Ibid.*, pp. 77–89.

[19] Edwards, 'The Church and the Jews', p. 50.

[20] R.N. Swanson, *Church and Society in Late Medieval England* (Oxford, 1989), pp. 236–7; Joan Greatrex, 'Monastic charity for Jewish converts: the requisition of corrodies by Henry III', in Wood, ed., *Christianity and Judaism*, pp. 133–45, at pp. 133–43.

during Henry III's reign, though they became more frequent under his successor, Edward I, between 1275 and the Expulsion in 1290. Nevertheless, the London House of Converts was apparently full by 1250, with the result that 'excess' converts had to be scattered among English monastic communities. In 1255, for example, the year in which 'little Hugh of Lincoln' was supposedly murdered by Jews, over 150 Jewish converts to Christianity were living in the houses of seven different religious orders, throughout England. Converts continued to be accommodated in this way up to the very end of legal Jewish life in medieval England, in 1290.[21]

While some details of the political and economic arrangements made for Jewish converts, by Church and Crown, may be established, it is much harder to discover the true nature of the 'conversions' that took place. There is, however, a possibility of knowing, at least, what guidelines existed for such cases. Under the rules set down by Pope Innocent III, in 1215, it was almost impossible for a Jew to be released from baptismal vows, even when the sacrament was administered under threat of violence and even death, as frequently happened on the continent during Crusades. Only physical resistance during the ceremony itself could secure subsequent release, and this was evidently a hard condition to fulfil. In 1236, Henry III ruled that the children of couples of mixed religion should be allowed freedom of choice. In general, though, English legislators in the thirteenth century, whether lay or clerical, seemed to have been more preoccupied with 'impurities', which might result from Christian contact with the remaining English Jews, than with the future fate of those Jews whose sins were supposedly washed away by baptism.[22]

Faith and doubt

Just as the monastic corrodies, used to support English Jewish converts, were similar to those offered to lay brothers, when they joined such communities, so ideas of 'conversion' drew their inspiration from earlier tradition, both monastic and lay, within the Catholic Church. As Karl Morrison has brilliantly shown, the first point to notice is that, contrary to later Protestant models, conversion to a full Christian life was seen, in the High Middle Ages, as a lengthy, even a lifelong, process, and not the matter of an instant. By the thirteenth century, the phenomenon of conversion, in general, tended to be associated with the religious life, so that the placing of converts from Judaism, either under the supervision and instruction of Dominican friars in Houses of Converts or as holders of corrodies in monasteries, would have seemed entirely appropriate. More ominously, though, it is also clear that one consequence of this view of conversion as process was an obsessive suspicion and fear of relapse.[23] While the rapid end to Jewish life in medieval England, brought about by Edward I's expulsion order in 1290, prevented the experiment of conversion from developing on a large scale and over a long period, the

[21] Greatrex, 'Monastic charity', p. 137.
[22] J.A. Watt, 'Jews and Christians in the Gregorian decretals', in Wood, ed., *Christianity and Judaism*, pp. 93–105, at pp. 99–100, 103.
[23] Karl F. Morrison, *Understanding Conversion* (Charlottesville and London, 1992).

problems of such a phenomenon were to be graphically displayed in the Iberian peninsula, after 1390.

Another feature of the Church's attitude towards conversion in the High Middle Ages, which is noted by Morrison, is the deep sense of insecurity and doubt that affected Christians, both when they viewed their own conversions and when they received converts from other faiths, such as Judaism and Islam.[24] In recent years, a number of historians, including this writer and Gavin Langmuir, have come to recognise the fact that 'For the religious person, doubt has always been an intrinsic part of faith', applying this notion in particular to medieval Christians, in their relationship with Jews, Judaism and Jewish converts to Catholic Christianity.[25] In the case of Jews, in the thirteenth century and later, four major doctrines seem to have caused difficulties, as they did for many of their Christian contemporaries. The three main difficult and 'doubtful' doctrines in question were the Incarnation of Jesus, including his Virgin birth and divinity, the cross on which Jesus was crucified for the salvation of the world, and the Eucharist or Mass, in which Jesus' sacrifice was remembered by the consumption of his body and blood in the forms of bread and wine. Unfortunately, there is little direct evidence of the effect of Christian worry about these beliefs and practices on Jews in thirteenth-century England, but there can be little doubt that Catholic teaching had an important and direct effect on both ecclesiastical and royal policy towards them in this period. The most direct and drastic effect on English Jews of such religious anxieties and fears was the accusation that members of their community had, on certain occasions, tortured and killed Christian children, generally boys, in imitation of the sufferings that had been inflicted on Jesus himself. The three most notorious English cases of such an accusation, at Norwich in 1147, Gloucester in 1168, and Lincoln in 1255, and especially the latter, were undoubtedly part of the religious and social preparation of Christian opinion for the subsequent expulsion order.[26]

Epilogue: Implications

Inevitably, it is not possible to separate England from the mainland of Western Europe in the period 1066–1290, in the context of the Church or in any other. Nor is it possible to disentangle Christianity and Judaism, as both sides discovered to their cost, in this period as well as later. This is certainly not the first effort to point to the two, Janus-like faces of certainty/doubt,

---

[24] Morrison, *Understanding Conversion*, pp. 21, 32, 49, 54, 119.

[25] Gavin I. Langmuir, 'Doubt in Christendom', in id., *Toward a Definition of Antisemitism* (Berkeley and Oxford, 1990), pp. 100–33 and id., 'Faith of Christians'; Edwards, 'Religious faith and doubt', p. 3; and id., 'Religious faith, doubt and atheism (with a contribution by C. John Sommerville)', *Past and Present*, 120 (1990), 152–61, reprinted in Edwards, *Religion and Society in Spain*, essay no. IIIa.

[26] Gavin Langmuir, 'Thomas of Monmouth: detector of ritual murder', *Speculum*, 59 (1984), 820–46, and id., 'The Knight's Tale of young Hugh of Lincoln', *ibid.*, 47 (1972), 459–82, both reprinted in id., *Toward a Definition of Antisemitism*, pp. 209–36 and 237–62 respectively; Joe Hillaby, 'The ritual child murder accusation: its dissemination and Harold of Gloucester', *JHS*, 34 (1994–6), 69–109; Edwards, 'The Church and the Jews', pp. 45–6. See also Anthony Bale's discussion in this volume, below, pp. 130–5.

defensiveness/aggression in Western Europe in this period. The consequences for Jews, though, both in England and on the continent, were clearly drastic and full of menace for future centuries – even if the direct 'action' was transferred across the Channel after 1290. The Parkes Centre at Southampton is, of course, concerned with the current situation of Jews and Christians. Nevertheless, as many have recognised, since James Parkes began his work in the 1920s, Jewish–Christian relations in the twentieth and twenty-first centuries cannot be understood, let alone improved, without a deep study of earlier periods of British and European history.

6

Medieval Anglo-Jewry: the Archaeological Evidence

DAVID A. HINTON

Certainly the Jew exhibited many curious characteristics to the ordinary medieval man. He had often a strange name; he spoke a strange tongue, and wrote with a strange writing; he ate different food; he had different legal customs; he belonged to a different religion. Almost any of these singularities, taken singly, might be found in other groups but there was no other group so widely scattered amongst the general population which possessed them all.[1]

Much attention is paid by archaeologists to the problems of defining and identifying different population groups through their material culture. This approach was developed by Gordon Childe for prehistory, but has been challenged and debated, not only by prehistorians, but also by early medievalists, who feel that ideas about migration into England have been based too much on Bede's tripartite division into Angles, Saxons and Jutes, and that this may have been a construct explaining identity in the later sixth or seventh century rather than one that was applicable in the fifth.[2] Rather different is the problem of identifying the undoubted presence of a minority group in England from the eleventh century onwards, and assessing whether the material culture of the Jews can be recognised, and its effect upon that of the majority of the population be estimated.[3]

It has been said that the Jews were the first migrants to come to England with neither a cross nor a sword in hand. William of Malmesbury reported that they had been introduced by William I from Rouen; they may originally have come as merchants and dealers, but changing and lending money was their main source of prosperity in the twelfth century.[4] Their legal status on their first

---

[1] J. Parkes, *The Jew in the Medieval Community* (2nd edn, New York, 1976), p. 239. It is appropriate to begin this paper with a quotation from the work of James Parkes, as it is being written in the building at the University of Southampton that bears his name, and much of the preparation for it was done using the resources of the Parkes Library.

[2] Among many, two useful articles are J. Hines, 'The becoming of the English: identity, material culture and language in early Anglo-Saxon England', *Anglo-Saxon Studies in Archaeology and History*, 7 (1994), 49–59 and B. Ward-Perkins, 'Why did the Anglo-Saxons not become more British?', *EHR*, 115 (2000), 513–33.

[3] When I first wrote this paper in 1989, I remarked that the difference was that for every word written on the archaeology of the Jews in England, there had been 10,000 written on the Jutes. I am grateful to Tony Kushner for not getting round to publishing the paper, as that purple phrase was probably indefensible then, and is certainly further from the truth today, as the 1990s references that follow will show.

[4] Richardson, *English Jewry* (see Abbreviations), p. 1; J. Hillaby, 'The London Jewry: William I to John', *JHS*, 33 (1992–4), 1–44, at 2; R.C. Stacey, 'Jewish lending and the medieval English

arrival was not set out in any surviving charter, but at least by the middle of the twelfth century they and their possessions were considered to be the king's, and they were free in everything except in their relationship with the Crown. Presumably, as royal possessions, they could not swear an oath of allegiance, so although they could hold land, they could not hold it for military service. Such restrictions would have prevented them from sharing the social goals both of the aristocracy and of indigenous merchants who might aspire to use their wealth ultimately to place their families within it.[5] Dietary regulations, if observed, excluded Jews from Gentile feasts, halls and the values of hall society.[6] Even before the further restrictions placed on them in the later twelfth century and in the thirteenth, therefore, Jews who held to their faith were prevented from social and political, as well as from religious, integration.

The material culture of the Jews[7]

Just as in the documents it is the richer Jews who make the most appearances, because of the scale of their dealings, so in the archaeological record it is the wealthier element who can most readily be recognised, since only the rich could afford such potentially durable things as stone buildings and inscribed tombstones. The former have been much studied; surviving stone houses in Lincoln and Norwich are ascribed to Jewish ownership on the basis of charters and other records, as there is nothing about their plan or style to distinguish them from the properties of rich Gentiles. Next to the 'Jew's House' in Lincoln, a building with a first-floor niche may have been a synagogue, but there are no other features that support the attribution.[8] Another, half-demolished, synagogue may now have been discovered in Guildford, behind the High Street. It had blind arcading created by columns with bases datable to the 1180s, stone benches and painted walls, so was clearly something very special.[9] Doubts over its function arise from the arcading, which goes all round the walls and does not seem to create a special niche on the east for an ark, and because unlike the

economy', in R. Britnell and B.M.S. Campbell, eds, *A Commercialising Economy: England 1086 to c. 1300* (Manchester, 1995), pp. 78–101, at pp. 78–84.

[5] C. Platt, *The English Medieval Town* (London, 1979), pp. 122–5. E. Miller and J. Hatcher, *Medieval England: Towns, Commerce and Crafts 1086–1348* (London, 1995), pp. 346–53, argue that ties between the wealthy townspeople and the local aristocracy were closer in the twelfth century than in the thirteenth.

[6] This did not only affect relationships, but participation in various modes of cultural behaviour: S. Dixon-Smith, 'The image and reality of alms-giving in the great halls of Henry III', *Journal of the British Archaeological Association*, 152 (1999), 79–96, shows how the distribution of food to the poor could be seen as a metaphor for the Mass.

[7] This section has benefited greatly from the paper by R.M.J. Isserlin, 'Building Jerusalem in the "Islands of the Sea": the archaeology of medieval Anglo-Jewry', in S. Kadish, ed., *Building Jerusalem: Jewish Architecture in Britain* (London and Portland, 1996), pp. 34–53, which discusses much of the archaeological record; I have tried to avoid duplication.

[8] *Ibid.*, pp. 40–5. A column in Norwich of similar date could perhaps also have come from a synagogue: B. Ayers, *Book of Norwich* (London, 1994), p. 47.

[9] Work by M. Alexander, J. Boas and K. Fryer, reported in *Medieval Archaeology*, 41 (1997), 290–2; a longer discussion is M. Alexander, 'A possible synagogue in Guildford', in G. de Boe and F. Verhaege, eds, *Religion and Belief in Medieval Europe: papers of the Medieval Europe 1997 Conference, Brugge*, IV (Bruges, 1997), pp. 201–12.

putative synagogue in Lincoln it is a semi-sunken chamber. If it is a Jewish building, it is a further example of the expense that some Jews went to; the use of Christian masons, and the architectural styles of the period, may 'reveal the desire of the Jews to legitimise their presence'[10] in the twelfth century, at least on the surface.

Houses and possible synagogues are no longer the only built survivals of the medieval Anglo-Jewry. A Hebrew inscription at what has been identified as a ritual bath or *mikveh* at Hotwells, not far from medieval Bristol's Jewish cemetery, has provided definite evidence for one specifically Jewish structure, although the actual function has recently been contested.[11] Two subterranean features found in the Jewry area of London may also have been baths; one in Gresham Street is described as a pit with two steps leading down into it, and could perhaps have been a strong-room, but the other, in Milk Street, has a curved wall and its identification as a pool seems more secure, despite there being no inscription.[12]

Hebrew texts were also used on tombstones, though few survive even in part,[13] and on such things as seals and tally sticks.[14] A long Hebrew inscription occurs on the Bodleian Bowl, found in a Suffolk stream in the seventeenth century; the text records that it was 'The gift of Joseph, son of the holy rabbi Yehiel . . .', one of whose sons, Samuel, lived in Colchester, and may have been an owner of the bowl in the thirteenth century. Two exceptionally large coin hoards found in Colchester have been associated with the Jews there;[15] they were found on what are now adjacent tenements in the High Street, but in the thirteenth century may have been a single property. Recent reassessment of the hoards attributes the earlier find to c.1237, the second to an original deposition in 1256, after which it was opened and perhaps had some coins removed, finally being made up with an additional parcel in 1268–78. The quantity, mint origins and relatively high weights of the coins that they contain suggest that they were financiers' hoards, and Jewish ownership is very likely. The lead containers in which the hoards were kept were more functional than a mere earthenware bottle or metal cauldron, used for many hoard burials. They may be 'forels', referred to in royal treasury documents, graded in size to hold specific amounts, and the way that they could be opened and have coins taken out and replaced provides an insight into the mechanics of dealing. Including a few forgeries, the second hoard had 12,160 coins in its first part, making 76 marks, and 1,916 in

[10] Isserlin, 'Building Jerusalem', p. 50.
[11] R.R. Emanuel and M.W. Ponsford, 'Jacob's Well, Bristol, Britain's only known ritual bath (*mikveh*)', *Transactions of the Bristol and Gloucestershire Archaeological Society*, 112 (1994), 73–86; S. Kadish, '"Eden in Albion": a history of the *mikveh* in Britain', in Kadish, ed., *Building Jerusalem*, pp. 101–54, at pp. 105–8. The identification is further discussed in I. Blair, J. Hillaby, I. Howell, R. Sermon and B. Watson, 'The discovery of two medieval *mikva'ot* in London and a reinterpretation of the Bristol *mikveh*', *JHS*, 37 (2002, 32–4).
[12] G. Pepper, 'An archaeology of the Jewry in medieval London', *London Archaeologist*, 7 (1992), 3–6; Kadish, '"Eden in Albion"', pp. 105–6; *The Guardian*, 25 October 2001; Blair et al., 'Discovery'. I am grateful to Richard Sermon for advice on this.
[13] M. Roberts, 'A Northampton Jewish tombstone, *c.* 1259 to 1290, recently rediscovered in Northampton Central Museum', *Medieval Archaeology*, 36 (1972), 173–8.
[14] *Anglo-Jewish Exhibition* (see Abbreviations), nos 3, 12 and 13. Isserlin, 'Building Jerusalem', p. 38, for some recent London finds.
[15] D. Stephenson, 'Colchester: a smaller medieval English Jewry', *Essex Archaeology and History*, 16 (1985), 48–52; Isserlin, 'Building Jerusalem', p. 38.

its second, 4d short of twelve marks. The 1909 hoard may have been in a
container able to carry £50 in pennies, but its actual contents are recorded only
as over 10,000 coins.[16]

The Colchester coin hoards have distinctive characteristics, but it is the
documents that make the specifically Jewish attribution so convincing. Other
forms of archaeological evidence may not be so amenable to detailed analysis;
food remains, for instance, become mixed between different periods and
different households, making it impossible under most circumstances to isolate
the bones and shells that are the refuse of a particular population group.[17] An
interesting attempt was made recently to try to identify Jewish elements among
the large quantities of medieval debris found in excavations in the Jewry area in
London. This was not based on artefacts that were exclusively Jewish, but on
those that might be particularly associated with Jews because of their beliefs
and activities; counters, scales, lead tokens and louvres were found to be in
greater proportions there than in other zones.[18] Unfortunately, the first three
categories are all trading items that would be needed by any well-to-do
merchant or dealer, and the fourth, louvres, is one likely to be associated
with any stone building with a tiled roof in a wealthy area. A fifth category,
lamps, actually occurred less frequently in the Jewry. There were no small
artefacts with Jewish inscriptions, a *shofar* from Leadenhall not being close to
the Jewry.[19] Such finds are very occasionally made, such as the lead disc with a
Hebrew inscription, thought to have been a synagogue token and copying the
English short-cross penny of 1180–1247, found in Winchester – not in Jewry
Street, but in the predominantly small-trade and manufacturing zone in the
lower part of the city.[20] A more spectacular discovery was the three-spouted
lamp found in Bristol's New Jewry, in 1976, and presumably therefore a
medieval object used in England, in contrast to the four-spouted lamp owned
by the Society of Antiquaries, which is recorded as dug up near Windsor in
1717, a context that leaves its origin obscure.[21]

Another category of material culture that might be expected in the archaeological record of the medieval Anglo-Jewry is the finger-ring, particularly as the
marriage ring was very distinctive in later centuries;[22] but despite the recent

[16] This information paraphrases M.M. Archibald and B.J. Crook, *English Medieval Coin Hoards I:
Cross and Crosslets, Short Cross and Long Cross Hoards* (British Museum Occasional Paper 87,
London, 2001), pp. 67–142. Only the hoard found in 1969 is analysed in detail, but the discussion
includes that found in 1902. (There is also a mention of a third lead container found on the same
site in 2000, frustratingly empty!) Stephenson's suggestion of Jewish ownership is reviewed and
accepted on pp. 94–6. The bias towards a London origin of many of the coins fits well with
Colchester Jews' known dealings with that city, and compensates for rejection of one minor
element in Stephenson's argument, that the number of continental and Scottish coins would
reflect Jewish dealings, since comparison with other English hoards does not seem to me to
suggest a higher proportion of such coins than in those.
[17] Isserlin, 'Building Jerusalem', p. 38.
[18] Pepper, 'Archaeology of the Jewry', pp. 3–6.
[19] Isserlin, 'Building Jerusalem', p. 37.
[20] D. Keene, *Survey of Medieval Winchester* (Oxford, 1985), p. 386; I am grateful to Professor
Martin Biddle for telling me of the synagogue interpretation.
[21] R.R. Emanuel, 'The Society of Antiquaries' sabbath lamp', *Antiquaries Journal*, 80 (2000), 308–
15; the Bristol lamp seems to be unpublished otherwise.
[22] O.M. Dalton, *Catalogue of the Finger-Rings . . . in the British Museum* (London, 1912), pp. xlix
and 189–94.

proliferation of metalwork discovered by detectorists no pre-Expulsion examples have been noted. Furthermore, the only Hebrew inscriptions found on rings are pseudo-cabbalistic, but have a Christian connotation, like AGLA, Latin letters used for *Atha Gebri Leilan Adonai* – 'Thou art mighty for ever, O Lord'.[23] Wearing inscribed rings may have been one form of distinguishing device that was not used by the English Jews, therefore. They would, however, have become increasingly distinctive in a negative way through jewellery, if they respected the rabbinical law proscribing the wearing of gemstones,[24] another increasing fashion in the thirteenth century, imbued with Christian belief and indeed initiated by churchmen. The Jews may have been less drawn generally to changes in fashion than their contemporaries, but in general wore the same dress.[25] One of the remarkable caricatures that occur in a few administrative records shows a female Jew in contemporary coif and wimple, and the costume worn by the men would not have looked out of place in an English street, except that one is wearing a pointed *pileum cornutum* hat, head-gear distinctive to the Jews; the others are in hoods that may have been less specific to their race, but which were perhaps worn in public at times when Gentiles might have gone bare-headed.[26]

The attitude of the Jews to Christian material culture seems to have been slightly ambivalent; their respect for the written text may account for their reluctance to handle books,[27] since pawns involving church treasures are recorded,[28] but they had no qualms over dealing in gems, including cameos. which if antique presumably carried images given Christian interpretations.[29] Gems were used on church plate long before they were commonly set into secular rings and brooches, and the likelihood that they would have to create Christian chalices and the like may have restrained Jews from working as goldsmiths and jewellers in the numbers that might be expected in view of the investment necessarily involved in the craft, even before the growing power of the guilds, and the exclusion of Jews from them, closed it to them.[30] Probably

[23] *Ibid.*, no. 866.

[24] G. Seidmann, 'Jewish marriage-rings', *Jewellery Studies*, 1 (1983–4), 41–4.

[25] C. Roth, 'A day in the life of a medieval English Jew', in id., *Essay and Portraits in Anglo-Jewish History* (Philadelphia, 1962), pp. 26–45, at p. 27.

[26] C. Roth, 'Portraits and caricatures of medieval English Jews', in id., *Essays and Portraits*, pp. 22–5; Lipman, *Norwich* (see Abbreviations), pp. 313–15 and figs 1 and 10. The most complex drawing shows a scene that is usually taken to be a reference to a stage setting, but an alternative is to see the context as Henry III's castle infiltrated by Jews and devils, with Isaac of Norwich crowned to make the point more explicit; two of the other named Jews would then be seated behind a table, draped along the front as in many Last Supper representations, and with a chequer-board top for accounting.

[27] C. Hilton, 'St Bartholomew's Hospital, London, and its Jewish connections', *JHS*, 30 (1987–8), 21–50, at 21–2.

[28] Hillaby, 'London Jewry', p. 11, for examples. This is despite the ban that is inferred to date at least from Henry II's charter: Richardson, *English Jewry*, p. 109. The ban placed on dealing in blood-stained garments may have arisen from the increasing incidence of child-murder accusations, discussed by J. Hillaby, 'The ritual child murder accusation: its dissemination and Harold of Gloucester', *JHS*, 34 (1994–6), 69–109.

[29] E.g., R.W. Lightbown, *Medieval European Jewellery* (London, 1992), p. 23; Keene, *Survey*, p. 324. An imposition on dealing in high-value jewellery without royal licence, cited by C. Roth, *The Jews of Medieval Oxford* (Oxford Historical Society, new series 9, Oxford, 1945–6), pp. 41–2, was perhaps more important for the fine than for the restriction.

[30] Richardson, *English Jewry*, pp. 25–7, cites a few examples, and Hillaby, 'London Jewry', p. 10,

more significant was that Jews do not seem to have been moneyers, an occupation often combined with goldsmithing, despite their dealing in coin and plate, often in very large amounts.[31] Moneyers had to have a royal licence, and well-established English seigneurial involvement in minting may have precluded outsiders from breaking in.[32]

Burials and topography

The archaeological record of the medieval Anglo-Jewry was enhanced in 1982–3 by the discovery and partial excavation of the Jewish cemetery in York, and by its exemplary publication.[33] Early doubts about its correct identification arose from three factors. No inscribed tombstones of the sort known from four other English sites were found, but this could be merely because they were not used in York, as traces of a few wooden grave-markers were observed. Secondly, iron coffin fittings had been used, which is not a modern Jewish practice. Finally, and perhaps most remarkably, the graves were aligned approximately south to south-east/north to north-east, rather than west–east. This alignment, which had already been recorded in Germany at Worms, may have been so that the bodies could rise to face an entrance gate.[34] In York, this would place the gate in a narrow passage that led between houses in Monkgate, one of the main roads into the city, which seems a more plausible explanation than that the alignment was imposed upon the Jews by Christian authorities anxious to stress their difference.[35] It was certainly a local not a state decision, since west–east burial was practised at the Jewish cemeteries in both London and Winchester, where three graves were found in 1955, others in 1974 and 1975, and a much larger group in 1996.[36]

---

records a king's goldsmith called Leo; I do not know of any further names in records published subsequently. See also R.I. Moore, *The Formation of a Persecuting Society* (Oxford, 1987), pp. 83–4.

[31] Stacey, 'Jewish lending', p. 82.

[32] P. Nightingale, 'Some London moneyers, and reflections on the organization of English mints in the eleventh and twelfth centuries', *Numismatic Chronicle*, 142 (1982), 34–50. There may have been occasional exceptions, such as 'David' of Thetford seems to imply: K.T. Streit, 'The expansion of the Jewish community in the reign of King Stephen', *Albion*, 25 (1993), 177–92, at 183; Hillaby, 'London Jewry', pp. 14–15, notes that Jews were drawn to towns that had mints, presumably though for dealing rather than moneying; this would explain the paucity of records of their being in such towns as Coventry and Dunwich. The suggestion that moneyers had to take an oath of allegiance to the king, which would not have been permissible for Jews, was made by Jacobs, *Jews* (see Abbreviations), pp. 393–5, but I have not been able to substantiate this.

[33] J.M. Lilley et al., *The Jewish Burial Ground at Jewbury* (Archaeology of York 12/3, York, 1994).

[34] P.V. Addyman, 'Circumstances of excavation and research', in *ibid.*, pp. 298–30; J.M. Lilley, 'The archaeology of Jewbury', in *ibid.*, pp. 316–60 at pp. 341–3, and ead., 'Interpretation of the excavated remains', in *ibid.*, pp. 360–94, at pp. 382, 383 and 370.

[35] R.B. Dobson, in his review of Lilley et al., *Jewbury*, *JHS*, 34 (1994–6), 237–41, noted at 239 the possibility of Christian control.

[36] W.F. Grimes, *The Excavation of Roman and Medieval London* (London, 1968), p. 181; J. Collis, *Winchester Excavations, Volume 2, 1949–1960* (Winchester, 1978), p. 248; summaries in *Medieval Archaeology*, 18 (1974), 200; 19 (1975), 44; and 41 (1997), 270. Some burials in Northampton's Jewish burial-ground have been excavated, but details have yet to be published: G. Foard, 'The early topography of Northampton and its suburbs', *Northamptonshire Archaeology*, 26 (1995), 109–22, at 120.

Other aspects of York's Jewbury cemetery conformed to expectations of a *Hortus Judeorum*. Its orderliness was one of its most noticeable features, a contrast to the intercutting of graves at parish churches like the city's St Helen's,[37] a typical urban graveyard in which respect for the bodies of the dead as individuals would be likely to last only as long as members of their families remained in the parish. Winchester's Jewry, like York's, made considerable use of coffins. One reason for this may have been the need to transport the dead from places far away from the few licensed cemeteries. Gentiles were moved in various containers that were lighter than wood, but their corpses might be disembowelled or defleshed first,[38] which might have been unacceptable to Jews. The York cemetery's alignment suggests that national and international uniformity was not as strong as supposed, however, and that modern practices in such details as the use of iron fittings for coffins cannot be automatically assumed also to have been medieval. This raises the wider question of the extent to which Jews adapted or were forced to adapt to local circumstances in other matters, such as food taboos.

The Winchester burials include a very high proportion of infants, so comparison of the population's ages, heights and diseases may not be directly comparable to the results obtained from York. Preliminary analysis suggests a similar access to a better than average diet, however.[39] In stature, there was a little difference between Jews buried in York and other townsfolk; the average Jewish male in particular was slightly shorter than his contemporaries, but the difference was too slight to have been noticeable in individuals. A close look at a Jew's head might have revealed minor differences around the eyes and mouth, and in the teeth; and the number of older women might have caused comment.[40] The number of successfully healed fractures is probably a tribute both to greater care in the community and to Jewish medical skills. The high proportion of broken leg-bones is curious, especially in a population group that suffered fewer injuries than most.[41] Riding falls, perhaps to be expected in skeletons of people who spent much time travelling, would have caused more arm and upper body injuries. What the Jewbury cemetery cannot reveal is whether the Jews had a distinctive swarthiness of skin, or whether any difference would have been no more than a contemporary might have attributed to exposure to the sun, like a peasant-farmer. The thirteenth-century caricatures emphasise other characteristics that would not show in skeletons – hook noses, beards and curly forelocks.[42] Popular belief was that the Jews had a distinctive smell, possibly from eating more garlic than most, or using chemicals to remove body hair.[43]

[37] Lilley, 'Interpretation', p. 365.
[38] R. Horrox, 'Purgatory, prayer and plague, 1150–1380', in P.C. Jupp and C. Gittings, eds, *Death in England: An Illustrated History* (Manchester, 1999), pp. 90–108, at pp. 95–7.
[39] Analysis by Dr Janet Henderson for the City of Winchester Archaeological Office; I owe the information to Mr Kenneth Qualmann.
[40] G. Stroud, 'The distinctiveness of the Jewbury population', in Lilley et al., *Jewish Burial Ground*, pp. 523–6, at pp. 525–6. The longevity of Jewish women has been attributed to their having had smaller families: R. Bartlett, *England under the Norman and Angevin Kings* (Oxford, 2000), p. 348.
[41] D.R. Brothwell and S. Browne, 'Pathology', in Lilley et al., *Jewish Burial Ground*, pp. 457–94, at pp. 480–6.
[42] Roth, 'Portraits and caricatures'.
[43] Mundill, *Solution* (see Abbreviations), p. 49.

Although the Jews were isolated from their Christian contemporaries in death, a matter of mutual choice, they were not confined to specific areas in their lives. Many towns had 'Jewries', but they were not ghettos;[44] other wealthy townsfolk lived in the same streets, and it has to be assumed that poorer Jews lived undocumented according to what they could afford.[45] The need for Jews to live close to a castle is well-documented; the only town without one that was licensed to have an *archa*, the chest in which Jewish records were kept, was Wilton, Wiltshire, because that was where the county court was normally held.[46] The Jewries were not necessarily adjacent to the castles; what mattered was that they should be in the best trading zone. Similarly, proximity to castles was not a major reason for the choice of Jewish cemeteries, although Winchester's backed on to the moat. More important was that they should be outside the town walls at some distance from buildings.[47] The topographical obliteration of York's Jewbury cemetery after 1290 is typical, because land just outside towns was too valuable to be left undeveloped,[48] as it might have been a hundred years later.

Contributing to the costs of maintenance of their cemeteries was but one of the extra costs involved in being a Jew. All the differences between Jews and Christians in Western Europe cited in the quotation at the start of this chapter would have been expensive to maintain – the special education needed to learn to write Hebrew, Aramaic, French and Greek,[49] foodstuffs that could not be bought in the ordinary market;[50] and the maintenance of a separate religious establishment. Whether this meant that poorer Jews were more likely to accept conversion, and thus to merge into the general population because they could not afford to maintain a lifestyle separate from it, seems to be unknown,[51] but to desert 'a status-group who were defined as outsiders and inferiors on the basis of their religion'[52] may have had more attraction for them.

---

[44] Isserlin, 'Building Jerusalem', p. 36, mentions the possibility of a palisade around the Jewry at Hereford, but this was not noted by Joe Hillaby, 'A magnate among the marchers: Hamo of Hereford, his family and clients, 1218–1253', *JHS*, 31 (1988–90), 23–82, at 55–6, and the idea may have arisen because properties on the north side of Jewry Lane would have been backed on to the city wall.

[45] See for instance maps of Winchester: Keene, *Survey*, fig. 46; of Oxford: Roth, *Jews of Oxford*, end map; and of Norwich: Lipman, *Norwich*, figs 12 and 13.

[46] V.D. Lipman, 'Jews and castles in medieval England', *TJHSE*, 28 (1981–2), 1–19.

[47] S. Rees Jones, 'Historical survey', in Lilley et al., *Jewbury*, pp. 301–16, at pp. 305–8; J. Barrow, 'Urban cemetery location in the high Middle Ages', in S. Bassett, ed., *Death in Towns: Urban Responses to the Dying and the Dead, 100–1600* (Leicester, 1992), pp. 78–100, at p. 94, notes that Norwich and Cambridge may have had intra-mural Jewish cemeteries despite prohibitions, though Rees Jones, p. 305, suggests that the former possibility may arise from confusion over *hortus* references; the Cambridge location depends upon finds of broken tombstones near the Guildhall.

[48] Rees Jones, 'Historical survey', p. 309.

[49] J. Hillaby, 'Beth miqdash me'at: the synagogues of medieval England', *JEH*, 44 (1993), 182–98, at 190–2.

[50] Isserlin, 'Building Jerusalem', pp. 37–8.

[51] R. Stacey, 'The conversion of the Jews to Christianity in thirteenth-century England', *Speculum*, 67 (1992), 263–83, notes that property of converts being forfeit to the king would have been a disincentive for the better-off.

[52] S.H. Rigby, *English Society in the Later Middle Ages* (Basingstoke, 1995), p. 284.

Castles and hinterlands

The castles to which the Jews looked for protection were usually the king's, but some were privately held, such as the Bigods' in Bungay, Suffolk, a town which the Jews had to leave in 1174 after the Bigods' power was undermined by Henry II[53] – quite literally, as the miners' tunnel can still be seen. Overseeing the Jews was one of several administrative roles taken on by urban castles in the twelfth and thirteenth centuries,[54] though no building is known to have been done specifically to receive them, the 'Jew's Tower' in Winchester being recorded as a name only some time after the structure had been built.[55] Nor was a defensible castle actually essential, for not only did Wilton not have one, but Bedford's was substantially reduced after 1224, and was probably useless for practical purposes.[56]

Bungay was not the only town that the Jews were forced to leave, and by the later thirteenth century their condition was made more precarious because of the influence of Queen Eleanor, who forced them from four of her towns, including Marlborough, Wiltshire, from which they were expelled in 1275. The queen had stayed in the castle in 1272 and 1274, and may have intended to continue to do so; certainly it remained as her property.[57] The thought that her own house might be a shelter for them, and that she might be 'polluted' by their proximity, would have been more than sufficient for her to have had them removed altogether. Another of her towns was Guildford, and it has been suggested that the putative synagogue there could have been systematically demolished and obliterated at that time.[58]

Even if no castle building is recorded as being specifically because of the need to provide for the Jews, it is worth considering whether their expulsion affected the need for castles to be maintained. In the relatively unimportant shire town of Dorchester, Dorset, the whole of the royal castle was sold in 1290.[59] Despite the date, however, and although there was a Jewish resident, there was no *archa* there,[60] and the diaspora is unlikely to have been a factor in the king's decision. One reason for the maintenance of castles was if they were places where royalty stayed, like Marlborough. Another was whether they were positioned where they could counter threats of invasion;[61] phrases such as 'we should not have to fear invasions by our enemies' that justified maintenance of Colchester in 1223 meant internal as much as external opposition, and Colchester's role diminished along with fear of political takeover by foreign kings, whatever threats of sea-borne raids meant for coastal sites. Typically, Colchester was reduced after

---

[53] Hillaby, 'London Jewry', p. 26, and D.J. Cathcart King, *Castellarium Anglicanum* (New York, 1983), p. 456.

[54] C. Drage, 'Urban castles', in J. Schofield and R. Leech, eds, *Urban Archaeology in Britain* (CBA Research Report 61, London, 1987), pp. 117–32, at pp. 123 and 127–8.

[55] Keene, *Survey*, p. 386.

[56] H.M. Colvin, ed., *History of the King's Works*, II (London, 1963), p. 559.

[57] J.H. Stevenson, 'The castles of Marlborough and Ludgershall in the Middle Ages', *Wiltshire Archaeological and Natural History Magazine*, 85 (1992), 70–9, at 77.

[58] Alexander, 'Possible synagogue', pp. 205 and 211–12.

[59] Colvin, ed., *King's Works*, p. 629; K.J. Penn, *Historic Towns in Dorset* (Dorset Natural History and Archaeological Society Monograph Series 1, Dorchester, 1980), p. 61.

[60] Mundill, *Solution*, p. 287.

[61] Drage, 'Urban castles', pp. 123, 125 and 127.

about 1307–8, though retained as a prison.[62] Most others were like Colchester, unless like York needed for particular reasons, in that case provisioning against the Scots. The Jews' expulsion would have removed one reason for maintenance, but not one that can be seen as establishing a pattern.

One recent discussion of the Jews in the years before 1290 has focused on their dealings in petty commodities, and with smaller land-holders and farmers. This makes it possible to see something of their involvement in some towns' hinterlands, not only in their streets.[63] They were brought into what may have been for them a new, rural, network, in which they offered an alternative source of credit to the established inter-vill pledging that put the poorer peasantry into obligation to their economic superiors.[64] Presumably the Jews did not travel around the local settlements – hawking money would scarcely have been a secure activity! Their willingness to make loans against future harvest produce presumably helped to draw people to the markets in which they operated.

There is so little information on market hinterlands in the Middle Ages that it may be useful to compare a very different form of evidence, supplies of pottery to the three towns for which Mundill has mapped the places that the Jews' debtors came from.[65] For two, Canterbury and Lincoln, there is published evidence on the sources of pottery used in them. In Lincoln, for instance, much of the excavated pottery was made in Lincoln, and the bulk of the rest came from Potterhanworth, with some probably from Fiskerton and Boston, and a little from further afield.[66] In other words, the supply into Lincoln does not at all reflect even all the main compass-points of the distribution of the places from which the debtors came. It would be interesting to know if the distribution out from Lincoln has a similarly limited range, or if the pottery spread as widely as the Jews' debtors,[67] revealing whether they were used to coming into the shire capital for their goods, and were extending their dealings, or if they were making special journeys.

For Hereford, there is evidence not only of what was used in the town, but work has also been published on pottery found within the county generally. Few of the Jews' debtors came from more than nineteen miles away from the town,[68] but they came from a wide circle around it. Much of the pottery used and broken in thirteenth-century Hereford came from kilns in or close by, and distribution of their wares seems to be nearly all to the west side of the River Wye; Malvernian wares are very similar, though with slightly more to the

---

[62] P.J. Drury, 'Aspects of the origins and development of Colchester Castle', *Archaeological Journal*, 139 (1982), 302–419, at 404.

[63] Mundill, *Solution*.

[64] E.g.. D. Postles, 'Personal pledging: medieval "reciprocity" or "symbolic capital"', *Journal of Interdisciplinary History*, 26 (1996), 419–35.

[65] Mundill, *Solution*, figs 4, 6 and 7.

[66] J. Young and A.G. Vince, *A Corpus of Anglo-Saxon and Medieval Pottery from Lincoln* (Oxford, 2002); I am grateful to Dr Vince for letting me have copies of the relevant chapters in advance of publication.

[67] Another network that bears comparison is that of the royal purveyance of grain for the Scottish campaigns of 1303–4, which have a similar spread apart from a zone of about five miles south of Lincoln, which supplied plenty of debtors but not much wheat: M. Haskell, 'Breaking the stalemate: the Scottish campaigns of Edward I, 1303–4', in M. Prestwich et al., eds, *Thirteenth-Century England VII* (Woodbridge, 1999), pp. 223–41, maps 2a and 2b.

[68] Mundill, *Solution*, p. 238.

north-east.[69] These patterns could so easily be changed by more excavation and fieldwork in the county that they cannot be taken as definitive, but they could at present be used to suggest that the Jews' clients who lived east of the Wye were getting much of their pottery from markets other than Hereford, and that in going into the regional capital they were stepping outside the normal petty commodity dealing of their district. As they were farmers who could reasonably expect to have surpluses of produce, they must have been among the better-off and more ambitious,[70] willing and able to travel extra distance to a larger town, and so not necessarily representative of the medieval majority. If there is any validity in this tenuous argument, it might be used to show that the Jews' network was not stimulating a flow of goods into and out of the markets where they dwelt, and that their disappearance would therefore have had no visible effect on the everyday lives of any but those few who borrowed from them.

Material culture used against the Jews

During the course of the thirteenth century, the Jews' position became increasingly parlous. Physical expression was given to antisemitism in 1215 by the barons who made their point about the Jews by breaking up their London houses and setting them in the City walls for all to see.[71] Burning of the chests that contained debt records similarly had practical purposes but used physical destruction as a metaphor. The notorious charges of coin-clipping may overtly have been accusations of offences against the currency, but involved a visible abuse that all could recognise.[72] Growing sensitivity about the human body, intervention in it for surgery and the concomitant shedding of blood created tensions about the Jews' established role as doctors and physicians.[73] Church liturgies that stressed the elevation of the Host at the Eucharist also led to the Jews' position worsening, as they were seen to have been responsible for the shedding of Christ's blood.[74]

The Church's stance against the Jews became more active in other ways, such

---

[69] These statements depend on two maps that are the work of Dr Vince and were published some years ago; errors in their interpretation, if any, are mine not his; see A. Vince, 'The medieval and post-medieval ceramic industry of the Malvern region: the study of a ware and its distribution', in D.P.S. Peacock, ed., *Pottery and Early Commerce* (London, 1977), fig. 8, and id., 'Part 2: the ceramic finds', in R. Shoesmith, ed., *Hereford City Excavations Volume 3: The Finds* (CBA Research Report 56, London, 1985), fig. 34.

[70] Mundill, *Solution*, pp. 220–4.

[71] Isserlin, 'Building Jerusalem', p. 42, corrects the misconception that these were broken tombstones, citing M.B. Honeybourne 'The pre-Expulsion cemetery of the Jews in London', *TJHSE*, 20 (1959–61), 145–59, at 153–4; see also Hillaby, 'London Jewry', p. 39; W. Johnson, 'Textual sources for the study of Jewish currency crimes in thirteenth-century England', *British Numismatic Journal*, 66 (1996), 21–32, at 23.

[72] D.C. Skerner, 'King Edward I's articles of inquest on the Jews and coin-clipping, 1279', *Historical Research*, 72 (1999), 1–26. Johnson, 'Textual sources', p. 28, points out that the medieval mind would have made a connection with circumcision, another physical expression of difference.

[73] Moore, *Formation*, pp. 150–1; Hillaby, 'London Jewry', pp. 8–9 for twelfth-century Jews practising medicine in England.

[74] M. Rubin, 'The Eucharist and the construction of medieval identities', in D. Aers, ed., *Culture and History 1350–1600* (Hemel Hempstead, 1992), pp. 43–63; ead., *Gentile Tales; the Narrative Assault on Late Medieval Jews* (New Haven, 1999).

as placing the friars into Jewries to be a constant and visible advocacy of conversion.[75] Restrictions on the sounds that were to be allowed to emanate from synagogues were decreed, not least so that they should not 'pollute' the friars' services.[76] An extreme form of extermination of all traces of heresy was the appropriation of synagogues for churches, in marked contrast to the twelfth-century tolerance that seemingly had allowed Bristol Jews to use the undercroft of a parish church.[77] Jews were not supposed to enter churches as a result of the Oxford Council of 1222, nor to build their own synagogues,[78] decrees that gave physical expression to religious intolerance. Physical confrontation was perpetuated in Oxford after a Jew supposedly attacked a Christian procession in 1268; the Jews had to pay for a replacement of the liturgical cross carried by the priest, but also more tellingly for a marble cross that was to be a constant reminder of the event, placed to cause the Jewish community maximum offence near their synagogue.[79]

Oxford's synagogue was set well back from the main street. Whereas the twelfth-century Lincoln synagogue, if correctly identified, was on a frontage, worship in the thirteenth century took place in back areas; partly this resulted from the conversion of private synagogues, on the rear of tenements, into public ones, but was also for discretion, to reduce the risk of violent interference and overt desecration – the Christian processions that increasingly targeted the Jewries would have sanctified the latter.[80] The placing of cemeteries shows a similar mixture of motives; rabbinical requirements for open ground away from buildings, state decrees that they should be extra-mural, the need for reasonable access, and probably an unspoken acceptance that public visibility might cause problems, combined to produce a suburban plot of land tucked away behind the built-up frontage of one of the principal routes leading out of the town, reached by a narrow alley. Winchester and York are examples, Northampton probably another;[81] even London's was reached only by a passage from Cripplegate, though it had a gate between houses on the lesser Red Cross Street.[82] These were liminal positions, physically expressing the Jews' place as outsiders, and often compared to hospitals, particularly lepers'. There is a significant difference, however, as the hospitals were deliberately made visible,[83] and their cemeteries were not necessarily hidden away out of sight.[84]

---

[75] Stacey, 'Conversion of Jews', pp. 263–4; Rigby, *English Society*, pp. 294–5.

[76] Hillaby, 'Beth miqdash me'at', pp. 186–90; id., 'The Worcester Jewry 1158–1290: portrait of a lost community', *Transactions of the Worcestershire Archaeological Society*, 12 (1990), 73–122, at 91–6.

[77] Isserlin, 'Building Jerusalem', p. 35.

[78] N. Vincent, 'Two papal letters on the wearing of the Jewish badge, 1221 and 1229', *JHS*, 34 (1994–6), 209–24, at 215–16.

[79] Stacey, 'Conversion of Jews', p. 265; Roth, *Jews of Oxford*, pp. 152–3.

[80] Stacey, 'Conversion of Jews', p. 264; Hillaby, 'Worcester Jewry', pp. 91–8.

[81] Keene, *Survey*, fig. 133; Rees Jones, 'Historical survey', fig. 304; Foard, 'Topography of Northampton', p. 116.

[82] Honeybourne, 'Pre-Expulsion cemetery', p. 146 and fig.

[83] R. Gilchrist, 'Christian bodies and souls, the archaeology of life and death in later medieval hospitals', in Bassett, ed., *Death in Towns*, pp. 101–18, at p. 115.

[84] I have found it difficult to substantiate this, as there are so few where the positions of both cemeteries and buildings around them are known in detail, but at least J. Magilton and F. Lee, 'The leper hospital of St James and St Mary Magdalene, Chichester', in C.A. Roberts et al., eds, *Burial Archaeology: Current Research, Methods and Developments* (BAR British Series 211,

After the Fourth Lateran Council in 1215, all European Jews were supposed to wear distinctive clothing and a badge; the latter was enforced in England in 1218, the synod held in Oxford in 1222 adding a few extra penalties and bans. It was to be of white textile or parchment, sewn onto the clothing, the design being a double rectangle, each round-topped, to represent the tablets of the Mosaic Law, or *tabula*.[85] The Jews were extremely reluctant to accept this imposition, partly no doubt because when wearing the badge they could not have hoped to melt imperceptibly into the general population when it suited them. There was probably also deep antipathy to wearing a cultural identifier that was forced on them;[86] the white *pileum cornutum* hat was originally a self-selected marker, worn with pride.[87] The badge was putting them on a par with heretics and prostitutes, and they were prepared to pay fines to avoid the stigma.[88]

In the thirteenth-century caricatures, two of the male Jews are shown wearing the *tabula* badge. One picture shows it worn at the breast, as it is on a Lincoln Cathedral sculpture,[89] but on the other it is closer to the stomach, possibly a derisory reference to gluttony. Jews probably lived frugally, but their caricaturists would not have known this, and their wealth would have made the assumption an obvious one to make. Perhaps the context of that particular drawing, alongside a Forest prosecution following a deer chase through the streets of Colchester, made it seem particularly appropriate. If the sin of gluttony was indeed intended in this drawing, it is to be set alongside both avarice, suggested in the Exchequer drawing by the devil at one end of the picture whose scales balance those held by a Jew at the other, and lust, suggested by the hats.[90]

From at least the late twelfth century, the wearing of badges and other markers was becoming increasingly familiar in English society, not least because of the crusaders whose activities helped to throw the Jews into the public gaze.[91] Most were of cloth, linen or parchment, sewn onto clothing, and therefore do not survive. In metal, the Folkingham Castle brooch with a coat of arms attributable to the 1150s/80s is the earliest known English example of the transfer of motifs from weapons and seals to badges.[92] Thereafter familiarity grew, from coats of arms to crusaders' crosses to pilgrimage insignia. No example of the *tabula* in metal is known, but that is not surprising if no-one

---

Oxford, 1989), pp. 249–65, at pp. 250 and 255–6, shows a cemetery apparently strung out along one of the principal roads into the city, with the hospital buildings closest to the gate.

[85] Roth, *History*[3] (see Abbreviations), p. 6. R. Mellinkoff, *Outcasts: Signs of Otherness in Northern European Art of the Later Middle Ages* (Berkeley, 1993), p. 101.

[86] Parkes, *Jew in the Medieval Community*, p. 239.

[87] This presumably changed over time, particularly as it came to be seen as an allegory of an erect penis and therefore suggested Jewish lust: M. Camille, '"For our devotion and pleasure": the sexual objects of Jean, duc de Berry', *Art History*, 24 (2001), 183. They are prominent in the Exchequer caricature: Roth, 'Portraits and caricatures'.

[88] Vincent, 'Two papal letters', p. 213.

[89] Roth, 'Portraits and caricatures', p. 25.

[90] *Ibid.*; Camille, '"Devotion and pleasure"'. It is not clear whether the only female Jew caricatured is wearing a badge or not; if one was intended, its shape, like a crescent moon worn at 90 degrees to its appearance in the sky, might possibly be an 'echo' of one of the scale-pans.

[91] E.g., Vincent, 'Papal letters', pp. 212–13.

[92] J. Cherry and J. Goodall, 'A twelfth-century gold brooch from Folkingham Castle, Lincolnshire', *Antiquaries Journal*, 65 (1985), 471–2.

wore it with pride and a desire for its permanence. Part of the significance of the caricatures in the thirteeenth-century documents is that they show how aware people had become of the symbolism of badges as identifiers of different groups within, or on the margins of, society.

The caricatures are especially interesting because they are not set-pieces in illustrated bibles and the like, but seem to be the work of bored clerks done for no higher reason than self-entertainment. Consequently they are expressive of the perception of the Jews in England among the lesser clergy, unlike the more formal twelfth- and thirteenth-century representations of the Crucifixion or Synagogue. They raise the possibility that other derisive representations may have been made. A chimney-pot or louvre found in Oxford, modelled as a bearded head with prominent nose wearing a pointed cap, is one possibility.[93] It may not have carried a specifically antisemitic message, however, as it may be no more than a cruder version of the stone 'face-pullers' found in obscure, unofficial positions in churches.[94] There are modelled faces on pottery jugs that could also be antisemitic caricatures, though as they occur on rims they do not usually show distinctive headgear; one with a long nose for a spout could be one,[95] a prominently hook-nosed Londoner another.[96] There are also recognisable knights, well-dressed ladies and even bishops, however, and the types are a European commonplace,[97] so virulent antisemitism at popular level is less likely than general mockery of social or economic superiors. There is nothing in these pottery grotesques to deny that 'the ordinary townsmen rubbed along with the Jews'.[98]

---

[93] I owe this suggestion to a delegate at a conference some years ago, whose name I do not know, and to whom I apologise if he reads this for my purloining his idea. The object is illustrated in D.A. Hinton, *Medieval Pottery of the Oxford Region* (Oxford, 1973), no. 19. I dated it then to the fourteenth century, which would make it post-Expulsion, but I am not sure how firmly that should now be taken.

[94] M. Camille, *Image on the Edge: The Margins of Medieval Art* (London, 1992), pp. 84–5.

[95] J. Musty, 'Pottery, tile and brick', in P. Saunders, ed., *Salisbury Museum Medieval Catalogue Part 3* (Salisbury, 2000), pp. 132–212, no. 182.

[96] B. Rackham, *Medieval English Pottery* (London, 1957), no. 47.

[97] E.g., H.-G. Stephan, 'Spätmittelalterliche Gesichtsgefasse aus Mitteleuropa', in D. Gaimster and M. Redknap, eds, *Everyday and Exotic Pottery from Europe: Studies in Honour of John G. Hurst* (Oxford, 1992), pp. 127–56.

[98] C. Richmond, 'Englishness and medieval Anglo-Jewry', in Tony Kushner, ed., *The Jewish Heritage in British History: Englishness and Jewishness* (London, 1992), pp. 42–59, at p. 53; Moore, *Formation of a Persecuting Society*, pp. 117–20. The most virulently antisemitic representations seem to come after the Expulsion, when knowledge of the reality was fading, e.g., the Holkham Bible: C.M. Kauffman, 'Art and popular culture: new themes in the Holkham Bible picture book', in D. Buckton and T.A. Heslop, eds, *Studies in Medieval Art and Architecture* (Stroud, 1994), pp. 46–69, and H. Schreckenberg, *The Jews in Christian Art. An Illustrated History* (London, 1996), p. 154; and the Tring tiles: Richmond, 'Englishness', p. 59. Antisemitism still received official as well as religious expression; as late as 1361, the order that Jews, like prostitutes, were to wear a distinctive badge was reaffirmed: S.M. Newton, *Fashion in the Age of the Black Prince* (Woodbridge, 1980), p. 121, n. 67. Material culture was also used against the Jews after the Expulsion by Edward I, who put royal sanction behind the cult of Little St Hugh at Lincoln by helping to finance the new shrine and having it embellished with the royal coat of arms: Richmond, 'Englishness', pp. 44–5, citing D. Stocker, 'The shrine of Little St Hugh', in T.A. Heslop and V. Sekules, eds, *Medieval Art and Architecture at Lincoln Cathedral* (British Archaeological Association Transactions 7, 1986), pp. 109–17.

Conclusion

It may have been in Winchester's 'Jew's Tower' that one of the most poignant records of Anglo-Jewry's suffering was to be found; transcribed by Selden in the seventeenth century, a Hebrew inscription recorded 'On Friday, Eve of the Sabbath in which the pericope *Emor* is read, all the Jews of the Land of the Isle were imprisoned. I, Asher, wrote this.' The date was 1287.[99] Three years later came the final Expulsion. It left little direct physical evidence; urban properties passed to new owners,[100] and the cemeteries were put to new purposes.[101] The Jews' departure caused no backlash from potential creditors unable to get loans; their late thirteenth-century role in dealing with lesser folk had no more integrated them within the population than their earlier negotiations with the barony had done. They had remained what they had always been, a group of outsiders. It can no longer be said of them, as it was in 1887, that 'The relics of their stay . . . are exceedingly scanty, as is natural when we reflect how few remains there are prior to the fourteenth century,'[102] partly because we have far more data from earlier centuries now, and partly because of the recognition of buildings associated with the Jews. Other aspects of their material culture do remain elusive, however. But the way that material culture was used both by them and against them to emphasise their group identity as 'other' is nevertheless an important indication of the way that people in general became increasingly aware of differences within society and the manner of their expression in the centuries after the Norman conquest.

---

[99] Roth, *History*[3], p. 273.

[100] Isserlin, 'Building Jerusalem', p. 36, cites Lipman, *Norwich*, pp. 123–4 and 176–7, for a building burnt in 1286 or 1290, but the account of the four-inch layer of charcoal reported in the 1930s is very vague, and such fire layers (if that is what it was) are very difficult to date with any precision; Ayers, *Book of Norwich*, does not take up the suggestion. The deliberate obliteration of the Guildford building, if indeed it was Jewish, would be a very extreme physical eradication: Alexander, 'Possible synagogue', p. 208. The non-recovery of the Colchester coin hoards may well be because they had to be left behind in 1290: Archibald and Cook, *English Medieval Coin Hoards*, p. 96.

[101] Empty graves in London's could indicate the removal of bodies for reburial overseas, but the dating is not secure: Grimes, *Excavation*, p. 181.

[102] *Anglo-Jewish Exhibition*, p. 3.

7

Women in the Medieval Anglo-Jewish Community

SUZANNE BARTLET

In a previous study, researching three medieval Jewish women of Winchester through the pipe rolls of the period and other contemporary documents,[1] I found that searching for the women of the medieval Anglo-Jewish community was a surprisingly fruitful exercise. Some of the methodological issues surrounding the study of Anglo-Jewish women apply equally to the men, although the former were less involved in the high-profile money deals that dominate the official records of the day. All of the original documentation was produced by non-Jewish authors whose main interest was in the wealth and business activities of the Jews. Colin Richmond estimates that only about one hundredth of the Jewish community were involved in moneylending,[2] while the rest rarely appear in the records. There are references throughout the pipe rolls to times when the king insisted that those Jews who were too poor to pay tallage or taxes were of no use to the Crown and should be expelled from the country. The earliest records referring to individual Jews by name began in the reign of King Henry II, but initially the records were sparse and inadequately maintained. Even those that do survive rarely mention Jewish women. More efficient documentation began in the reign of King Richard I, following the coronation riots of 1190 during which the records of debts were destroyed and with them a considerable amount of potential income to the king. As a result a more detailed system of recording monetary transactions administered by a Jewish Exchequer was established. This was followed by a growing bureaucracy that recorded the decisions of the king, the law courts and other financial incomes such as fines or duty payable for the more everyday activities of marriage, moving around the country or inheritance. This documentation constitutes the main source of information about the Anglo-Jewry for all historians of the period.

The upsurge of interest in the medieval Anglo-Jewish community at the end of the nineteenth century (described by Joe Hillaby above, p. 15) led to initial comments, most notably by Israel Abrahams, on the status of women within Jewish culture, as visible in the legal and fiscal texts.[3] In the light of more recent

---

[1] Suzanne Bartlet, 'Three Jewish businesswomen in thirteenth-century Winchester', *JCH*, 3 (2000), 31–54.

[2] C. Richmond, 'Englishness and medieval Anglo-Jewry', in Tony Kushner, ed., *The Jewish Heritage in British History: Englishness and Jewishness* (London, 1992), pp. 42–59, at p. 53.

[3] Israel Abrahams, *Jewish Life in the Middle Ages* (London, 1896, reprinted Philadelphia, 1911), p. 115 onwards.

research some of the earlier speculations and assumptions have been called into question. Stacey found some historians such as Powicke, Lipman and Roth repeating an error of dating by Stokes that put the 1244 tallage figures as happening in 1219. Katz found Roth to be 'full of mistakes, undocumented assertions and numerous gaps'.[4] In his favour it should be noted that when Roth found out he had made a mistake he did not hesitate to identify it, but there is plenty of factual reporting in Roth's books that is dependable, and it should be remembered that we are only operating within the limits of our current knowledge as Roth did in the middle of the last century.

Some of the most productive researchers have concentrated on a single theme of either place or subject. The medieval Jewries of Oxford, Norwich, London, the Midlands, Southwest England, Canterbury and York have been among the communities researched and, although not specifically women's histories, such studies have uncovered a lot of information about individual rich business women (Barrie Dobson reviews the York evidence below, pp. 153–6). Stacey and Mundill have, respectively, concentrated on Jewish commercial dealings with the Christian community and the Expulsion in 1290. Zefira Entin Rokeah has written extensively about crime and punishment among medieval Anglo-Jews. Approaching the rolls and other contemporary documents in search of a single theme can uncover new interpretations of the material, or the hidden meaning in some of the pipe roll entries. The thematic approach has shed new light on the ordinary lives of Jewish women.[5]

More recent accounts of medieval Anglo-Jewish women are scarce. Tellingly, in Cheryl Tallan's comprehensive bibliography of sources for medieval Jewish women, only four or five refer to English Jewry while a further twelve provide useful background information about their religious lives.[6] Seeing that most English Jews originated from France and that many English customs were also Norman French in origin, it makes sense to look at the accounts of French Jewry. The dissolution of the Angevin empire from the

---

[4] R.C. Stacey, 'Royal taxation and the social structure of medieval Anglo-Jewry: the tallages of 1239–1242', *HUCA*, 56 (1986), 175–249, at 190, n. 62. D.S. Katz, 'Marginalization of English modern Anglo-Jewish history', in Kushner, ed., *Jewish Heritage*, pp. 60–77, at p. 61.

[5] Regional studies: Cecil Roth, *The Jews of Medieval Oxford* (Oxford, Oxford Historical Society new series no. 9, 1945–6); Lipman, *Norwich* (see Abbreviations); J. Hillaby, 'London: the thirteenth-century Jewry revisited', *JHS*, 32 (1990–2), 89–158 and id., 'The London Jewry: William I to John', *JHS*, 33 (1992–4), 1–44; id., 'Hereford gold: Irish, Welsh and English land. The Jewish community at Hereford and its clients, 1179–1253, Part 1', *TWNFC*, 44 (1984), 358–419; 'Part 2', *ibid.*, 45 (1985), 193–270; id., 'A magnate among the marchers: Hamo of Hereford, his family and clients, 1218–1253', *JHS*, 31 (1988–90), 23–82; id., 'The Hereford Jewry, part 3: Aaron le Blund and the last decades of the Hereford Jewry, 1253–1290', *TWNFC*, 46 (1990), 432–87; id., 'The Worcester Jewry 1158–1290: portrait of a lost community', *Transactions of the Worcestershire Archaeological Society*, 3rd series 12 (1990), 73–122; id., 'Testimony from the margin: the Gloucester Jewry and its neighbours, c. 1159–1290', *JHS*, 37 (2002), 41–112; M. Adler, 'Jews of Canterbury', *TJHSE*, 7 (1911–14), 19–96; R.B. Dobson, *The Jews of Medieval York and the Massacre of March 1190* (Borthwick Papers, no. 45, York, 1974); id., 'The decline and expulsion of the medieval Jews at York', *TJHSE*, 26 (1974–8), 34–52. Thematic studies include: Stacey, 'Royal taxation'; Z.E. Rokeah, 'Some accounts of condemned Jews' property in the Pipe and Chancellor's Rolls: part 1', *Bulletin of the Institute of Jewish Studies*, 1 (1973), 19–42; part 2, *ibid.*, 2 (1974), 59–82; part 3, *ibid.*, 3 (1975), 41–66, and ead., 'Money and the hangman in late thirteenth-century England: Jews, Christians and coinage offences alleged and real: part 1', *JHS*, 31 (1988–90), 83–109; part 2, *ibid.*, 32 (1990–2), 159–218.

[6] Tallan's resource list is now downloadable from http://www.brandeis.edu/hirjw/pdf/tallan.pdf

beginning of the thirteenth century, though signalling increased political division between the two countries, does not appear to have meant the isolation of their Jewish communities. There is evidence of an appeal of one English divorcee to the Paris Beth Din in 1242, suggesting that many still regarded it as the senior religious arbitrator.[7] At times of danger English Jews took shelter with their co-religionists across the Channel, evacuating their children and their nurses there for shelter in 1265, and ultimately attempting to settle there after the Expulsion in 1290. Grossman, however, maintains that Jewish women in Germany had more social rights than any of their counterparts in Europe,[8] itself evidence of the variations that existed between Ashkenazic communities. There were signs that the English community was assimilating at a different rate and in differing ways from those on the continent. For example, Kisch, tracing the wearing of the *tabula*, the Jewish badge ordered by successive Lateran Councils, found that assimilation of dress had been almost total in England, northern France, Sicily and Spain, while Ruben's examination of the wearing of the *pilum*, the pointed straw hat worn by continental Jews, found it was no longer in use in England. It is thought that the lack of distinction in dress was the reason that the king introduced the wearing of the *tabula* to England soon after the Third Lateran Council in 1179 had demanded it, England being the first country to do so.[9] Despite several attempts to enforce this rule throughout the century, it still was not universally worn by the Expulsion in 1290.

Another potentially enlightening source of information can be from Jewish religious practices or teachings of the period. Maimonides (1135–1204) issued a long list of the requirements and duties of a married couple towards each other. This included the *ketuba* or dowry, property, furniture, a separate lavatory, the right of the wife to visit her parents once a month, and for either of them to bar the house to the other's relatives. It also covered sexual rights, specifying that she was not a captive woman to be forced to submit.[10] While this gives a clear picture of ideal family life, it is only an interpretation of the traditions of Jewish Law by a Sephardic scholar, and there is nothing to say that it had been generally adopted by the Anglo-Jewish community, or if anyone followed it to the letter. Some of the requirements of Rabbi Gershom, writing in about 1000 C.E. with regard to the rights of the divorced wife, were still not being followed by English Jewry in the mid-thirteenth century.[11]

Neither can it be assumed that religious practices or customs of today applied then. An instance of this is the current Ashkenazi custom that a baby should not be named for a living relative. Dr Rokeah believes the custom only dates from the nineteenth century, and the pipe rolls are full of examples proving that this was not followed in medieval England. Another instance of a possible variation from present customs is that of an attack on Bessa, a

[7] I. Epstein, 'Pre-expulsion England in the *responsa*', *TJHSE*, 14 (1935–9), 187–205, at 202.

[8] A.M. Grossman, 'Medieval rabbinic views on wife-beating, 800–1300', *JH*, 5 (1991), 53–62, at 59.

[9] G. Kisch, 'The yellow badge in history', *Historia Judaica*, 4 (1942), 95–144; A. Ruben, *The History of Jewish Costume* (London, 1973), p. 95.

[10] Maimonides, 'The Book of Women', quoted in Emilie Amt, ed., *Womens' Lives in Medieval Europe* (New York and London, 1993), chapter XII.

[11] Roth, *Jews of Medieval Oxford*, p. 52.

pregnant wife (see below, p. 125), who was dragged to the ground by her hair, which raises the question of why she was not wearing a *sheitl*, the wig that devout married women are now required to wear on their shaven heads. Maimonides also refers to the need for married women to cover their hair, which again suggests that *sheitls* are an innovation from Eastern Europe.

Other contemporary English sources include monastic cartularies, and the accounts of writers such as Matthew Paris, Roger of Wendover and William of Newburgh, but they are produced from a Christian viewpoint and only very rarely mention Jewish women. Nevertheless they reflect the beliefs and opinions of their time, and can give us some sense of the hostile attitudes facing the Jewish community. It must also be emphasised that those same accounts reflected the chroniclers' own prejudices, and this applies equally to the clerks writing up the court rolls, who were for the most part members of religious orders. Rigg says of them, 'They strove to be veracious, their accuracy on the whole is remarkable' but 'they had little sympathy or charity to spare for the Jewish people'.[12] Some showed their antipathy in caricatures drawn in the margins of the Jews appearing before them in court;[13] others by the way they reported the cases. Their recording abilities varied considerably: sometimes they used extremely poor Latin, while in others poor understanding of court procedures was apparent. For our purposes, the incompleteness of many records presents a real obstacle: Rigg suspected that many clerks made notes in court intending to write the report properly at their leisure, which in the event they could not, and so there are incomplete reports, such as 'The Sheriff appeared . . .' and nothing else.[14]

However, the modern editors of the pipe rolls have also to share the blame for obscuring medieval Jewish women. They thought fit to omit lists of debts and pledges, deeming them of little interest but depriving researchers of possible evidence of the whereabouts or even the continuing existence of the male and female individuals being traced. 'Lists of debts taken into the King's hands which consisting merely of names and figures are here omitted', followed by the bald entry 'lists of essoins', have the unrealised potential of essential information contained nowhere else. Fortunately, most of the original Latin documents are extant in the Public Record Office.[15] The Exchequer Rolls also have large gaps, one of them lasting thirteen years in the mid-thirteenth century, when the actual records were destroyed during the Barons' Wars.[16] Occasionally a little of the missing information can be traced by retrospective inference contained in later records, but this does not happen often. Large numbers of records kept in the Tower of London were destroyed during the Peasants' Revolt in 1381, while a valuable collection of Jewish tallies recording medieval Jewish debts were burnt in the fire that destroyed the Houses of Parliament in the nineteenth century.

---

[12] Rigg, *Select Pleas* (see Abbreviations), p. xv.
[13] Cecil Roth, *Essays and Portraits in Anglo-Jewish History* (London, 1962).
[14] *CPREJ*, V, p. 49.
[15] *CPREJ*, I, p. 82.
[16] H.P. Stokes, 'Records of mss and documents possessed by the Jews in England before the expulsion', *TJHSE*, 8 (1915–17), 78–97, at 87.

Identification: Names and naming practices

Tracing individual Jewish men and women from the rolls does have its own particular difficulties. The courts conducted their written business mostly in Latin, but a few accounts are in Norman French. While the nobility and court spoke a dialect of Norman French,[17] Jews among themselves spoke in Hebrew, and their signatures on the wooden tallies and chirographs that were the records of their business were mostly in that language. The more sophisticated members of the community had to translate for their monoglot colleagues in court, and sometimes were called upon by the authorities to identify the handwriting of Hebrew signatures. The absence of an agreed convention as to the spelling of the names of people and places can lead to much confusion for the researcher. In a single-sentence account of one court appearance, for example, Benedict is also spelt 'Benettus' and 'Beneton', which can lead to confusion as to whether one or three people are involved in this case.[18] Southamptonshire was the official title of Hampshire, but 'Southampton', which appeared at the beginning of some of the cases, has misled historians to think that the case was heard in the city itself, and that a sizable Jewish community continued there although they had been expelled in 1236, with a few individuals subsequently being allowed to have houses there for business activities.[19]

The same lack of conformity in spelling sometimes produces different names or can even alter the gender of the individual. Remembering that most women did not themselves appear in court may have added to the clerk's confusion. Belia of Bedford is called 'Bely' in one report, and her son becomes 'his brother'.[20] Jewish men had a Hebrew name, but wealthy businessmen dealing with Christians and appearing in court frequently might adopt Christian equivalents, Baruch becoming Benedict, Moyshe Moses and so on. Surnames were rarely used among Jews, the patronymic taking its place, although sometimes, if their mother was better known, her name was used instead. If both parents were successful dealers then either or both parental names were used. The sons of a remarried widow's first husband may have used their stepfather's name. An example of this is when the sons of Belia of Bedford are sometimes fils Deulebeny, their biological father who died in 1235, but with the passage of time they used their better-known stepfather, Pictavin's name. This may illustrate the need to obtain business credibility by association with a well-known individual, or possibly the head of their consortium. It should be pointed out that sons of wealthy Christian mothers who inherited their estate from their mother also often used a matronymic. Where surnames occur such as L'Eveske,[21] Le Blund and Crespin, they are usually associated with business consortia.

Jewish names often included a toponym, but whereas Christian toponyms refer to the place in which they were born, and frequently continued to live, Jewish toponyms mostly allude to their main area of business. In some cases

[17] M. Prestwich, *The Three Edwards: War and State in England 1272–1377* (7th edn, London, 1980), p. 137.
[18] *CPR 1272–81*, p. 113.
[19] A. Saltman, *The Jewish Question in 1655. Studies in Prynne's Demurrer* (Bar-Ilan U.P., 1995), p. 153.
[20] *CPR 1266–72*, p. 21.
[21] Sometimes translated as 'Episcopus'; today it would be Cohen.

when they move to another town their toponym changes too; as when David of Lincoln became 'of Oxford' and, on one occasion 'of London'. Licoricia of Winchester, early in her documentary career, was 'of Canterbury'. Those of foreign origin can sometimes be identified in this way, as in 'Isaac of Tchernigoff' or 'Josce of Calais', who is also called 'the French' on occasion. There are many Isaacs, Jacobs and Abrahams, the names sometimes recurring among their sons and grandsons, which makes for some considerable difficulty in sorting them out, as in a court case involving 'Samuel son of Sampson and Sampson son of Samuel'.[22] When there are more than one of the same name living in a city, they are distinguished by descriptive nicknames, such as 'the bearded one'.[23].

The identification of Jewish women named in the rolls is a little simpler. They signed their Hebrew names on tallies and bonds, but in the documents the wealthiest businesswomen used anglicised versions. Those still using their Hebrew names are more difficult to distinguish from each other. There are several Hannahs or Hennas, Sarahs or Sarras, and Leahs, and like the men, where more than one lived in the same town they might be distinguished from each other by nicknames, such as 'Sara the fair' and 'Sara the short' of Canterbury.[24] Other versions or diminutives of a popular name are sometimes used in the same family. Bellasez, sometimes called Belaset, could also be Belia or Bella; and was 'Belacot of Winchester' yet another version? Antera or Anchera could use the nominal derivative Chere or Chera for other members of her family. Antera Quatrebuches is called by all of these versions at various times by court clerks.[25] The rare use of a surname in this case might have indicated a consortium originally of four members.

More distinctive was a shared fashion in the first quarter of the thirteenth century among upper-class Christian and Jewish women for very florid French names. Among Jews appeared Almonda, Saffronia, Comtessa, Preciosa and Licoricia. These names were rarely duplicated elsewhere in the community, and this makes tracing them much easier. Patronymics were only added for the unmarried, and many used their mother's name when she was a reputable business woman or they were acting in partnership with her. When they were widowed their altered status was referred to by the phrase 'que fuit uxor'(was the wife of) or sometimes by the word 'vidua' (widow). Once they married they were identified as the wife or widow of their husband, this part of their name changing whenever they remarried. As most make their first appearence in the rolls as wives and widows, information as to the families from whom they originated can be lost.

A woman's toponym might be the same as her husband's, but when she became a successful businesswoman in her own right she, like the better-known businessmen, would be known just as 'Belaset of Wallingford', or 'Licoricia of Winchester'. An added complication is that those who converted also changed their names, adopting that of a Christian sponsor, or patron, so that there were several converts called Henry after the king. An 'Emma the convert' was in

[22] *CPREJ*, IV, p. 118.
[23] *Close Rolls 1234–7*, pp. 50–2: 'Benedict cum barbe'.
[24] Adler, 'Jews of Canterbury'.
[25] M. Adler, 'Jewish tallies of the thirteenth century', *MJHSE*, 2 (1935), 8–24, at 15 and 18.

conflict with Chera of Winchester over six tenements in the city. There are several cases in the rolls concerning the marital property or *ketuba* of wives who converted when their husbands did not, and vice versa. Where they did convert it can be difficult to continue tracing them.

Women and business

The tallage or taxation rolls give many clues to women's business activities. They also mention by name women not involved in moneylending but wealthy enough to qualify as taxpayers. These are mostly single women or wealthy widows who, because they have no business activities, are never mentioned elsewhere. The records suggest that the most successful medieval Jewish businesswomen were mostly either married or widowed, although this may be an issue of visibility: single women would have worked through their fathers or brothers, or in a family firm, which was sometimes headed by a matriarch. No woman, Jewish or Christian, was supposed to sign any form or agreement, or appear in courts of law unrepresented by a male attorney, but there is evidence that both religious groups had outstanding women who were exceptions to the rule. Dobson quotes Adler as saying that a Jewish woman could prosecute Jews and Christians and could find mainpernors or sureties for herself.[26] The account of the trials of Licoricia of Winchester make it clear that she was actually in the court as the accused, although she may not have testified in person. Although Dobson and Adler thought Jewesses had greater legal freedom, some Christian women appear to be carrying on their business in a similar way with the same freedoms. When attorneys were named they are often identifiable as a relative, but there were many Jews and Christians who hired out their services as attorneys to anyone, regardless of religion, who was unable to attend court themselves either because of the gender prohibition or owing to distance or pressure of business.

Once women married their ability to operate for themselves varied with their husband's attitude, and while they mostly vanish from the records of the Exchequer, a considerable number appear to have taken a very active role in their husband's business. They might be co-defendants when their husbands are accused of trespass or offences against the laws relating to moneylending or damaging the coinage, but they are also named as partners in the ownership of property. Their appearance as joint owners of houses or land, or even as owning property in their own right may indicate a close partnership, but might also be associated with their dowry arrangements. In some cases their sole property ownership may have been a way of evading a mid-century ruling that Jews were not allowed to own property other than that in which they lived, or rented to other co-religionists. Belassez, the wife of Benedict of Winchester, was named as the co-owner of a fully stocked 39-acre estate in the Sutton Hundreds.[27] There can be little doubt that many

---

[26] R.B. Dobson, 'The role of Jewish women in medieval England', in D. Wood, ed., *Christianity and Judaism* (= *SCH* 29, Oxford, 1992), pp. 145–68, at p. 156.
[27] Z.E. Rokeah, 'Crime and Jews in late 13th-century England, part 1', *HUCA*, 55 (1984), 95–158, at 100.

wives were invisible partners, acquiring considerable business expertise as backroom girls. Belia is first mentioned as a widow of a few weeks who was able to start dealing at once although her inheritance from her husband was not settled for at least two years.[28] Clearly she had access to money of her own apart from her *ketuba* or dowry, which would have been delayed in being paid out.

If wives shared their husbands' success then they were also subject to imprisonment and mistreatment in bad times. They could be used as hostages, as in the case of the wife and children of Samaritanus of Winchester, who were held while he tried to find the tallage he owed.[29] Throughout a whole series of imprisonments and trials over the next few years, his wife was named with him. Judea, the wife of Abraham Russell, found herself alone abroad after her husband died as a fugitive, and her family and friends had to pay twenty gold talents for her to be allowed to return to England, as she had lost all of her husband's chattels, which were impounded by the Crown when he was out-lawed.[30] In pre-tallage imprisonment to extort the expected payments, wives and children would be brought to prison at their own expense.[31]

Although evidence of the activities of the majority of women therefore has to be looked for elsewhere, it is possible to glean from reported incidents facets of their everyday life, and from edicts banning certain activities the fact that they were involved in them. Examples of this include an edict banning Christians from buying Jewish food, which demonstrates that such commerce went on.[32] The requirement that no Christian should become a servant of a Jew, issued by the Third Lateran Council, was clearly ignored throughout the remainder of their stay in England. Bishop Swinfield of Hereford in 1286 threatened his congregation with excommunication if they attended a Jewish wedding, which reveals that inter-religious relationships could be friendly, particularly as his threats were ignored.[33]

Information about women's clothes or possessions is also alluded to in the records, although seldom directly. When their chattels were confiscated after a finding of guilt, or when they were suing the Christian custodians of their goods, which had been handed over for safekeeping in times of danger, the lists can give some reference to the clothes they wore. Robes of bluet, shawls from Rouen, a cape of perse with silver and gold tassels, tunics and supertunics of shot silk trimmed with rabbit fur, another dyed blood red and trimmed with squirrel fur and valued at five marks are listed among the many court cases where items given into the safekeeping of Christian friends and neighbours have vanished. The use of rabbit fur, given that rabbit is not considered to be kosher for eating purposes, raises the likelihood that these were pledged items, but some of them would have been worn by the wealthier Jewish women. Under Maimonides' requirements it seems that the minimum expectations were of a new robe every year, the old one being kept for wear during menstruation.[34] In 1245 two Jewish

[28] *Close Rolls 1234–7*, p. 230.
[29] Saltman, *Jewish Question*, p. 163.
[30] *Ibid.*, p. 195.
[31] *CPREJ*, III, pp. 103–4.
[32] A. Corcos, 'Extracts from the Close Rolls', *TJHSE*, 4 (1899–1901), 202–19, at 212, dated 1/12/81.
[33] Dobson, 'Role of Jewish women', p. 159.
[34] Maimonides, 'The Book of Women'.

women who converted were supplied by the king with robes of green or blue with panels of rabbit fur in the front.[35]

Jewish women and the life-cycle

The absence of birth dates can thwart attempts to trace the family of an individual woman, the age at which she married or in what order her children were born. Most documents recording stages in the life-cycle focused on property exchanges. Judith Baskin suggests that girls were betrothed very young, often at the ages of eight or nine, and married at eleven or twelve to a similarly aged husband, despite Talmudic prohibitions.[36] The betrothal contract of Belassez's daughter (see below, p. 126) gives a clear picture of what was covered in such agreements. The clause concerning failure to complete the marriage contract indicates that betrothals did not invariably end in marriage. Epstein states that English Jewry had adopted a more modern attitude towards betrothal being a lesser bond, although any default on the arrangement made the *ketuba* forfeit.[37] He exempts child marriage from this, although it is clear from the Belassez document that this was not always the case. Nonetheless Grossman maintains that early marriage was common throughout Jewry in the eleventh to thirteenth centuries.[38] That arranged on behalf of his daughter by Yomtob ben Moses indicates that some girls had more freedom of choice than others. He promised 'compliance as far as he can sway his daughter's actions'.[39] Generally it was only widows secure in their independence who had some control over future spouses. Spinsters were more at the marital mercy of fathers and brothers who were responsible for them.

Some women were betrothed while very young. We cannot know their exact age as this is never recorded. Isaac ben Reb Menachem betrothed his daughter when she was still very young to Morel of England in the 1170s. Unfortunately, he did not specify which of his three daughters was affianced. Morel subsequently had to divorce all three rather than be accused of bigamy.[40] Although the betrothal contract between the daughter of Belassez and the son of Benjamin fil Josce stipulates a four-year delay before marriage, we still cannot know when the permitted minimum age was.[41] Even presuming that the *Bar Mitzva* at age thirteen may have been crucial for the groom, there was no female equivalent that may have approximated to the menarche, although Dobson states that eligibility to pay tallage commenced at twelve for both sexes.[42] The age of legal adulthood for appearing in court or for carrying on a moneylending business might also have been useful as a possible indicator of the birth date, but this is not known.

---

[35] *CLR III*, p. 70.
[36] J.R. Baskin, 'Jewish women in the middle ages', in J.R. Baskin, ed., *Jewish Women in Historical Perspective* (Detroit, 1991), pp. 94–114, at p. 102.
[37] Epstein, 'Pre-expulsion England', p. 198. Judith was subsequently given permission to remarry after her husband was reported killed by a non-Jew: *ibid.*, p. 192.
[38] Grossman, 'Medieval rabbinic views', p. 57.
[39] Davis, *Deeds* (see Abbreviations), p. 33.
[40] Jacobs, *Jews*, p. 53.
[41] *Ibid.*
[42] Dobson, 'Role of Jewish women', p. 151.

Wives may have taken their own money with them into the marriage aside from the *ketuba* or agreed dowry, which was nominally £50 of their own and £50 from their new husband.[43] Sometimes this could be a dwelling promised to her in her own right when the marriage ended. What is clear is that the total of £100 'as is the custom of the isle' was not a hard and fast sum. In most cases it would have been used by the husband, and her *ketuba* would only have come to her on widowhood, if then, but it is clear that some wives had their own money.

Recent archaeological evidence from York (also discussed by Hinton and Dobson in this volume, pp. 102–3 and 148–9) allowed a comparison of the skeletons in the Jewbury cemetery with those from the Christian burial places of the same period, and revealed differences between the two communities. Jewish women survived longer into old age, and infant mortality rates were less among Jews. It has been speculated that this may have been owing to the different nutrition, and also the higher standard of hygiene and cleanliness practised among religious Jews. Men were required to bathe before attending religious services, and women to bathe after child-bearing and menstruation. It was also discovered that Jews were shorter in stature, and while the incidence of rickets and tuberculosis seem to have been approximately the same in both communities, anaemia occurred much less frequently among Jewish infants. The latest medical techniques communicated from the continent to Jewish doctors and midwives could also have contributed to these variations. Certainly there was evidence of expert surgery in the survival of some of the most severely wounded Jews whose wounds manifested signs of healing before dying much later. Jewish family sizes can only be guessed at. Dobson thought that families with more than three or four children were probably a rarity, but my own research has shown larger families documented among the wealthier Jews. Pregnancy is only occasionally recorded in the rolls when it involved fiscal payments: the wealthy Abigail, pregnant wife of Salle of Canterbury, paid for various comforts while her husband was absent abroad. Her nurse was fed with the sheriff's lamb at Easter, which seems to imply that her nurse was Christian, although this was forbidden several times during the century. Abigail also paid him for some other unspecified help, and ten marks for ten days' help as she lay in childbed.[44]

A common assumption is that the eldest son was most involved in his mother's business activities, but this does not allow for his level of competence or their personal relationships. There are plenty of entries that recount profound disagreement between mother and son or stepson. These seem mostly to be about her *ketuba* when she was widowed. She did not automatically inherit all her husband's property, but was only entitled to the amount agreed between them when they married. Usually the property included the house in which she lived. If it was agreed that she inherit more than this, it was expected that she return this to her deceased husband's children should she remarry. Any of her own money that she took into a

---

[43] Cheryl Tallan, 'Opportunities for medieval northern European Jewish widows in the public and domestic spheres', in L. Mirrer, ed., *Upon My Husband's Death: Widows in the Literature and Histories of Medieval Europe* (Ann Arbor, 1992), pp. 115–27.

[44] J.M. Lilley, G. Stroud, B.R. Brothwell and M.H. Williamson, eds, *The Jewish Burial Ground at Jewbury* (York Archaeological Trust, 1994); Dobson, 'Role of Jewish women', p. 152; *CPREJ*, IV, p. 146, n. 60 and p. 147, nn. 73 and 74.

marriage was generally regarded as her property. Disputes arose when her son or stepsons claimed their full legal entitlement. Leah widow of Benedict of Bristol was in dispute with her stepson, Mosse, and also had to pay her own children ten bezants for an agreement and another twenty marks for having her fair share of her husband's chattels and debts.[45] The records also contain as much evidence of good relations with sons and stepsons. Other associated information can be deduced from the roll entries. That Licoricia inherited all of David of Oxford's estate after paying the king his usual third indicates that there were no children by his divorced wife.[46] Like Christian women, Jewish mothers sometimes had to fine with the king to retain custody of their children. Avegaye, widow of Jacob, paid the king two hundred marks for the custody of her sons. Where there were young children left fatherless, guardians would be appointed, often from among male family members. Fines also reveal more mundane concerns: Bone the daughter of Josce of Canterbury paid two shillings for permission to go to her husband at Cheriton.[47]

Once widowed, medieval Jewish businesswomen came into their own. Dobson calls them the most liberated, independent and influential of women, with more freedoms and protection than their Christian counterparts, who might be married off by their lord to whomever he chose, unless he agreed to accept a bribe from the unwilling bride. Such independence was limited: Gentilla the Jewess is recorded owing £15 for permission not to marry a certain Jew.[48] Many of the wealthiest Jewish widows seemed to have remarried, sometimes more than once, carefully choosing older, rich husbands and accumulating more wealth with every bereavement. At a time when mortality rates were high it seems that the healthiest survivors married several times. This applied equally to Christians as evidenced during the following century when '27% of the married M.P.s were the second, third, fourth and even fifth husbands of their wives'.[49] Muriel of London paid a fine of £100 to marry Isaac 'as has been spoken between them'. They were both widowed and wished to form a partnership, which the king was always reluctant to accept as it reduced his chances of getting an instant inheritance when one of them died.[50] Others, such as Pictavin of Bedford, Belia's second husband, and David of Oxford, husband of Licoricia, allowed their wives to continue their business activities for themselves.

As widows some women headed or established their own family firms. Their sons could supply the male partners or attorneys essential for the continuation of their business, while their unmarried daughters could deal for themselves within the firm. Sons-in-laws, daughters-in-law, step-children from a previous marriage and nephews are mentioned as operating within these consortia, and there is plenty of evidence of members of the next generation continuing to work together long after the original head of the firm had died. Membership of the firms did not debar individuals from continuing to work alone or with other partners. The evidence of the names of their children, and of their attorneys

[45] Jacobs, *Jews*, pp. 95 and 97.
[46] *CPR 1232–47*, p. 478.
[47] Jacobs, *Jews*, p. 75; *CPREJ*, IV, p. 143.
[48] *CPREJ*, IV, p. 28.
[49] C. Rawcliffe, *Medicine and Society in Later Medieval England* (Stroud, 1997), p. 5.
[50] Jacobs, *Jews*, p. 29.

when they are mentioned, can give valuable leads to identifying and distin-guishing individual women. Clients can also supply an identifying link although there seems to be a tendency among the clerks to continue using the original names on the bond long after that has changed owing to remarriage or widowhood.

When a widow remarried her new husband might claim all her first husband's chattels for himself if there were no children counterclaiming. In a colourful account of a case that came before the Master of Jewish Law, Milla the widow of Saulot Motun disputed the claim of Samuel of Bolum that she was his wife by reason of 'contract and commerce between them'. The reason underlying his claim was that he ordered her not to dispose of any of her chattels without his consent. The court found that Milla was not married or tied to him in any way.[51] Some indication of her wealth might be deduced by a later record of her selling a debt of 100s to Elias ben Moses, but this could also have been an indicator of financial difficulties because her son's guardian, Aaron, gave her 4 ells of land in his courtyard by way of relief.[52] Other widows were snatched into marriage within days of losing their first husband. Porun widow of Josce fil Abraham of Worcester was quickly married by Isaac of Berkhamsted, who not only acquired all of her late husband's bonds and chattels, but three years later carried off her ex-father-in-law's estate before it could be assessed for the king's share.[53]

Imprisonment and protection

The fines of a third of property that the king demanded on the death of any man or wealthy businesswoman provide plenty of evidence of their property and possessions, but other entries in the rolls tell of more ordinary life against the upheavals of general imprisonments, which frequently occurred. Two pregnant wives imprisoned in the Tower of London at the time of the coin-clipping trials of 1278/9 had fines of 20s each paid by their respective husbands for permission to be 'at large', that is, free to leave the Tower. The lists of fines paid to Sergeant of the Tower during that period (discussed above, p. 60, by Robin Mundill) reveals that many wives were jailed with their husbands, who paid so that they might be free of chains and other restrictions. There are entries showing that the prisoners tried to carry on normal life as much as possible. Some of the poorer prisoners paid for permission to act as servants to their wealthier co-religionists. Whole communities from various cities were housed there. It must be assumed that these included the wives and families of the men.

There is also evidence that Christian men and women attempted to come into the Tower to continue business dealings with the prisoners. Some of this may have been caused by anxiety about their pledged property, which the king would confiscate when the creditor was condemned. Others, including several women, were caught bringing in silver and coins to exchange.[54] Einbinder

[51] *CPREJ*, II, p. 152.
[52] *CPREJ*, I, p. 154.
[53] *CPREJ*, II, p. 21.
[54] *CPREJ*, IV, pp. 171–94.

suggests that some women would have felt more comfortable dealing with women, and there might well have been a 'kitchen-door' element about the loans brokered by the 'invisible' wives of Jewish moneylenders.[55] Certainly they seemed to have been more inclined to arrange the safekeeping of their property with Christian neighbours in times of danger, as evidenced by the many subsequent court cases when they tried in vain to retrieve it.

When danger threatened there were places where the Jewish community could shelter. In the early thirteenth century women and children could be housed in monasteries. although this was not allowed later on.[56] Otherwise they could seek safety in the castles and prisons designated for that purpose. In the absence of any records listing those killed in attacks on Jewries it is not possible to trace the deaths of individual women except where they are subsequently referred to in property assessments for the king's third. Benedict of Winchester and his first wife Bellassez were attacked during the period before the Barons' Wars by a mob led by the Prior of St Swithuns. The attack must have been severe because the Prior had to pay Benedict £100 in compensation.[57] Jewish women were recorded as the victims of Christians and Jews. In 1277 two murders took place in Winchester. The well-documented case of Licoricia, who seems to have fallen prey to a poor saddler in the course of theft, is contrasted by the rather bald report of the murder of Pucelle the widow of Bonavye of Newbury.[58] That they occurred in the same year could indicate a level of violence in the community at that time. Similarly, there are cases of violence and family feud within the Jewish community. In 1244 Bessa the wife of Elias of Warwick was beaten up by Leo, his wife Henna, his daughters Antera and Sigge and his sister Muriel. The attack was so severe that Bessa miscarried. The whole Elias family was exiled from Warwick for life.[59] Even death might bring its costs: there is evidence of Jews being transported over long distances for burial, reflected in the pontage charged for carrying a Jewish corpse over bridges.

Conclusions

It is hard to trace any Anglo-Jewish woman's life continuously through the surviving legal records. For example, court cases, while they throw up valuable evidence of business dealings and family networks over a number of years, often end up disappearing without any final verdict. This has little to do with inefficiency of the reporters. The fact is that court cases were conducted in this way, with the jury members, witnesses, the accused, the plaintiff, and their mainpernors who guaranteed their appearence, taking it in turns not to appear and in some cases no-one came at all. It may have been a means of delaying justice either until the whole thing lapsed or the participants came to an out-of-court settlement. Where fines are recorded repeatedly in the various pipe rolls

[55] S.L. Einbinder, 'Pulcellina of Blois: romantic myths and narrative conventions', *JH*, 12 (1998), 29–46, at 37.
[56] Roth, *History*[2], p. 11.
[57] *CPR 1266–72*, p. 400.
[58] Licoricia: *CPREJ*, III, p. 293; Pucelle: *CPREJ*, V, p. 185.
[59] *CPREJ*, I, pp. 103–4.

confusion can arise over whether they refer to more than one occasion or are the same fine being repeated until it is paid up.[60]

Perhaps the most difficult aspect of modern studies of Jewish medieval women is the fact that they contain suppositions and expectations arising from recorded laws and customs of the times. There are many instances where modern religious practices are assumed to have been in existence then, or that the laws were accepted and followed in their entirety by the whole community, but the records are full of exceptions and individuals who do not conform. Rigg makes the point that 'we are liable to attribute much more logic and rigidity to medieval institutions . . . than they ever possessed'.[61] This, and the necessity of using legal records created for entirely different purposes than our own, means that the history of Anglo-Jewish women has yet to be written, and may never be known in its entirety.

Appendix: the Betrothal Document of Belassez (1271)
(from Davis, *Deeds*, pp. 298–9)

Lincoln,1271.
On Friday, the 3rd. Shabat [February] 5031/1271, Judah fil' Milo, Abraham fil' Josce and Josce fil' Joshua having received a preliminary 'God speed you' from a *minyan* [required minimum congregation] of ten, undertook the functions of a *Bethdin* [an official tribunal] to arrange, determine and attest the following transaction between Benjamin fil' Josce Yechiel on the one part, and Belle-assez, the daughter of the *Rav* Benedict fil' Mag. Mosse on the other. Belle-assez undertakes to marry her daughter Judith to Aaron the son of Benjamin, giving as a wedding gift to the young bridegroom 20 marks sterling and a precious volume containing the whole twenty-four books of the Hebrew bible, written on calfskin, properly provided with punctuation, Targum, Haphtaroth and Masora. . . . The young folk being too youthful to marry yet, the father of the bridegroom undertakes to take charge of the book and to keep it 'for the use of the children'. Belle-assez also delivers into the hands of the father these 20 marks sterling, to be lent out at interest to Gentiles, until Aaron is grown up. In lieu of this, at the period of Aaron's marriage to Judith, Benjamin under-takes to give them £20 sterling, and more if more has accrued out of the original 20 marks by way of interest meanwhile. Out of this sum also, he is to provide both bride and groom with wedding apparel befitting their station, both Sabbath and weekday clothing and to make the wedding feast all out of the same proceeds. He has to put no further claim on Belaset the mother.

The wedding is arranged to take place in the month of Adar [end of February], 1275, unless some impediment publically well known arise. If such difficulty occur, the nuptials are to take place within one month after the lapse of such impediment. Benjamin mortgages all his chattels and property, real and personal, as a guarentee that he will perform his part of the covenant. Should the affair not proceed prosperously, Benjamin refusing at a future date to marry his son, he is to restore the precious volume or to retain it

[60] Rokeah, 'Money and the hangman, part 1', p. 97.
[61] *CPREJ*, III, p. xviii.

at his pleasure, giving six marks in exchange. With regard to the 20 marks Benjamin is believed on oath as to what he might have gained from them in the course of time and undertakes to refund one half of the amount, reserving the other half to himself. The parties, each and either, then enter into a solemn compact and oath of the law, holding a sacred emblem in their hands and swear to perform their respective shares of the covenant. They thereupon place a partnership deposit or fine in the hands of the *Bethdin*, amounting to 100 shillings sterling, with the following undertaking. Should Aaron ever refuse to marry Judith and settle on her £100 'as is the custom of the isle', or should the father refuse his consent to the match, the deposit is to go absolutely to the mother of the jilted bride, or vice versa she is to lose it. Etc.

8

Fictions of Judaism in England before 1290

ANTHONY BALE

This chapter will introduce and survey some images of Jews from England dating from before 1290, the year of the expulsion of the Anglo-Jewish community by Edward I. I wish to demonstrate the role of art and literature in the development of antisemitic discourses, examining how the fantastical grotesqueries of antisemitism accompanied the practicalities of anti-Jewish persecution. I will also focus on the fluid 'uses' and meanings of antisemitic images or *topoi*; antisemitism was the product of many and changing circumstances, and medieval English interpretations and definitions of Judaism are diverse. Moreover, the persecution of the Jews was often an attendant, secondary element in the dissemination of these images; their primary purpose was often to bolster Christian identity and to 'use' the Jews, or the idea of Judaism, to ask difficult, dangerous or radical questions, as John Edwards has highlighted above, pp. 93–4.

Throughout this chapter 'antisemitism' will be my preferred term. The term is admittedly a modern one applied retrospectively, but the fact that the label did not exist does not mean that antisemitism was absent; it simply had not yet been categorised.[1] As will be demonstrated, medieval texts display the 'standard' antisemitic features of abjection, corruption, flexible notions of superiority and crude categorisations of Jewish physical difference. To be 'anti-Jewish' is to attack the real faith and culture of Judaism and those who identify as Jews. Conversely, antisemitism is constituted by imaginative and imaginary slanders forced on to those identified as Jews; antisemitism can flourish without 'real' Jews as it is not concerned with reporting material reality. As Jean-Paul Sartre wittily but incisively wrote, '[i]f the Jew did not exist, the anti-Semite would invent him.'[2] However, antisemitism and anti-Judaism are not unrelated categories; one encourages and feeds off the other. The fantasies, fears and preoccupations of antisemites have led to sadly real attacks on Jews and their communities. But, as Sartre's quotation usefully suggests, in our attempts to understand the development of antisemitic images our concern should be as much with the motivations of the antisemite as with the Jews the antisemite claims to depict. I do not wish to suggest that antisemitism is merely a fascinating rhetorical posture; we must always be mindful of the victims of the discourses we will encounter in the following pages. The *topoi* of antisemitism were used – in a sermon, a poem, an image – to discuss topics like

---

[1] The term is a nineteenth-century invention: a useful introduction to the history and theory of antisemitism is Milton Shain, *Antisemitism* (London, 1998).

[2] Jean-Paul Sartre, *Anti-Semite and Jew*, tr. George F. Bleeker (New York, 1965), p. 13.

national crisis, the Crown, sexual identity, financial disaster: to place blame, to explore selfhood and to make memory. And yet the attribution of blame to the Jews sometimes resulted in the 'real' manifestation of violence and oppression, arising from the original antisemitic utterance in which Jews were only an allusion, a figure, a vanishing reference-point.[3]

Christian culture, in the medieval Latin West, insistently discussed Judaism. At each cultural *stratum* – from marginal doodles to theological tracts – ideas about Jews appear with a remarkable regularity and pervasiveness. Yet the Jewish *topos* is rarely the main concern of the texts in which it appears; it is usually the disavowed discontents, the shady outsider lingering at the margin or embedded deep within the text. The Jew (meaning both the Jew as found in medieval Christian representations and the actual 'Jew-on-the-street' of medieval England) was rarely given a subjective or independent space in which to move. Instead, the Jew impinged on somebody else's story, a pawn or a stooge to be shuffled, reconfigured, elided, in whatever was found to be the most meaningful way. At a basic level, stories about Jews often focused on violent (or sometimes sexual) attacks on Christians or Christian symbols, articulating concerns and fears about Jewish–Christian physical, spatial and theological contacts.

Writing ritual murder

As a starting-point we might usefully consider the myth of Jewish ritual murder, the phenomenally widespread allegation that Jews kill Christian children as part of 'Jewish' practice.[4] The allegation was probably invented in twelfth-century England (although this has been hotly contested by Israel Yuval, who has given the allegation a German pedigree);[5] certainly it was in medieval England that the boy-saints of ritual murder were first venerated in cults that were sponsored and developed by ecclesiastical authorities. Cults were instituted around the miraculous corpses of William of Norwich (putatively murdered in 1144), Harold of Gloucester (1168), Robert of Bury St Edmunds (1181) and Hugh of Lincoln (1255), and there were many other instances – for example, at Winchester (1225 and 1232) and at London (1244) – in which some form of the allegation was raised but failed to take any lasting hold on local imaginations.[6] From what we know, the story was broadly similar

---

[3] On the place of antisemitism in medieval European Christian culture, see the introductory chapters of David Nirenberg, *Communities of Violence: Persecution of Minorities in the Middle Ages* (Princeton, 1996) and Miri Rubin, *Gentile Tales: The Narrative Assault on Late Medieval Jews* (New Haven, 1999).

[4] The blood libel (the idea that Jews seek Christian blood as part of their Jewish praxis) is little different and should be considered as a ritual murder allegation.

[5] Israel Jacob Yuval, '"Vengeance and damnation, blood and defamation": from Jewish martyrdom to blood libel accusations', *Zion*, 58 (1993), 33–90. Yuval argues that the ritual murder allegation arose out of Jewish self-sacrifices ('*kiddush ha-shem*') during the First Crusade (1096). The subsequent edition of *Zion* contains (often angry) responses to Yuval's controversial thesis.

[6] Norwich: John McCulloh, 'Jewish ritual murder: William of Norwich, Thomas of Monmouth, and the early dissemination of the myth', *Speculum*, 72 (1997), 698–740. Gloucester: Joe Hillaby, 'The ritual child murder accusation: its dissemination and Harold of Gloucester', *JHS*, 34 (1996), 69–109. Bury: Anthony P. Bale, '"House devil, town saint": antisemitism and hagiography in medieval Suffolk', in Sheila Delany, ed., *Chaucer and the Jews: Sources, Contexts, Meanings* (New

in each case: the Jews abducted a young, pious Christian boy and cruelly murdered him, usually in a mockery or perversion of the Crucifixion. Miracles were performed either at the boy's corpse, grave or shrine. In Norwich, Gloucester, Bury and Lincoln shrines were erected, with limited success, in the respective churches and formal cults initiated, with *vitae*, miracle-lists, ecclesiastical art, custodians and so on.

There is little evidence that any of these cults (except, perhaps, that at Lincoln) enjoyed 'popular' devotion on a substantial level and oblations at the shrines were erratic (for instance, William's shrine received 423s 4d in 1277, but this had diminished to the negligible sum of 6d by 1341). Moreover, each cult was fuelled by steadfast 'marketing' by particular agents (seen most clearly in Thomas of Monmouth's desperate attempts to spread the word concerning William). Further still, none of these cults arose out of anti-Jewish policy, popular antisemitism or child-murders (although these elements possibly preceded and accompanied the cults) but out of competing claims and rivalries between several of the wealthiest and most prestigious Benedictine houses in medieval England. Thus it is more useful to think of ritual murder as a textually generated 'event' (or perhaps 'non-event' that can only happen once the story has been written and told), rather than as a historical 'crime' with victims, criminals and a body of evidence (although if we are looking for victims, it was the Jews who were usually punished for crimes they almost certainly did not commit).[7] It is clear that Thomas of Monmouth, the cynical hagiographer of William of Norwich, tried and tried and tried again to make the narrative 'work'. Well into the 1160s and 70s, some thirty years after William's 'murder', Thomas and the monks at Norwich were collecting miracle stories and trying new ways (such as the dedication in 1168 of the 'Chapel of St William in the Wood') to invigorate the cult and make it lucrative. This process was based around Thomas's written testimonials.[8]

The development of the cult of William of Norwich was, to a significant extent, an attempt to garner the financial benefits of having a local saint's cult; at Lincoln, the Lincolnshire nobleman John of Lexinton was instrumental in developing the Little Hugh story for the same reason. At Norwich the invention of William was also probably a rebuke to nearby Bury St Edmunds, where the cult of St Edmund had recently been energetically developed, and Ely, where the cult of St Withburga was nurtured. In turn, Bury St Edmunds developed the cult of little Robert (in the form of a written *vita* or miracle-list by Jocelin of Brakelond and a chapel in the abbey) as an answer, or snub, to Norwich.

More generally, ritual murder allegations developed from and responded to changes in Christian piety, their imagery fed by the burgeoning *exempla*

York, 2002) pp. 185–210. Lincoln: Gavin Langmuir, 'The Knight's Tale of Young Hugh of Lincoln', *Speculum*, 47 (1972), 459–82. The baffling case of Adam of Bristol, which also has its origins in the late twelfth century, is possibly derived from parish drama: Christoph Cluse, '"Fabula ineptissima": die Ritualmordlegende um Adam von Bristol nach der Handschrift London, British Library, Harley 957', *Aschkenas* 5 (1995), 293–330. On other minor cases, Roth, *History*[3] (see Abbreviations).

[7] Gifts to William's shrine: M.R. James and Augustus Jessop, eds, *Thomas of Monmouth, The Life and Miracles of St William of Norwich* (Cambridge, 1895), p. lxxxiii. A new edition of Thomas's work is due from Oxford University Press, edited by Willis Johnson. This is not necessarily to say that the children concerned were not murdered, or that they were not murdered by Jews.

[8] Thomas of Monmouth, *Life and Miracles of St William*.

tradition. *Exempla* (pithy, moral tales used to illustrate a point of Christian teaching) emerged from an indistinct coalescence of biblical, folklore and pagan narratives and were easily adapted to reflect local stimuli and changes in piety. Medieval *exempla* that vilify Jews and Judaism are numerous and their manifestations in European texts and art are ubiquitous.[9] Early collections, such as those of Anselm of Bury St Edmunds (c.1100), Petrus Alphonsus (*fl.* 1106), Caesarius of Heisterbach (c.1180–1240), Odo of Cheriton (d. 1247), and the widespread *Alphabet of Tales* and *Gesta Romanorum*, feature various stories of outrages committed by Jews, usually against little boys, crucifixes or icons, or the Eucharist, or concerning the figure of the Jewish daughter, sometimes deadly, sometimes noble (and a distant precursor of Marlowe's Abigail and Shakespeare's Jessica).[10] Such narratives include the story of the Jewish boy of Bourges, put in an oven by his father as punishment for attending church;[11] the story of the Jew who offered the Host to an ass, who knelt before it rather than eat it (from the thirteenth-century *Speculum Laicorum*); the tale of a Jew who threw the Host into a pig-trough, but the pigs refused to eat it; the story of a Jew who wore the Host in his shoe, and was killed by a knight for doing so; the story of Jewess who gave birth to a baby girl rather than the Messiah, as her seducer had led her to expect (included in the *Alphabet of Tales* and Caesarius of Heisterbach); the tale of a Jewess who fell in love with a Christian boy, overcoming her father's violent objections (which also dates back to Caesarius).[12] Latin and vernacular *exempla* were produced and transmitted in medieval England, and the imagery of ritual murder narratives, if not the actual allegation itself, is closely derived from such tales. The Jews in ritual murder allegations abuse the boy's body in the same way that elsewhere they are said to abuse Christian symbols. Indeed, the ritual murder victim's body might be thought of *as* a symbol or icon, a version of the sacramental, edible Christ-child, so common in medieval devotion.[13]

The murderous Jew and the corpse of the Christ-child or pseudo-Christ-child are pervasive images in this devotional arena and reflect not only increasing anti-Jewish sentiment but also the burgeoning cult of the saints, Marian devotion, Eucharistic and sacramental piety, the rise of the vernacular and the concomitant religious concerns of the laity. Such factors should also be considered against the backdrop of the vigorous policies of conversion and repression which characterised the papacy of Innocent III (pope from 1198 to 1216) and in particular the Fourth Lateran Council (of 1215), which stressed sacramental and doctrinal orthodoxy and branded Jews with a distinctive costume. This last act, instituted in England in 1218, might itself be seen as a way of turning real Jews into symbols or signs, subject to a meaning imposed on the Jewish body.

In short, the allegation of ritual murder, and the ensuing devotion to the

---

[9] Joan Young Gregg, *Devils, Women and Jews: Reflections of the Other in Medieval Sermon Stories* (Albany, 1997).

[10] For an index to such stories, see Fredric Tübach, *Index Exemplorum: a Handbook of Medieval Religious Tales* (Helsinki, 1969).

[11] Rubin, *Gentile Tales*, pp. 7–39.

[12] Tübach, *Index Exemplorum*, nos 2641; 2687; 2802; 2807; 2804 and 2805.

[13] Leah Sinanoglou, 'The Christ child as sacrifice: a medieval tradition and the Corpus Christi play', *Speculum*, 48 (1973), 491–509.

martyr's body, was primarily a way of crafting a devotional Christian polity rather than a way of persecuting England's Jews. However, the fiction of ritual murder was unequivocally part of anti-Jewish persecution: Langmuir has shown how the Hugh of Lincoln affair in 1255 cost many Jewish lives, while the story of Robert of Bury likely had a part in fuelling the anti-Jewish violence there in 1190, which culminated in the expulsion of the Jews from the town.[14] In this way the ritual murder allegation, and similar 'chimerical' fictions, might be seen as part of the '*imaginary* screen of . . . myths' about Jews which enables the 'neutralisation' of horrific actions towards them, the 'plague of fantasies' about which Slavoj Žižek has eloquently written.[15]

This is only the briefest of sketches of the circumstances of the ritual murder allegation in medieval England; the salient point here is that the allegation did not spread by itself but seems to have been transmitted by books and oral reports trafficked between prestigious Benedictine houses by two or three enterprising monks and their associates: at Norwich, Thomas of Monmouth and bishop William Turbe; at Gloucester, the author of the St Peters chronicle; at Bury St Edmunds, Jocelin of Brakelond; at Lincoln, a coalescence of ecclesiastic (Henry de Lexinton, bishop of Lincoln), aristocratic (John de Lexinton, who 'investigated' the Hugh of Lincoln affair) and royal (Henry III). There is nothing particularly antisemitic about the Benedictine rule; what is important is the Benedictine emphasis on textual production and literacy. As Jeremy Cohen has shown, in general it was the mendicant orders – in England, principally the Dominicans and Franciscans – that were responsible for the development of antisemitic ideology and discourse in the twelfth and thirteenth centuries.[16] This was clearly not the case with the ritual murder allegation in England, although it is difficult to offer a conclusive reason why. In general terms, the friars were more interested in effecting social changes through preaching (for example, the degradation of Jewish communities) whereas the Benedictines sought to develop hagiographic culture with a concomitant emphasis on literacy and the value of book-production.

Richard of Devizes' 1190s *Cronicon*, a witty satire of historical writing and of antisemitic rumours, graphically demonstrates the fictional, referential and inherently literary nature of the ritual murder allegation. The *Cronicon* was written at the Benedictine abbey of St Swithun, Winchester, of which Richard was a monk. It charts the first years of the reign of Richard I (r. 1189–99) and his failed crusade to the Holy Land. The *Cronicon* is framed by incidents related to Jews, at its opening an account of the massacre of the Jews of London at Richard I's coronation and towards the end a lengthy ritual murder allegation, against a French Jew in Winchester.[17] Richard cannot have failed to notice the steadfast efforts of his Benedictine confreres at Norwich, Gloucester and Bury to develop boy-martyr cults. The *Cronicon*'s ritual murder allegation is depicted as the crass fantasy of a young Christian boy, a friend of the putative victim who had travelled from France to Winchester, who accuses the Jew thus:

[14] Langmuir, 'Knight's Tale', pp. 479–81; Jacobs, *Jews*, p. 75.

[15] Slavoj Žižek, *The Plague of Fantasies* (London, 1997), p. 55.

[16] Jeremy Cohen, *The Friars and the Jews: the Evolution of Medieval Anti-Judaism* (Ithaca, 1982).

[17] Richard's *Cronicon* and its playfulness regarding the Jewish trope are more fully discussed in Anthony P. Bale, 'Richard of Devizes and fictions of Judaism', *JCH*, 3 (2001), 55–72.

'You son of a dirty whore', he said, 'you thief, you traitor, you devil, you have crucified my friend! Alas, why haven't I the strength of a man? I would tear you to pieces with my hands!'[18]

Encouraged by the crowd, the boy goes on,

> '"O you men who gather together," he said, "see if there is a grief like unto my grief" [Lamentations 1.12]. This Jew is a devil; this man has torn the heart out of my breast; this man has cut the throat of my only friend, and I presume he has eaten him, too. A certain son of the devil, a French Jew – I do not understand or know what it is all about – that Jew gave my companion a fatal letter to this man. He came to this city, led or, rather, misled by him. He often worked for this Jew here, and he was last seen in his house.'[19]

The ritual murder allegation here is explicitly performative, staged for the crowd and encouraged by it.[20] It is the Christian boy's fantasies that cast the Jew as murderer, and the interpretative void or gap of the missing and incomprehensible Hebrew letter is foregrounded.[21] The boy's speech usurps the Jew's text (Lamentations), strikingly adopting the idiom of Old Testament grief to interpret the medieval (non-)event, one of many ways in which Richard of Devizes forges subtle connections between medieval Christians and the Jews they despise and aspire to reject.

In the *Cronicon* the ritual murder passage offers a veiled comment on, and parallel to, Richard I's crusade. Like the little boy's journey from France to Winchester, the crusading journey from England to Jerusalem never reached its climax or *telos*, instead becoming a fractured failure, discredited and falling far short of the fiction of Christian totality by which it is represented. Moreover, Richard's story is itself derived from a mid-twelfth-century French exemplary text (in Paris, Bibliothèque Nationale MS Lat. 3177, fols 143v–145v), which glosses the scanty documentary evidence of sinister rumours in Winchester about 1193 (an entry in the pipe roll, which states that the Winchester Jews were questioned on unknown charges and were fined 35s 1d, hardly the punishment for ritual murder).[22] Richard's account of Jewish/Christian relations in the 1190s is referential, intertextual, drawing on the shared image of the little boy, current in English Benedictine circles in the second half of the twelfth century (the myth of ritual murder) and northern European religious culture more generally (the icon of the little boy), and deriving its meaning from the satirical commentary it offers on Richard I's crusade. The Jewish passages of the *Cronicon* are not separate from the culture that spawned them, but intertwined at every level – literary, political, authorial, devotional.

The fiction and rumour of ritual murder persisted in Winchester for some time after the 1190s. In 1225 the allegation was again raised at Winchester but, ludicrously, the female victim was found alive and well and the charge could

---

[18] J.T. Appleby, ed. and tr., *Richard of Devizes, Cronicon* (Oxford, 1963), p. 68.

[19] *Ibid.*, pp. 68–9.

[20] Discussed by Michael Jones, ' "The place of the Jews": anti-Judaism and theatricality in medieval culture', *Exemplaria*, 12 (2000), 327–59.

[21] A common theme in medieval iconography is pseudo-Hebrew lettering, on which see Ruth Mellinkoff, *Outcasts: Signs of Otherness in Northern European Art of the Late Middle Ages*, vol. 1 (Berkeley, 1993), pp. 95–108.

[22] The French manuscript, *exemplum* and documentary evidence are discussed more fully in Bale, 'Richard of Devizes'.

not stand.[23] In the same year the Jews were implicated in the murder of one William fitz Richard fitz Gervase; four of the Jews were acquitted and two were found guilty.[24] This new impetus to make the narrative work may have been part of the crusading fervour of the then bishop of Winchester, Peter des Roches (d. 1238), for in 1225 Frederick II declared a crusade, which commenced in 1227 with des Roches as one of its three leaders.[25]

Des Roches was almost certainly involved in a further recapitulation of the allegation at Winchester, in 1232. A year-old baby, one Stephen, was found at St Swithun's, dismembered, castrated, his eyes and heart removed. Despite the apparent culpability of the boy's mother – she fled Winchester – suspicion fell on a Jew, Abraham Pinch (d. 1235), who had been implicated in the 1225 allegations and was the son of the prolific businesswoman Chera. As Nicholas Vincent has suggested, the allegation was part of a programme of anti-Jewish (financial) and antisemitic (demonising) measures instituted by des Roches on his return from Crusade in 1231, a money-raising tactic to pay for Henry III's abortive incursions into northern France and a symbolic assertion of his own authority.[26]

Like any narrative, the idea, the rumour, of ritual murder could be shuffled and rewritten, found useful and meaningful at divergent times. The reappearances of the ritual murder myth in Winchester in 1192, 1225 and 1232 show the pervasive durability of the fiction (which could survive in some form even without a dead body) and the transformations it could undergo, from irony to sincerity, contingent on a larger narrative encompassing Church, Crown and Crusade.

Christian historiography and derogatory discourse

Indeed, the myth of ritual murder was transmitted and kept alive through books rather than worship or devotion. While written *vitae* and miracle-lists are known to have existed for William of Norwich (Thomas of Monmouth's *vita*) and Robert of Bury (a now-lost hagiographic document, mentioned by its author Jocelin of Brakelond), Christian historiography kept the myths alive. Medieval history was a narrative plot, a set of events that could be organised, interpreted, moralised and interpolated according to their resonance to the present day of the author. Crucial to the enterprise of the medieval historian was the construction of identity – be it personal, local, corporate or religious. Equally crucial was that history offered a moral exemplar. Medieval historians, both before and after the expulsion of the Jews, insistently discussed Judaism and its place in the formation of English identity. For instance, the chronicle of the Benedictine abbey of St Peter at Gloucester provides the only firm evidence of the cult of Harold of Gloucester;[27] consequently we can see Harold's cult as

---

[23] Roth, *History of the Jews*, p. 273; Hillaby, 'Ritual child murder', p. 90; *Rot. Litt. Claus.* (see Abbreviations), II, p. 53b.

[24] *Rot. Litt. Claus.*, II, pp. 50b, 51b.

[25] David Abulafia, *Frederick II: A Medieval Emperor* (London, 1988), pp. 164–201.

[26] On Chera, see Suzanne Bartlet, 'Three Jewish businesswomen in thirteenth-century Winchester', *JCH*, 3 (2000), 31–54. Nicholas Vincent, 'Jews, Poitevins, and the bishop of Winchester', in D. Wood, ed., *Christianity and Judaism* (= *SCH* 29, Oxford, 1992), pp. 119–32.

[27] Hillaby, 'Ritual child murder', p. 83. Hillaby writes that 'the evidence against [a successful, formal] cult is overwhelming'.

part of the creation of a spiritually distinctive, up-to-date public devotional identity at Gloucester. Again, the *purposes* to which the *image* of the little boy's body could be put were more important than the presence (or absence) of a *corpus delicti*. Likewise, the cult of Robert of Bury is glancingly noted in chronicles from as far apart as Essex (Ralph of Coggeshall) and the Scottish borders (Melrose), the common link between these two houses being their Cistercian foundation.

A particularly instructive and graphic example of medieval historians' role in the fictionalisation of English Jewry comes from the celebrated *Chronica Majora* of Matthew Paris (c.1200–1259), who wrote at the Benedictine monastery at St Alban's (Hertfordshire), one of the most powerful and wealthy houses in the country and the centre for royal historiography. Among many passages on Judaism and individual English Jews Matthew includes the following, relating to the important Jewish financier Abraham of Berkhamsted:

> There was a certain quite rich Jew, Abraham by name but not in faith, who lived and had property in Berkhamsted and Wallingford. He was friendly with Earl Richard [of Cornwall] for some improper reason or other. He had a beautiful and faithful wife called Floria. In order to dishonour Christ the more, this Jew bought a nicely carved and painted statue of the blessed Virgin, as usual nursing her son at her bosom. This image the Jew set up in his latrine and, what is thoroughly dishonourable and ignominious to mention, as it were in blasphemy of the Blessed Virgin, he inflicted a most filthy and unmentionable thing on it, daily and nightly, and ordered his wife to do the same. Noticing this after some days, by reason of her sex, she felt sorry and, going there secretly washed the dirt from the face of the disgracefully defiled statue. When the Jew her husband found out the truth of this, he impiously and secretly suffocated his wife. However, these crimes were discovered and the Jew, clearly proved guilty, although there were other grounds for putting him to death, was thrust into the foulest dungeon in the Tower of London. In a bid to be freed, he promised most positively that he would prove all the Jews in England to be the basest traitors.

A marginal comment continues the story thus:

> Thereupon he was basely accused by almost all the English Jews, who tried to put him to death, but Earl Richard spoke up for him. So the Jews, accusing him of clipping coins and other serious crimes, offered the earl a thousand marks to stop protecting him, which however the earl refused because the Jew was said to be his. This Jew Abraham then paid the king seven hundred marks so that, with the help of the earl, he could be freed from the life imprisonment to which he had been condemned.[28]

This extract from the *Chronica Majora* crystallises a number of significant trends in earlier English writing about Judaism. First, it makes a scatological slander integral to the narrative, clearly identifying Abraham the Jew with an excremental trope. Such images are commonplace: in the late twelfth-century ritual murder story of Adam of Bristol the boy's murderer, Samuel the Jew, likewise murders Adam in his latrine (he had, allegedly, already murdered three

---

[28] Richard Vaughan, ed. and tr., *The Chronicle of Matthew Paris: Monastic Life in the Thirteenth Century* (Gloucester, 1984), pp. 142–3. Richard of Cornwall (1209–72) was the second son of King John and brother of Henry III. He had very close economic links with the English Jewish community.

boys there that year) and in the Anglo-Norman *Hugues de Lincoln* ballad the Jews bury the boy in manure.[29] In the story of the Jew of Tewkesbury, a Jew falls into a public cesspit on a Saturday and refuses to extract himself out of reverence for Jewish law, making excretion cognate with the Jewish Sabbath.[30] Famously, in the 'miracle of the boy singer', which developed in early thirteenth-century England and was later developed by Chaucer as 'The Prioress's Tale', a little Christian boy is tossed by Jews into a privy.[31] Such images are not only used to create a sense of physical disgust and bodily corruption, although this is certainly part of their task. The perceived Jewish preference for excrement counterpoints the 'correct' culture of Christian feeding and regeneration, exemplified by the Eucharistic wafer. The Eucharist – transformed in incorporation and beyond digestion – is positive; excrement – literal, worldly, earthbound, temporal – is negative. In Eucharistic terms, the Jew is the accident to the Christian substance.[32] In this case the holy milk inherent in Matthew's image of the statue of the Virgin nursing her son at her bosom contrasts with Abraham's heretical excretion, in turn juxtaposing the decorous holy family with Abraham's dysfunctional, homicidal domestic set-up. In common with other antisemitic narratives, the real villain is the Jewish male; Jewish women are considered more pliant, more easily brought to faith.[33]

Another common image is the 'bad', current Jew as contrasted with the 'good', antique Hebrew, here achieved through playing on Abraham's name, 'Abraham by name but not in faith'. The antiheroes of similar stories are likewise frequently given Hebrew names – Samuel in the Adam of Bristol story, Solomon in the Jew of Tewkesbury narrative – as if to mark and highlight their departure from the models of good conduct encoded in the Old Testament.[34] The continued existence of Jewry denies the retrospective, typological role of the Jews envisaged in Christianity. The naming of characters like Abraham, Samuel and Solomon suggests that Jews retain the image of the Old Law, rather than its substance or typological validity.[35]

Most importantly, Matthew's brief *exemplum* of Abraham of Berkhamsted slyly suggests that the Jew has improper connections to vectors of power and goes on to replace the reality of Abraham of Berkhamsted's money-lending with the fictional icon-desecration story. For, as Gavin Langmuir long ago

---

[29] Cluse, '"Fabula ineptissima"'; F.X. Michel, *Hugues de Lincoln, receuil des balades anglo-normande et écossoises relatives au meurtre de cet enfant commis par les juifs en MCCLV* (Paris, 1834).

[30] Anthony P. Bale, 'Framing antisemitic *exempla*: locating the Jew of Tewkesbury', *Mediaevalia*, 20 (2001), 19–47.

[31] The earliest known text of this miracle is Oxford, Corpus Christi College MS 32, f. 92r, which dates from c.1215 and comes from the Oxford or Gloucestershire area.

[32] On these terms and the status of the Eucharist, see Miri Rubin, *Corpus Christi: the Eucharist in Late Medieval Culture* (Cambridge, 1991); on the 'scandal of digestion', Piero Camporesi, 'The consecrated Host: a wondrous excess', in Michael Feher, Ramona Nadaff and Nadia Tazi, eds, *Zone 3.1: Fragments for a History of the Human Body* (New York, 1989), pp. 220–38.

[33] Gregg, *Devils, Women and Jews*, pp. 187–9; Rubin, *Gentile Tales*, pp. 71–7.

[34] Medieval English Jews tended to have Hebrew, Anglo-Norman and Latin names (e.g., Hebrew 'Chaim' became Anglo-Norman 'Vives'). At present the most complete guide is Eleazar ha-Levi, 'Jewish naming convention in Angevin England', at the website www.sca.org/heraldry/laurel/names/Jewish.html.

[35] Jeremy Cohen, *Living Letters of the Law: Ideas of the Jew in Medieval Christianity* (Berkeley, 1999), discusses the Augustinian pedigree of such notions.

pointed out, the 'real' Abraham was indeed in trouble in the 1250s, both for financial misdeeds and for murdering his wife.[36] The outcome was that Abraham was granted to Richard of Cornwall so that Richard, like other members of the royal family, also had a 'personal' Jew. Debts owed to Abraham (totalling some £1,800) were collected and passed to Richard. The important process here is not so much the element of slander under way, but the process of fictionalisation and glossing. Mundane, technical, realistic, indeed real, charges against Abraham were overlaid and redetermined in fantastical (or 'chimerical') terms.[37] The political or criminal charges (site specific, temporally specific, personally specific) were glossed by a fantasy of heretical opposition, of collective and timeless malevolence and of physical disgust.

Moreover, the story of Abraham of Berkhamsted gains added resonances in narrative context. Following the story is an account of a group of Armenian Christian pilgrims in England:

> And at the same time certain Armenian brethren, fugitives from the Tartar [i.e., Mongol] invasions, arrived as pilgrims in England. When they came to St Ives one of them was taken ill and unfortunately died in that town. He was reverently buried next to St Ivo's spring, the water of which is said to have great virtue. These brethren were of most honest life and amazing abstinence, being always in prayer, with rugged, honest faces and beards. The one who died was their leader and master, George by name, and he is thought to have been a most holy man and a bishop; he now began to perform miracles.[38]

The Armenians' story clearly contrasts with that of Abraham ('at the same time') and relativises categories of alterity, otherness. The handsome Armenians – foreigners fleeing an attack on Christendom – wash correctly and work miracles. These passages from the _Chronica Majora_ collapse easy binarisms of English:-alien, self:other, us:them, and instead suggest that it was not difference that made Jews threatening to medieval Englishmen, but rather the Jews' possible interaction and familiarity with the structures and images of medieval England that caused concern.

In this way, the Jewish trope problematises the ostensibly authoritative Christian chronicle; the historical conceit seems to founder, challenged by crises in authority it cannot accommodate. The Abraham of Berkhamsted _exemplum_ queries Christian symbols and leads the Christian reader into forbidden areas of heretical desire. A clear example of such anxiety is furnished by William of Newburgh's account of the massacre of the London Jews at Richard I's coronation in 1189:

> The first day of his reign of the most illustrious King Richard was marked by this hitherto unheard of event in the royal city [i.e., Westminster], both by the uncompleted destruction of a notoriously perfidious people, and by a new confidence of the Christians against the enemies of the Cross. Clearly this was a presage of the advancement of Christianity in Richard's own time, not only according to the rule which prescribes that ambiguous readings be derived in the better rather than the worse sense, but even according to the most appropriate meaning.[39]

---

[36] Langmuir, 'Knight's Tale', p. 463.
[37] Gavin Langmuir, _Toward a Definition of Antisemitism_ (Berkeley, 1990), pp. 311–52.
[38] _Chronicle of Matthew Paris_, p. 143.
[39] Translation from Nancy Partner, _Serious Entertainments: The Writing of History in Twelfth-Century England_ (Chicago, 1977), p. 226.

Here Newburgh explicitly subjects his account to a favourable or 'better' interpretation even while expressing unease about the event. As Nancy Partner has observed, this is the only time in his history that Newburgh is forced to resort to a rule of historical interpretation.[40] Based around the concept of 'the rule' of Christian historiographic hermeneutics and 'ambiguous readings', Newburgh's text strives to master the meaning of the past and the (Christian) narrative into which it must be accommodated. The iconoclastic and bloody nature of the event, and the shock of its newness, left Newburgh without an exemplar by which to comprehend the incident within a Christian frame of reference ('this hitherto unheard of event'). It is thus not surprising that when he came to write about the self-slaughter of the Jews of York in 1190 Newburgh used Josephus's account of the mass-suicide of the zealots at Masada to understand and interpret the catastrophe.[41] The current validity of Judaism is refracted through its relation to the past and through its use to the Christian present; the reality of Jewish life (and death) is subjected to its literary role.

The possibility of philosemitism

Could the variety of reactions to Judaism in medieval England have included positive, or at least equanimous, responses? Marc Saperstein's attempts to find positive interplay between Judaism and Christianity have led only to the rather bare and axiomatic conclusion that 'there was more to Jewish history than a progression of uninterrupted persecution and suffering';[42] most of Saperstein's evidence comes from the post-Expulsion period, in particular from the preacher John Bromyard (d. c.1352), so real Jews were hardly being defended or promoted. However, Judaism in pre-expulsion England was the object of discursive doctrinal scrutiny rather than of repulsion alone. Of course, 'Old Testament' 'Hebrews' (as opposed to post-biblical Jews, a distinction first posited by Eusebius of Caesarea) remained ubiquitous subjects of Christian analysis and veneration; images of characters such as Noah, Abraham, Moses, Jesse and David are likely to be found in any medieval cathedral. Where these figures are distinguished by a pointed 'Jewish' hat the purpose may not have been mockery for, as Ruth Mellinkoff has shown, such headgear does not have a stable iconographic meaning.[43] Even so, such depictions often foreground the physical difference of the Jews, caricaturing long faces and noses, dark beards, sunken eyes and stooping posture – for instance, the image of Simeon in the twelfth-century 'Winchester Psalter' (London, British Library Cotton MS Nero C.liv, f. 15r) or the paintings of Nicodemus at the Chapel of the Holy Sepulchre, Winchester Cathedral (c.1189 and c.1230).

Meanwhile, the field of Hebrew scholarship did sometimes bring medieval English Christians into non-adversarial contact with Jews and Judaism. In her

[40] *Ibid.*, pp. 226–7.
[41] R.B. Dobson, *The Jews of Medieval York and the Massacre of March 1190* (Borthwick Papers, no. 45, York, 1974).
[42] Marc Saperstein, 'Jews and Christians: some positive images', *Harvard Theological Review*, 79 (1986), 236–46.
[43] For instance, there is an ambiguous artistic crossover between Jews' hats and bishops' mitres, or Jews' prayer-shawls and monks' hoods: Mellinkoff, *Outcasts*, vol. 1, pp. 59–94.

recent and important work on Hebrew scholarship in pre-Expulsion England, Judith Olszowy-Schlanger avers that Christian scholars had to rely on Jews or Jewish converts in order to have any access to the details of Hebrew linguistics and grammar.[44] There were certainly English Christian scholars, for instance, Herbert of Bosham (*fl.* 1162–86), Stephen Langton (c.1155–1228) and Nicholas Trivet (c.1258–1328), who achieved a quite formidable level of skill in Hebrew during the period of virulent anti-Jewish policy and antisemitic stereotyping that led up to the pogroms of 1190 and Expulsion of 1290.[45] Yet we must be cautious about attributing 'philosemitic' motivations to such scholarship; it was emphatically Christian (rather than ecumenical) in nature and was little concerned with bettering the medieval position of the Jews. An instructive case in point is the celebrated onetime bishop of Lincoln, Robert Grosseteste (c.1175–1253). Grosseteste possibly owned Hebrew books and certainly commissioned a Latin translation of the Hebrew psalter.[46] Grosseteste's interest in Hebrew is not reflected in his treatment of the Jews: he was archdeacon of Leicester in the year the Jews were expelled from the city (1231) and in his letter of the same year to the Countess of Winchester, Margaret de Quinci (c.1208–1258), Grosseteste repeated the Augustinian position that it is a Christian duty to hold Jews captive and to punish them for their sin of the Crucifixion.[47] The letter rebuked de Quinci for allowing the refugee Jews to come to Winchester and settle there. In the thirteenth century the Lincoln ritual murder martyr, Little Hugh, was buried next to Grosseteste at Lincoln Cathedral, as if symbolically glossing the latter's ambiguous Hebraism with the more common, powerful and durable ritual murder fiction.[48]

The Jewish–Christian disputation also appears to offer the Jew a space in which to speak, or be spoken for. The disputation form has received considerable academic attention from scholars such as Anna Sapir Abulafia, Robert Chazan and Hyam Maccoby;[49] disputations were known in medieval England (famously, Gilbert Crispin, abbot of Westminster, claimed his written disputation derived from an actual encounter). In the present context it is imperative to reiterate that the disputation, whether 'real', staged or textually generated, does not offer the Jew (or indeed the Christian) a subjective space. Rather the

[44] Judith Olszowy-Schlanger, 'The knowledge and practice of Hebrew grammar among Christian scholars in pre-expulsion England: the evidence of "bilingual" Hebrew–Latin manuscripts', in Nicholas de Lange, ed., *Hebrew Scholarship and the Medieval World* (Cambridge, 2001), pp. 107–28.

[45] Beryl Smalley, *The Study of the Bible in the Middle Ages* (Oxford, 1941); Raphael Loewe, 'The mediaeval Christian Hebraists of England: the *Superscriptio Lincolniensis*', *HUCA*, 28 (1957), 205–52.

[46] David J. Wasserstein, 'Grosseteste, the Jews and medieval Christian Hebraism', in James McEvoy, ed., *Robert Grosseteste: New Perspectives on his Thought and Scholarship* (Turnhout, 1995), pp. 357–76.

[47] The letter (Grosseteste's 'epistola V') is printed in modern English translation in Lee M. Friedman, *Robert Grosseteste and the Jews* (Cambridge, MA, 1934), pp. 12–18.

[48] R.I. Moore, *The Formation of a Persecuting Society: Power and Deviance in Western Europe, 950–1250* (Oxford, 1987), pp. 36–7.

[49] Anna Sapir Abulafia, 'An attempt by Gilbert Crispin, abbot of Westminster, at rational argument in the Jewish–Christian debate', *Studia Monastica*, 26 (1984), 55–74; Robert Chazan, *Daggers of Faith: Thirteenth-Century Christian Missionizing and Jewish Response* (Berkeley, 1989); Hyam Maccoby, *Judaism on Trial: Jewish–Christian Disputations in the Middle Ages* (Rutherford, 1982).

disputants' identities are forged with regard to each other and, as rhetorical creations, offer only partial reports. Whether esteemed or disesteemed the Jew's choices are conversion or execution, and the Jew remains defined as a Jew; his space is relative to the Christian concerns about which he disputes. For example, Gilbert's Jew suggests that Christians 'adore images and rejoice in their idols. For [they] figure God Himself as a wretch hanging on the beam of the cross transfixed with nails,' a powerful interrogation of the meaning and efficacy of Christian devotional practice.[50] Even Gilbert's moderate tone in his disputation maintains the Jew as the stooge through which Christian anxieties might be tested.

Blind beasts?

Perhaps the most substantial 'commentary' on Judaism in England before 1290 is found in an unlikely place: the bestiary. The bestiary draws together the theological (Isidore of Seville), the scientific (Aristotle) and something between the two (*Physiologus*) to illustrate points of Christian doxology.[51] The bestiary offers us clear evidence that Jews' bodies (as well as the Jewish religion) were thought of as degraded and corrupt entities, foreshadowing later antisemitic material and a 'racial' conception of Judaism. The principal 'Jewish' animals are the owl, the hyena and the bonnacon, each of which was a body incompatible with Christian notions of cleanness, deportment and piety. All three were imagined as Jewish animals with a preference for the scatological or anal.

The owl (usually the night-owl or *noctua*, night-crow or *nicticorax*, or common owl, *bubo*) was reviled partly for its theological or scriptural baseness: by flying at night it symbolises the Jews 'who, when our Lord came to save them, rejected Him, saying "We have no king except Caesar"', and preferred the darkness to the light', and was said to be attacked by the small, righteous Christian daybirds.[52] Accompanying these charges, the owl was also said to hover around graves and, recapitulating the scatological slanders so ubiquitous in the antisemitic exemplary tradition, the bird was said to roost in its own droppings, 'just as the sinner brings all who dwell with him into disrepute through the example of his dishonourable behaviour'.[53]

Likewise, the hyena (*yena*) was said to dwell in graveyards (like the owl), to feed on corpses and to have an hermaphrodite body. In the Aberdeen Bestiary (f. 11v) the hyena is clearly marked by circumcision as it mounts a corpse; in the Bodley 764 bestiary the animal attacks the placid naked body of a young

---

[50] Salient extracts from Gilbert's disputation are reproduced at www.fordham.edu/ halsall/source/1196crispin-jews.html and in Jacobs, *Jews*. Gilbert's complete works are edited by Anna Sapir Abulafia and G.R. Evans, *The Works of Gilbert Crispin, Abbot of Westminster* (London, 1986).

[51] Debra Hassig, *Medieval Bestiaries: Text, Image, Ideology* (Cambridge, 1995).

[52] Richard Barber, *Bestiary. Being an English Version of the Bodleian Library, Oxford, MS Bodley 764* (Woodbridge, 1999), pp. 147–8. Barber's translation and the wonderful Aberdeen Bestiary project (www.clues.abdn.ac.uk:8080/besttest/firstpag.html) are the most accessible bestiary texts and, for convenience, have been used here. The biblical reference is to John 19.15 and John 3.19.

[53] Barber, *Bestiary*, p. 149. For more detail on the owl, see Mariko Miyazaki, 'Misericord owls and medieval anti-semitism', in Debra Hassig, ed., *The Mark of the Beast: the Medieval Bestiary in Art, Life and Literature* (New York, 1999), pp. 23–50.

woman against the backdrop of a massive church edifice. The animal is a freak of nature and a deceitful snare based once again around incorrect forms of incorporation ('the hyena also [imitates] human vomit and devours the dogs it has enticed with faked sounds of retching'). These images of disgust and physical grotesquery are quite separate from the theological moralisation given after the physical description:

> The children of Israel are like this beast; at first they served the living God but later fell prey to riches and easy living and worshipped idols. Hence the prophets likened the Jewish people to an unclean beast, saying 'Mine heritage is become as the hyena's lair' [Jeremiah 12.8]. Every one among us who serves riches and an easy life is like this animal, for they are neither men nor women, that is, neither believer nor unbelievers, but certainly belong to those of whom Solomon [St James] says 'a double-minded man, unstable in all his ways' [James 1.8]. The Lord said of them: 'Ye cannot serve God and Mammon' [Matthew 6.24].[54]

The moralisation focuses on the beast's ambiguous gender, interpreted as religious hybridity, rather than vomiting, uneucharistic necrophagous appetite, and genital display. As can be seen time and time again, physical images of (often sexualised) disgust overlay the religious critique of Jewish–Christian difference.

The fabulous bonnacon, said to reside in Asia, has perhaps the most corrupt body of these Jewish animals: it has bowels from which it emits excremental fumes that burn anything they touch.[55] The bonnacon is not explicitly said to be Jewish but is contrasted in illustrations with the panther (*pantera*), the Christ-like animal with, crucially, sweet-smelling breath.[56] The calf (representing the 'lascivious Jews'), the hoopoe (which is also said to nest in its own excrement) and the pig are also tainted with antisemitic notions.[57] Such invective strives to identify physical manifestations of religious difference and represents early attempts to develop a kind of racial theory of Judaism, based around the imputed corruption of the Jewish body.

Conclusions

The fictionalisation of medieval Anglo-Jewry must be seen in terms of cultural power, the coercion of texts and images in the articulation of dominance and subjection. 'Popular antisemitism' – the everyday and widespread image of the Jew – was not *sui generis* or somehow spontaneous but came directly from narratives and images disseminated from the clergy (the provenance that all the artefacts we have surveyed have in common). The Jewish *topos* allowed the discussion of taboo subjects – child-murder, excrement, the efficacy of the Eucharist – and are poised between the ostensible fixity of orthodoxy and the realms of fantasy, imagination and desire to which they appeal. The develop-

[54] Barber, *Bestiary*, pp. 46–7.
[55] *Ibid.*, p. 47.
[56] Hassig, *Medieval Bestiaries*, pp. 156–66, offers an intelligent discussion of the antisemitism implicit in images of the panther and its followers, and describes the bonnacon as the panther's 'antithetical counterpart'.
[57] See Barber, *Bestiary*, pp. 93 and 171; Claudine Fabre-Vassas, *The Singular Beast: Jews, Christians and the Pig*, tr. Carol Volk (New York, 1997).

ment of antisemitic imagery was undoubtedly a part of Christian preaching and book-production and played an important component in developing the social cohesion and corporate identity that allowed horrific actions against the English Jews, culminating in their Expulsion of 1290.

However, the time-frame of this chapter is ultimately a false one. The radical *punctum* of 1290 affected a group of people who had been absent from, or had little access to, what was being said about them for many years; the material reality of the English Jewish community had long been lost in the net of stereotyping, vitriol, slander and fantasy by which they were depicted, glossed, interpreted. Jewish life in medieval England stopped but English Christian antisemitism continued and, indeed, flourished. Old themes were embellished (for instance, the cult of Robert of Bury certainly continued until at least the mid-sixteenth century in the sphere of popular devotional iconography) and texts remained concerned with the interrogation of Christian symbols via a staged Jewish presence (as is clearly the case in the late-medieval Croxton *Play of the Sacrament* in which the Jewish characters test the Eucharist). The post-Expulsion development of antisemitic imagery cannot only be attributed to the 'convenient' absence of Jews, for Judaism had long been a stimulus for the Christian imagination; as St Jerome (c.342–420), famed for his development of Christian exegetics and the *lectio divina*, wrote of the synagogue,

> If you call it a brothel, a den of vice, the Devil's refuge, Satan's fortress, a place to deprave the soul, an abyss of every conceivable disaster or whatever else you will, you are still saying less than it deserves.[58]

The representational challenge of Judaism defies even the greatest Christian interpreter. Judaism offers a hermeneutic gap (the unsayable, the unnameable) at the very point at which it is represented: the act of definition ('If you call it . . .') is accompanied by the failure of definition ('you are still saying less than it deserves'). Yet the idea of Judaism is a stimulus for imagination and rhetoric, the filling of the hermeneutic gap with lurid, if captivating and forbidden, material. If 'naming is norming', if definition is incorporation, containment or subjection, then Christian representations of Jews repeatedly resist such containment. Instead these images problematise their own categories through fantasies of what their authors were not, or did not want to be.

Yet fantasy and projection should not be divorced from the real world; indeed it might be said that it is through fantasy and projection that we make sense of the world.[59] These fictions of Judaism often had calamitous and dreadful consequences for the Jews living in England and were a contributory part of ongoing persecution of lived lives. We might close with an elegiac artefact, which negotiates the unhappy traffic, both real and symbolic, between Jew and gentile in medieval England. Cambridge, Pembroke College MS 59 is a thirteenth-century Latin gloss on the book of Isaiah. It was used by the monks at Bury St Edmunds and produced in the *scriptorium* there. The binding of the book was stiffened with leaves from a *siddur*, a Hebrew prayer-book, dating

---

[58] Quoted in Friedrich Heer, *God's First Love: Christians and Jews Over Two Thousand Years*, tr. Geoffrey Skelton (London, 1970), p. 37.

[59] To quote Jean Baudrillard, 'we forget a little too easily that the whole of our reality is filtered through the media, including tragic events of the past'. *The Transparency of Evil: Essays on Extreme Phenomena* (London, 1993), p. 90.

from the end of the twelfth century and written in a French hand.[60] The binding of the book was completed at the abbey at Bury and it is likely that, as Abrahams concludes, 'the leaf was obtained from the Bury synagogue after [the expulsion of the Jews from Bury in] 1190, and that it had been in actual use there before that date.'[61] The book is a moving articulation of the fundamental 'supporting' role of the idea of Judaism inherent in medieval Christian culture and of the 'violence' and destruction – material and figurative – surrounding the Jewish image. As the Christian book glosses Isaiah, the Jewish use of the book is obliterated; the Hebrew leaf strengthens the Latin book, even as its own meaning is obscured, erased and destroyed.

[60] See Moses Abrahams, 'Leaf from an English *Siddur* of the twelfth entury', *Jews' College Jubilee Volume* (London, 1906), pp. 109–13. Abrahams first drew attention to the book and its provenance.

[61] *Ibid.*, p. 113.

9

The Medieval York Jewry Reconsidered

BARRIE DOBSON

In perhaps the most moving poetic elegy in English on the notorious massacre of the Jews on Friday, 16 March 1190, John Silkin's 'Astringencies: The Coldness', the obvious moral was drawn some forty years ago. 'Absence of Jews/ Through hatred, or indifference,/ A gap they slip through, a conscience/ That corrodes more deeply since it is/ Forgotten – this deadens York'.[1] No doubt so; but it is at least some consolation that complete indifference to the grim fate of the Jews of medieval York is less common within the city now than it was a generation ago. It may still well be, to quote Silkin's poem again, that 'The event/ Has the frigid persistence of a growth in the flesh'; but contemporary attitudes to the medieval Jewish minority have undoubtedly changed a great deal in York in the last twenty years. Needless to say, that transformation owes much less to the researches of professional historians than to the dramatic expansion of interest in medieval Jewry among Christians and Jews alike. Somewhat ironically, it was only after the small eighty-year-old Hebrew synagogue in Aldwark closed its doors for ever in 1975 that the massacre of the York Jews on *Shabbat-ha-Gadol* has come to fill its present symbolic role as the supreme example on English soil of the evils of anti-semitism and of the need for reconciliation between Christians and Jews.[2]

Perhaps the critical date in the transition from deliberate oblivion to posthumous respect towards the Jews of York was Tuesday, 31 October 1978, when a memorial tablet was unveiled at the foot of Clifford's Tower by the President of the Jewish Historical Society of England in the company of Chief Rabbi Jakobovits, Archbishop Stuart Blanch of York as well as the Lord Mayor, the Dean of York and many others.[3] Even better attended were the events which accompanied the octocentenary of the 'Clifford's Tower Commemoration', held at various points in the city between 15 and 18 March 1990. The Jews of medieval York can never have been mourned so eloquently before as in a series of cantatas and litanies, all especially composed 'as pleas for tolerance in an unstable world'.[4] After centuries during which the atrocities that

---

[1] *Richard Murphy, Jon Silkin, Nathaniel Tarn* (Penguin Modern Poets, 7, Harmondsworth, 1965), pp. 43–4. For John Silkin's later and even more impassioned poem of indignation on the 1190 massacre, see 'The Malabestia', collected in his *The Principle of Water* (London, 1974), pp. 83–7.

[2] *VCH Yorkshire, The City of York* (London, 1961), p. 419; cf. G. Alderman, *Modern British Jewry* (new edn, Oxford, 1998), p. 26.

[3] The cost of preparing the tablet was raised from private subscriptions co-ordinated by the Jewish Historical Society of England. Equally crucial in erecting the memorial was the co-operation of the then Ancient Monuments Division of the Department of the Environment.

[4] G. Hunter et al., eds, *Clifford's Tower Commemoration, York, 15–18 March 1990: A Programme and Handbook* (York, 1990), pp. 95–113.

victimised the York Jews in 1190 have been deliberately remembered as infrequently as possible, they have accordingly at last found a place in whatever 'English Heritage' is supposed to be. Thus in the Ministry of Public Building and Work's official *Guide to Clifford's Tower, York Castle* by B.H. St J. O'Neill, published in 1943, the events of March 1190 are mentioned but – almost perversely – without any reference to the fact that Jews were killed there. By complete contrast, the current English Heritage Guide to *Clifford's Tower and the Jews of Medieval York* discusses the massacre in considerable detail but ignores the architectural history of Clifford's Tower almost completely.[5]

The transformation of the complex experience of the medieval Jewry into the simplified language of English Heritage and modern mass tourism ('The tragic story of the Jews of York offers a mesmerising glimpse of England in the first year of Richard the Lion-Heart's reign') is not perhaps to be deplored but is equally not without its dangers.[6] How far has our detailed historical knowledge and understanding of the York Jewry really been advanced and transformed in recent years? Perhaps the most honest answer is not enough. It is true that with a few exceptions I would not personally wish to recant the conclusions on the subject I published a quarter of a century ago. To my relief, most of what I wrote about the York Jewry and the massacre of March 1190, I would probably still write now.[7] However, there is no doubt that the extremely well-documented business activities of the leading York Jewish financiers of the thirteenth century deserve much more detailed and subtle analysis than they have ever received. Similarly, the recent publication of more plea-rolls of the Exchequer of the Jews and other sources makes it clear that Jewish social life in the city, especially during the final generation before the Expulsion of 1290, still has many revelations to offer its future historian. This chapter will in fact conclude with some comments on the last melancholy phase of the York Jewry, a period when it was increasingly dominated by bereaved widows. Needless to say, much the most significant contribution to the history of the York Jewry in the last two decades is the admirable report of the excavation of the Jewish Cemetery at Jewbury north of the city walls in 1982–3.[8] But a documentary historian is bound to be especially conscious that the medieval York Jewry would still repay the painstakingly thorough treatment of available sources that has transformed the history of several other medieval Jewish communities in recent years, not least at the hands of other contributors to this book. Thanks to their labours and perceptions the long period of comparative inactivity in medieval Jewish studies that followed the late Cecil Roth's death in 1970 seems at last over.[9]

As Roth himself pointed out, the York massacre of March 1190 was the only

---

[5] B.H. St J. O'Neill, *Clifford's Tower, York Castle* (H.M.S.O., 1943); K. Jeffrey, *Clifford's Tower and the Jews of Medieval York* (English Heritage, 1995).

[6] P. Taylor, 'Brutal Truth', *Heritage Today: the magazine of English Heritage* (June 2001), pp. 43–7. A 'Jewish Heritage Walk' through York is now regularly available for visitors to the city: M. Zaidner, ed., *Jewish Travel Guide 2001* (London and Portland, 2001), p. 243.

[7] R.B. Dobson, *The Jews of Medieval York and the Massacre of March 1190* (Borthwick Papers, no. 45, York, 1974), p. 47.

[8] J. Lilley et al., eds, *The Jewish Burial Ground at Jewbury* (York Archaeological Trust, 12/3, 1994); J. Lilley, 'Jewbury Update', *Archaeology in York, Interim*, 17 (1992), 25–33.

[9] A. Newman, 'The historiography of Anglo-Jewry, 1892–1992', *JHS*, 33 (1992–94), 215–18; R.B. Dobson, 'The Jews of medieval Cambridge', *JHS*, 32 (1990–92), 1–24.

episode in the history of medieval Anglo-Jewry to be recorded in some detail in contemporary Jewish as well as Christian sources.[10] Although the former are presented in the age-old language and format of Hebraic martyrology, they are in many ways more reliable than are the rhetorical accounts provided by the galaxy of Christian chroniclers of the atrocity. That said, the celebrated set-piece account of the massacre by William, canon of the Augustinian priory of Newburgh twelve miles north of York, seems even more penetrating and revealing than it always did. Recent study of Newburgh's chronicles has shown how very close were William of Newburgh's contacts with the royal court, not least because he seems to have been in communication with that other Yorkshire historian and man of affairs, Master Roger, rector of Howden in the East Riding.[11] Accordingly, Newburgh's influential suggestion that the York massacre was less an instinctive outbreak of racial hatred than the outcome of a political conspiracy on a grand scale, directed by 'certain persons of higher rank who owed large sums to those impious usurers, the Jews', continues to carry conviction. Somewhat less certain, but plausible enough to win Bishop William Stubbs's cautious support over a century ago, is the even more conspiratorial interpretation that in 1190 a group of Yorkshire barons led by Richard Malebisse and members of the Percy family – and in league with Bishop Hugh du Puiset of Durham – deliberately attacked the York Jews as a protest against what they took, with some justice, to be their own financial exploitation at the hands of the Angevin government.[12]

Not that William of Newburgh's narration of events at York in 1190 always provides a thoroughly reliable account of the course of events in that tumultuous year. Indeed, it now seems that he is most revealing when most at a loss as to how to explain the apparently inexplicable. As Professor Peter Biller has pointed out, for Newburgh the Jews of York probably did deserve due divine judgement because of their pride and insolence towards Christians.[13] On the other hand, the Christian persecutors who acted as the agents of that divine judgement were motivated by avarice and unspeakable cruelty. How could Divine Providence be manifested through the actions of evil men? William of Newburgh wrestles with this and other allied moral problems without coming to any conclusion that seems to satisfy himself. Eager to blame the Jews themselves if he can, he invoked what he regarded as their innate tendency towards self-immolation. 'Whoever reads "The History of the Jewish War" by Josephus understands well enough that madness of this kind, arising from ancient superstition, has continued down to our own times, whenever any heavy misfortune has fallen upon them'.[14] But in Newburgh's view such Jewish 'madness' could not at all excuse from outright condemnation the Christians who killed the surviving Jews at the foot of Clifford's Tower on

---

[10] Roth, *History*³ (see Abbreviations), pp. 22–5.

[11] A. Gransden, 'Roger of Howden' and 'William of Newburgh' in L. Boia, ed., *Great Historians from Antiquity to 1800: an International Dictionary* (New York, 1989), pp. 124–5, 130–2; D.J. Corner, 'The *Gesta Henrici Secundi* and *Chronica* of Roger, parson of Howden', *BIHR*, 56 (1983), 126–44.

[12] W. Stubbs, *Historical Introductions to the Rolls Series* (London, 1902), pp. 218–19; Dobson, *Jews of Medieval York*, pp. 31–7.

[13] P. Biller, 'William of Newburgh's account of the massacre', in *Clifford's Tower Commemoration*, pp. 31–2.

[14] *Newburgh* (see Abbreviations), I, pp. 318–22.

the morning of 17 March. 'Their first crime was that of shedding human blood like water, without lawful authority; their second, that of acting barbarously, through the blackness of malice rather than the zeal for justice; their third, that of refusing the grace of Christ to those Jews who sought it.' Here we seem to hear that rarest of voices to find expression in surviving sources, the voice of an intelligent and compassionate Christian clerk who is genuinely confused and distressed at his society's treatment of the Jews. William of Newburgh's profound uncertainties about the correct ideological relationship between Gentiles and their Jewish neighbours are all the more revealing because they were probably shared by large numbers of Christians in York and elsewhere who never had the means or opportunity to articulate similar attitudes.[15]

At first sight ideological relations between Jews and Christians would not seem likely to be a topic much illuminated by the famous Jewbury archaeo-logical excavations of 1982–3. The opportunity to examine that site emerged at very short notice; and in conditions of considerable haste the York Archaeo-logical Trust was able to investigate only approximately a half of the burial ground. It was accordingly a very considerable achievement that when published in 1994 the excavation report should be such a striking demonstra-tion of modern high-quality cemetery excavation techniques. One of that report's greatest virtues was that it rarely tried to prove too much; and it already seems clear that the Jewbury excavation is more important for the questions it raises than the ones it answers. Thus despite the valiant labours of Jane McComish (then Lilley) and her colleagues to resolve the various topographical issues at stake, it has proved not at all easy to locate the most probable boundaries of the burial ground and to estimate the number of Jewish skeletons, especially those of children, which may have eluded the attention of the York archaeologists in the early 1980s.[16] This issue was in some ways the most difficult problem faced by Professor Mark Williamson in his ingenious attempt to use statistical evidence to calculate the probable size of the medieval York Jewry: 260 for the total population and 159 for children over 14 years of age. Although these are not at all implausible figures, they suffer – like most of the conclusions drawn from the study of the 475 or so inhumations discovered at Jewbury – from the lack of any other comparable large-scale excavation of medieval Jewish cemeteries.[17]

However, there can be no doubt that one of the most important conse-quences of the Jewbury excavation is that it has dispelled the previous myth of uniformity in Jewish burial practice throughout medieval Christendom. Thus in the York cemetery the great majority of the burials were within nailed rectangular wooden coffins or boxes, making it clear that the later Jewish practice of using entirely wooden coffins could not have been in force in thirteenth-century York.[18] More disappointing was the complete absence of

[15] *Newburgh*, I, pp. 320–2; R. Davies, 'The medieval Jews of York', *Yorkshire Archaeological Journal*, 3 (1875), 148–97.

[16] J.M. Lilley, 'The archaeology of Jewbury', in ead., ed., *Jewish Burial Ground*, pp. 316–60.

[17] J.M. Lilley, 'Interpretation of excavated remains'; M.H. Williamson, 'Multivariate studies of the population'; id., 'The size of the medieval Jewish population of York', in *ibid.*, pp. 360–5, 450–7 and 526–38 respectively. For what little additional work has been done, see David Hinton's chapter, above, pp. 102–4.

[18] J.M. Lilley, 'Coffins', in *ibid.*, pp. 382–3.

grave goods or Hebraic tombstones at Jewbury, despite the fact that the latter are not uncommon at many continental, and especially Spanish, medieval Jewish sites. However, the most controversial feature of the Jewbury graveyard is the way in which the great majority of the bodies were aligned not towards the east but apparently quite deliberately towards the north or north-east. Was this unorthodox orientation of the corpses at Jewbury a reflection of the Jews' own preferred burial practices? There seems to be no trace in any medieval English Jewry of the burial confraternities that flourished in fourteenth-century Catalonian Jewish communities.[19] Perhaps English Jews whose activities were so exceptionally closely regulated by the Crown and their Gentile neighbours while alive may have been subjected to careful supervision by Christians after their decease. In that case who more likely to oversee the burials of Jews at Jewbury than such Christian royally appointed clerks as the significantly named Jacobus de Cimiterio? The crown clerk of the Jewish chirograph chest at York during the 1270s, this Jacobus was not only a speculator in Jewish real property but also supervised the financial operations, with a colleague, of that chest or *archa* in great detail.[20] Perhaps another large medieval Jewish cemetery excavation may resolve this and other problems one day; but meanwhile it seems sensible to suppose that the burial practices revealed at Jewbury are unlikely to have been entirely immune from Christian control.

Nor can the Jewbury excavation report, fascinating though its findings are (especially perhaps in the field of dental pathology), do much to enhance understanding of the demographic and financial attrition that gradually overtook the Jewish community in York. However, it still seems incontrovertible that after the halcyon years of the first half of Henry III's reign, the prosperity of the York Jewry began to decline, quite dramatically, after the death of the spectacularly wealthy Leo *Episcopus* or *Le Eveske* in 1243. Leo's son Samuel, was obliged to pay a relief to the Crown of no less than 7,000 marks, a higher sum than that recorded for any other English Jew.[21] Leo's even more famous son-in-law, Aaron of York, had been at the height of his own enormous fortunes during the period when he was arch-presbyter of the English Jews between 1236 and 1243; but despite his connections with the royal court and his great resilience he could hardly withstand the 'double blows' of the 20,000-mark tallage of 1241–2 and the subsequent 60,000-mark tallage of 1244–50, which effectively 'ruined the Jewish magnates of England'.[22] I once suggested that 1255, the year in which Matthew Paris stated that Aaron of York's wealth 'entirely evaporated' probably marked the 'watershed' in the history of medieval Anglo-Jewry. I now concede that in York as elsewhere the real watershed in both the financial affairs of the Jewry and its relations with its Christians neighbours had probably arrived, to progressively ruinous effect, in the previous decade.[23]

---

[19] R.I. Burns, *Jews in the Notarial Culture: Latinate Wills in Mediterranean Spain, 1250–1350* (Berkeley, 1996), p. 26. It can go without saying that the papacy prohibited the burial of Jews (and usurers) in a church: S. Grayzel, *The Church and the Jews in the XIIIth Century*, ed. K.R. Stow (Detroit, 1989), II, p. 281.

[20] *CPREJ*, II, pp. 2, 30, 62, 89, 103, 156, 173; *CPR 1272–81*, p. 67.

[21] T. Madox, *The History and Antiquities of the Exchequer* (London, 1769), I, p. 225; R.B. Dobson, 'The decline and expulsion of the medieval Jews of York', *TJHSE*, 26 (1974–8), 34–52, at 35.

[22] R. Stacey, *Politics, Policy and Finance under Henry III, 1216–1245* (Oxford, 1987), pp. 153–5.

[23] For the suggestion that Aaron of York was the Croesus of Henry III's England, whose career 'can be interpreted as a microcosm of the history of the English Jewry as a whole', see Dobson,

Nor can the last two generations of York Jews have been in much doubt as to their increasing geographical isolation. With the possible exception of Chester, the only other northern town to possess a Jewish community, Newcastle-upon-Tyne, successfully petitioned for the removal of its Jews as early as 1234.[24] There is no direct evidence that the York Jewry ever established significant long-term satellite communities elsewhere in Yorkshire or the north of England. Admittedly, the difficult issue of interpreting the toponymic surnames held by a handful of English Jews remains perhaps even more obstinately open than it always was. Robin Mundill's thought-provoking list of 'Places of Jewish Settlement between 1262 and 1290', largely based on toponyms, certainly includes ten Yorkshire place-names, ranging from quite large towns (Beverley and Scarborough) to very small villages (Brodsworth and Colton).[25] Admittedly, little about the mysterious history of Jewish settlement in Angevin England can be safely said to be impossible; but it still seems most likely that the Jews of northern England may have sometimes conducted business outside York (hence the toponymics) but were usually resident in the city itself. It was from this metropolitan urban base that they satisfied a demand for credit and liquid capital, which stemmed less from York itself than from Yorkshire rural society.

It is an even greater irony of the history of the medieval English Jews that their communities tend to be much better documented in their final declining years than at the height of their fortunes and influence. Such a generalisation undoubtedly applies to York, where there can be no doubt that the many unpublished taxation records as well as the last plea-rolls of the Exchequer of the Jews will in due course make it possible to recreate the life of the Jewish minority in much greater depth than at present.[26] There seems no doubt, in other words, that it is for the years (1262–90) described by Robin Mundill as the period of 'Experiment and Expulsion' that future research is likely to be most revealing.[27] Indeed, Mundill's own remarkably learned book is the best possible testimony to the detail with which that period can be analysed and reassessed. In the case of the York Jewry itself some entries from the latest published volume of the great series of *Plea Rolls of the Exchequer of the Jews* may serve to confirm this ubiquitous tendency for original evidence to accumulate as Jewish communities became more fragile and insecure. One possible point of reference is a date in late April 1278 when the already small

---

'Decline and expulsion', p. 36. See also R.C. Stacey, '1240–1260: a watershed in Anglo-Jewish relations?', *Historical Research*, 61 (1988), 135–50.

[24] G.D. Guttentag, 'The beginnings of the Newcastle Jewish community', *TJHSE*, 25 (1973–5), 1–24; Chester Record Office, Shakerley Charter, 639r (an undated charter of c.1200 in which 'Hugo Judeus' transfers property to the monks of Poulton before the Justiciar of Chester). I owe this last, intriguing reference to the generosity of Mrs Diana Dunn.

[25] Mundill, *Solution* (see Abbreviations), pp. 286–90; the evidence is discussed in *ibid.*, pp. 16–24.

[26] See, e.g., the many references to York Jews in Z.E. Rokeah, *Medieval English Jews and Royal Officials: Entries of Jewish Interest in the English Memoranda Rolls, 1266–1293* (Jerusalem, 2000); ead., 'Some accounts of condemned Jews' property in the Pipe and Chancellor's Rolls', *Bulletin of Institute of Jewish Studies*, 1 (1973), 19–42; 2 (1974), 59–82; 3 (1975), 41–66.

[27] Mundill, *Solution*, pp. 146–208; J. Hillaby, 'The Worcester Jewry, 1158–1290: portrait of a lost community', *Transactions of the Worcestershire Archaeological Society*, 3rd series 12 (1990), 73–122; id., 'London: the thirteenth-century Jewry revisited', *JHS*, 32 (1990–2), 89–158.

and attenuated Jewry of the city of York was visited by one of the most notorious of all royal Justices of the English Jews, Hamo Hauteyn. Hamo is now best known for the fact that he was soon to be the Justice placed in charge of those investigations into fraudulent coin-clipping, which led to the mass hanging of many Jews throughout the country and ultimately to his own disgrace and dismissal (in 1286) for gross peculation.[28]

According to the Memoranda section of the Plea Roll of the Exchequer of the Jews for the Hilary Term of 1278, Hamo's visit to the York Jewry in that year was a routine affair. However, it immediately reminds us – if reminder were necessary – of how very closely regulated the Jews of thirteenth-century England were. Never in the field of medieval history, to adapt Cecil Roth's own adaptation of a celebrated phrase of Winston Churchill, is it possible to know so much about so few as it is about the Jews of Angevin and Plantagenet England.[29] In fact, record survives of only four York cases brought before Hamo Hauteyn in 1278, of varying interest and importance but all revealing the insecurity of the Jews of the city twelve years before their final expulsion overseas.[30]

First, a York Jew called Pictavin, son of Urs, together with his wife Ermita, paid a fine of two bezants to the king 'to excuse themselves from some [unspecified] infamy (*infamia*) of which they had been accused by a certain thief imprisoned in York' (*per quendam latronem in Ebor' incarceratum*). English Jews had naturally long been at serious risk of being placed in the king's mercy as a result of malicious and unsubstantiated allegations; but there seems no doubt that at York, as in other Jewries, their legal position was much more vulnerable by the 1270s than ever before.[31]

Rather less to be expected was Hamo's action on the same day of placing not a Jew but a Christian at the king's mercy, no less a figure indeed than Alexander de Kyrketon, then sheriff of Yorkshire, because he had failed to appear before him or send a representative to his court. The overriding authority of the royally appointed Justices of the Jews – of whom there were normally between two and five in office at any given time – in the persecution and exploitation of the Jews has never received all the attention it deserves. In 1257 the royal justices in eyre had been instructed that Jews were to plead and to be sued only before their own Justices. As Hamo's own career demonstrates, the office of Justice of the Jews offered only too many opportunities for financial corruption.[32]

Thirdly, and more intriguingly, a certain Meyrot of Stamford, sergeant (*serviens*) of the *judaismo* of York, was placed in mercy by Justice Hamo 'because he did not have the book of Judaic law on which all the Jews could take their oath' (*quia non habuit librum legis judaice super quem judei potuerunt*

---

[28] Roth, *History*[3], p. 79; cf. *CPREJ*, V, pp. 44, 137, 575–7, 859 and 887–8.

[29] C. Roth, *The Jews of Medieval Oxford* (Oxford, Oxford Historical Society new series no. 9, 1945–6), p. iii.

[30] *CPREJ*, V, p. 46.

[31] F. Pollock and F.W. Maitland, *The History of English Law before the Time of Edward I*, 2 vols (2nd edn, Cambridge, 1898), II, pp. 468–71; Roth, *History*[3], pp. 76–85. Despite his considered view that Edward I's later 'experiment' met with 'partial success' in helping some Jews to make a living, the most recent historian of the English Jewry (Mundill, *Solution*, pp. 100–8 and 247–8) has no doubt that it was in a deplorable economic state by the late 1260s.

[32] Roth, *History*[3], pp. 29–30, 76–80 and 112–15.

sacramentum suum). The reference to this mysterious law book is all the more welcome because in a previous allusion to the volume in question, I accepted the much less likely reading of *librum regalis* ('royal book').[33] Needless to say, no such oath book survives for any medieval English Jewish community; but the fact that such volumes existed adds a valuable new insight into the mysterious internal constitutional arrangements that preserved the inner cohesion of Jewish communities despite the intense centrifugal pressures upon them. An organised and partly self-governing 'commune of the Jews of York' had emerged by at least 1208.[34] Little is known about its operations; but it would have been perfectly logical – and comparable to the oaths made by Christian townsmen when they took up the freedom of their borough – for Jews to have sworn oaths on a book containing sections of the Torah.

Fourthly and finally, the 1278 Plea Roll of the Exchequer of the Jews preserves the details of an inquisition taken before Hamo and a group of Christians and Jews on Friday, 26 April 1278 concerning the goods and chattels of three Jews, namely, Benedict son of Josce, Peter son of Sampson and Leon son of Meyr, all members of the York Jewry and now all deceased.[35] The jurors swore on oath that Benedict son of Josce had died at Doncaster, leaving no chattels except for a moiety of a house in London, of whose value they were ignorant. As for Peter son of Sampson, he had chattels to the value of 10s, which were now in the hands of his wife Floria. Finally, the jurors swore that Leo son of Meyr had no chattels except for a house in Micklegate, York, which was worth 16s a year and was now held by his wife, also named Flora. The latter, so Hamo determined, could be allowed to continue living in the Micklegate house; but she had henceforward to render a third part of its annual value, that is 5s 4d a year, to the royal Exchequer of the Jews. Of these three dead York Jews, only Benedict son of Josce seems to have been an outstandingly wealthy member of the community. As long before as 1238 he had been an heir, together with Aaron of York, of one of the city's very richest Jews, Samuel son of Josce. Since then he had been heavily involved in complex business transactions with the Cistercian abbey of Meaux and the Gilbertine priory of Watton. By the late 1260s his fortunes were in marked decline, and he died in 1274, shortly after being charged with failure to pay his liability to tallage.[36]

Nothing is yet known for certain of the circumstances under which Benedict son of Josce, Peter son of Sampson and Leo son of Meyr had all met their deaths by 1278. However, there is abundant evidence that throughout the country the lives of adult Jewish males were at greater risk in the late 1270s and early 1280s than at the time of the Expulsion: 'in many ways 1279 might be regarded as a more fateful year for the medieval York Jewry than either 1190 or 1290.'[37] With the solitary exception of the remarkably well-connected entre-

[33] *CPREJ*, V, p. 46; Dobson, *Jews of Medieval York*, p. 39, n. 127.

[34] A '*commune Judeorum Eboraci*', capable of offering security to suspected Jews, is first recorded in 1208 during the course of a case in which Milo, a York Jew, was accused of murdering his wife because of his affair with another Jewess called Belina: Jacobs, *Jews* (see Abbreviations), p. 233.

[35] *CPREJ*, V, p. 46.

[36] *CPREJ*, I, pp. 151, 161, 220, 224, 266; II, pp. 20, 155, 185; *Close Rolls 1264–8*, pp. 480–1.

[37] Dobson, 'Decline and expulsion', p. 43. In November 1279 the site of what had almost certainly always been the most important York synagogue (*schola*), located between Coney Street and the

preneur, Bonamy of York, the power and authority of the Jewish financial potentates never recovered from the coin-clipping allegations of 1276–9 and the subsequent hangings of prominent York Jews.[38] As already implied, in its final and declining years the York Jewry was increasingly dominated by women and (above all) by the widows of Jews whose lives had been brought prematurely to a close. To an extent I failed to appreciate sufficiently when I first encountered the sources for the history of the York Jewry, the contribution of women to the financial as well as social welfare of their families was very critical indeed. Here – to conclude this chapter – is an inadequate attempt to make some amends for unjustified neglect. As the Reverend Michael Adler demonstrated many years ago, the history of Jewish women in medieval England is certainly obscure, but it is by no means completely impenetrable.[39]

It is certainly true that at first sight the public history of medieval Anglo-Jewry can only be written in terms of the credit transactions of a comparatively small handful of outstandingly wealthy financial potentates or magnates. Nor is it hard to understand why such financial and economic ascendancy would have carried with it a patriarchal dominance over Jewish religious and family affairs too. Almost a century ago when contemplating the mythic resonances of selecting a Jew, Leopold Bloom, as the 'hero' of *Ulysses*, James Joyce expressed his fascination for the way that 'A Jew is both king and priest in his own family'.[40] There seems every probability that Joyce's remark was much truer of twelfth-century England than of early twentieth-century Dublin. On the evidence available the authority of the medieval Jewish *paterfamilias* was all the greater because of the absence of a separate priestly caste of the sort that obtained in contemporary Christian society. As outstanding Jewish financiers were likely to be the spiritual as well as economic leaders of their communities, it seems for example not at all psychologically implausible that they should have persuaded so many female members of their flock to self-martyrdom on the night of *Shabbat ha-Gadol* in March 1190. In less hideous circumstances, the Jewish woman's role in the liturgical life of her community was also much more limited than that of her menfolk. Naturally debarred from such masculine rites of passage as circumcision and the *Bar Mitzva*, she passively observed acts of corporate worship in the synagogue behind a *mehitsa* or screen.[41]

Nevertheless the medieval English Jewess was undoubtedly a more influential and even formidable figure than her Christian counterpart. The Jewish towns-woman in York as elsewhere in Christendom was able to hold lands and houses

River Ouse, was granted by Queen Eleanor to John Sampson and Roger Basy, two future mayors of York. It was probably replaced by a second much more modest synagogue situated in a Jewish private house: Mundill, *Solution*, p. 31.

[38] Z.E. Rokeah, 'Money and the hangman in late thirteenth-century England: Jews, Christians and coinage offences alleged and real', *JHS*, 31 (1988–90), 83–109; 32 (1992–4), 159–218.

[39] M. Adler, 'The Jewish woman in medieval England', in *Jews of Medieval England* (London, 1939), pp. 17–45; R.B. Dobson, 'The role of Jewish women in medieval England', in D. Wood, ed., *Christianity and Judaism* (= *SCH* 29, Oxford, 1992), pp. 145–68. See further Bartlet's chapter in this volume, above, pp. 113–27.

[40] R. Ellmann, *James Joyce* (London, 1966), p. 384; R.B. Dobson, 'A minority within a minority: the Jewesses of thirteenth-century England', in S.J. Ridyard and R.G. Benson, eds, *Minorities and Barbarians in Medieval Life and Thought* (= *Sewanee Mediaeval Studies*, 7, 1996), 27–48.

[41] I. Abrahams, *Jewish Life in the Middle Ages* (London, 1896), pp. 25–7; Roth, *History*³, p. 125. See also E. Cohen-Harris, 'Where did medieval Jewish women stand? Visual sources, halakhic writings and architecture', *Conservative Judaism*, 52 (2000), 3–13.

in her own right, accountable to no overlord except the king himself.[42] She could also manage a large money-lending business, either under her own name or sometimes in association with her husband or sons. Although the extent to which English Jewesses could speak, write or understand Hebrew remains a controversial issue, there must have been many of them, like Henna widow of Aaron of York in 1270, who could 'sign her Hebrew character'.[43] Because a Jewish wife could also lend money on the security of all kinds of rents, estates and valuables, she may well have been even more active in the poorly documented (and thus much underestimated) business of urban pawnbroking than her husband.[44] As a widow, a Jewess (like Henna in 1270) could hope to receive a royal licence to acquire a substantial dowry in chattels and real property provided by her late husband 'in keeping with the law and custom of the Jewry'.[45] She was also entitled not only to collect her late husband's debts but to continue to manage his business in her own right. She could implead both Jews and Gentiles at law, either before the Justices of the Jews or elsewhere. She might even, like Belassez of York in 1277, falsify documents and forge seals.[46] Naturally such comparative independence had its hazards as well as its advantages. By the second half of the thirteenth century the Jewesses of York were sharing in the tribulations of their menfolk. They too were subjected to heavy tallages; and they too might be arrested, not infrequently, on charges of coin-clipping. By the terms of the Statute of Jewry of 1275 Jewish females as well as males were obliged to wear the *tabula*, 'a badge on the outer garment, that is to say, in the form of two tables joined, of yellow felt, of the length of six inches, and of the breadth of three inches'.[47] But the medieval Jewess might suffer worse fates still, most obviously imprisonment, hanging or even murder.

Murder was in fact the eventual end of the most celebrated Jewess in medieval English history, Licoricia of Winchester. The death of her first husband, David of Oxford, in 1244 presented Licoricia with the *damnosa hereditas* of the greatest fortune ever enjoyed by a Jewish widow in thirteenth-century England. After her wealth had been subjected to remorseless tallaging during the 1250s, she was imprisoned in 1258 on the grounds that she had stolen a valuable ring destined for none other than Henry III himself. Allegedly too ill to move in 1270, she was apparently murdered at Winchester seven years later as a result of an obscure local conspiracy.[48] More representative of the plight of the wealthy Jewish widow than the ill-starred later career of this exotic 'Grande Dame of the pre-Expulsion community' was that of the best-

---

[42] *CPREJ*, I, pp. 186, 224, 271; II, pp. 31, 78, 102; Adler, 'Jewish Woman', pp. 17–45.

[43] *CPREJ*, I, p. 270.

[44] For the revealing case of two London Jews, Isaac of Warwick and his wife, Ivetta, who for security's sake deposited their valuables, including a casket of jewels and six silver spoons probably received in pawn, with a neighbouring Christian couple in 1267, see Rigg, *Select Pleas*, pp. 33, 38, 108–9.

[45] Rokeah, *Medieval English Jews*, p. 59. For the 'prominence in business' of Oxford Jewesses, see Roth, *Jews of Medieval Oxford*, pp. 35–6.

[46] *CCR 1272–9*, p. 487.

[47] Mundill, *Solution*, p. 292.

[48] *CPREJ*, I, pp. 120, 186, 227; III, pp. 248, 293; Rigg, *Select Pleas*, pp. 19–20 and 27–8. Licoricia's career is discussed in further detail by Suzanne Bartlet, 'Three Jewish businesswomen in thirteenth-century Winchester', *JCH*, 3 (2000), 31–54.

documented York Jewess of the middle ages, Henna, widow of Aaron of York. Henna came of patrician Jewish stock for she was the daughter of Leo *Episcopus* or *Le Eveske*, one of the six richest Jews in the kingdom during the early minority of Henry III and extremely active in Jewish national affairs for the rest of his life.[49] As has been noticed already, on Leo's death (probably in 1243) most of his extensive property, much of it in Micklegate and Coney Street, passed to his son, Henna's brother, Samuel, and finally, on Samuel's death, to herself. The date of her marriage to Aaron of York has still not been established; but there can be little doubt that she was acting as his business partner during the meagre years after relentless royal tallages throughout the 1250s reduced him to a position of increasing penury.[50]

Aaron of York's death in 1268 automatically propelled Henna into a position of great prominence in the York Jewry. By the Hilary Term of 1270 the Treasurer and Barons of the Exchequer confirmed that she was entitled to the lands and chattels assigned to her as her dowry by her deceased husband.[51] According to the Jewish Plea Rolls, it seems likely that her most substantial revenues stemmed from urban properties, many of them in the city of York, which she had inherited either from her husband or from her brother. Henna was certainly leasing houses in Coney Street in the centre of York by 1272; and for a time she seems to have been very effective in staving off infringements on her property rights by frequent recourse to litigation. Unfortunately, however, the early years of her widowhood coincided with the new royal provisions '*super terris et feodis Judeorum*' of July 1271, which forced many Jews to surrender their urban tenements and messuages. An inquest held at York in February 1274 shows that Henna together with seven other Jews had been compelled to sell large numbers of city properties to Christian purchasers.[52] During the immediately following years Henna was subject to several small fines; and on 10 June 1280 she and her son by Aaron, Elias, sold what was probably their only surviving house in Coney Street to a Christian named Henry de Brylaunde. Both Henna and her son Elias thereupon seem to disappear from the records, not at all untypically of the last generation of York Jews.[53]

By 1280, a decade before Edward I's expulsion of all English Jews from his kingdom, it accordingly seems that the great kindred network of Aaron of York, the most impressive of its sort that York had ever seen, had been destroyed beyond repair. Aaron's own nephew, Josce le Jovene, a very considerable moneylender to Fountains Abbey, was hanged for an unspecified felony in 1279 or 1280; and it was at about the same time (before July 1280 in any case) that Aaron's daughter, Aucerra, who had already lost one husband, discovered that she was widowed again: her second husband Lumbard had been hanged too.[54] Despite the energetic entrepreneurial activity of the last positively wealthy Jew of York, Bonamy, at a national level, it seems that the York *archa* had ceased to fulfil any significant economic function by the close

[49] Rigg, *Select Pleas*, p. 52; *CPREJ*, I, p. 224.
[50] *CPREJ*, I, pp. 181, 186, 210–11 and 271; II, pp. 31, 78, 102, 173 and 278.
[51] Rokeah, *Medieval English Jews*, p. 59.
[52] *CPREJ*, II, pp. 155–6; Dobson, 'Decline and expulsion', p. 43.
[53] *CPR 1272–81*, p. 380.
[54] *CCR 1279–88*, p. 28.

of the 1280s. To the extent that money transactions continued in the city, they were now dominated by a handful of plutocratic figures more likely to come from the London Jewry rather than from York itself.[55] Only one Jewess, Sara, mother of Josce son of Benedict, held a house in York to the very end in the summer of 1290, the last of the resilient women who had protected and sustained their families and community in York against increasingly cruel and overwhelming odds. But not perhaps quite the last survivor. Even in the case of the sombre history of the Jews of medieval England intolerance had the very occasional limit, towards wives as well as their money-lending husbands. As the York Jewry was being dismantled in late August 1290, Edward I ordered the men of the Cinque Ports 'not to molest Bonamy of York, and Josce his son, Jews of York, and other Jews of the same city quitting the town within the time fixed, with their wives, children, households and goods'.[56] Bonamy's extended family found its way to the temporary security of the court of Philip the Fair. But in Edwardian England female courage, tenacity and endeavour were no longer enough.

---

[55] Mundill, *Solution*, pp. 157–8. For a brief account of the remarkable career of Bonamy of York, the final English Jewish moneylender of substance, see Dobson, 'Decline and expulsion', pp. 45–6.

[56] R.W. Mundill, 'The Jewish entries from the Patent Rolls, 1272–92', *JHS*, 32 (1990–92), 25–88, at 86. Despite a proclamation that all Jews who fled from England to France in 1290 should be expelled from the realm (J. Strayer, *The Reign of Philip the Fair* (Princeton, 1980), p. 235) Bonamy and his family apparently remained in or near Paris for several years, the last authenticated Jews of medieval York – and of medieval England too.

Bibliography

1 Primary Sources: unpublished or directly cited

Chester:

Record Office: Shakerley Charter, 639r.

Lincoln:

Public Library: Ross, John, *Annales Lincolniae* (unpublished MS).

London:

British Library, Additional Manuscripts 24511, fols 48–9; 62534, fols 257v–258r; Additional Roll 19299; Lansdowne MSS 826, 4, fols 28–64.

Public Record Office (PRO), C/47/9/48–50; C62/66; C62/67; Exchequer of the Jews class E9: documents cited in this volume are E9/1–5; E9/12; E9/22; E9/23; E9/34; E9/35; E9/36; E9/38; E9/64; E9/66; E13/3; E101/249/13, 15, 17, 29, 31; E101/250/1–12; E143/1/3; E159/33, 42, 45, 47, 49, 50, 59, 64; E401/4–6, 1567, 1572–82.

St Paul's Cathedral Library, Liber L(WD.4), ff. 47r–50v.

Westminster Abbey, Muniments (WAM), 6079, 6709, 6712, 6713, 6716, 6719, 6725, 6746, 6792, 6794, 6811 6869, 6906, 6921, 6926, 6948, 6951, 6980, 6981, 9001, 9002, 9010, 9067.

Paris:

Bibliothèque Nationale, MS Lat. 3177, fols 143v–145v.

2 Primary Sources: editions and translations

Abrahams, I., 'The Northampton "Donum" of 1194', *MJHSE*, 1 (1925), lix–lxxiv.

—— and H.P. Stokes and H. Loewe, eds, *Starrs and Jewish Charters preserved in the British Museum with illustrative documents, translations and notes*, 3 vols (London, 1930–2).

Anderson, A.O., tr., *Early Sources of Scottish History, A.D. 500–1206* (Edinburgh, 1922).

Appleby, J.T., ed. and tr., *Richard of Devizes: Cronicon* (Oxford, 1963).

Ballard, A., ed., *British Borough Charters 1042–1216* (Cambridge, 1913).

—— and J. Tait, eds, *British Borough Charters 1216–1307* (Cambridge, 1923).

Barber, Richard, *Bestiary. Being an English Version of the Bodleian Library, Oxford, MS Bodley 764* (Woodbridge, 1999).

Beit-Arié, M., *The Only Dated Medieval Hebrew Manuscript written in England (1189 C.E.) and the Problem of pre-Expulsion Anglo-Hebrew Manuscripts* (London, 1985).

Benton, J., ed., *Self and Society in Medieval France: the Memoirs of Aboot Guibert of Nogent* (New York, 1970).

Berry, H.F., ed., *Statute Rolls of the Parliament of Ireland, King John to Henry V* (Dublin, 1907).

Biddle, M., ed., *Winchester in the Early Middle Ages: an Edition and Discussion of the Winton Domesday* (Oxford, 1976).

Brewer, J.S., J.F. Dimock and G.F. Warner, eds, *Giraldus Cambrensis Opera*, 8 vols (RS 21, London, 1861–91).

Butler, H.E., ed. and tr., *Jocelin of Brakelond: Chronicle* (Edinburgh, 1949).

Calendar of Charter Rolls, I: Henry III 1226–57 (London, 1903); *II: Henry III and Edward I, 1257–1300* (London, 1906).

Calendar of the Close Rolls of the Reign of Edward I, 1272–9 (London, 1900); *1279–88* (London, 1902); *1288–96* (London, 1904).

Calendar of Fine Rolls, 1272–1307 (London, 1911).

Calendar of the Liberate Rolls, I: Henry III, 1226–1240 (London, 1916); *II: Henry III, 1240–5* (London, 1930); *III: Henry III, 1245–51* (London, 1937); *IV: Henry III, 1251–60* (London, 1959); *V: Henry III, 1260–7* (London, 1961); *VI: Henry III, 1267–72* (London, 1964).

Calendar of the Patent Rolls of the Reign of Henry III, 1232–47 (London, 1906); *1247–58* (London, 1908); *1258–66* (London, 1910); *1266–72* (London, 1913); *Calendar of the Patent Rolls of the Reign of Edward I, 1272–81* (London, 1901); *1281–1292* (London, 1893).

Calendar of the Plea Rolls of the Exchequer of the Jews, I: 1218–1272, ed. J.M. Rigg (London, 1905), *II: Edward I, 1273–5*, ed. J.M. Rigg (Edinburgh, 1910), *III: Edward I, 1275–77*, ed. H. Jenkinson (London, 1929), *IV: Henry III, 1272 and Edward I, 1275–7*, ed. H.G. Richardson (London, 1972), *V: Edward I, 1277–9*, ed. S. Cohen, rev. P. Brand (London, 1992).

Chew, H.M., and M. Weinbaum, eds, *The London Eyre of 1244* (London, 1970).

Close Rolls of the Reign of Henry III, 1227–31 (London, 1902); *1231–4* (London, 1905); *1234–7* (London, 1908); *1237–42* (London, 1911); *1242–7* (London, 1916); *1247–51* (London, 1922); *1251–3* (London, 1927); *1253–4* (London, 1929); *1254–6* (London, 1931); *1256–9* (London, 1932); *1259–61* (London, 1934); *1261–4* (London, 1936); *1264–8* (London, 1937); *1268–72* (London, 1938).

Corcos, A., 'Extracts from the Close Rolls', *TJHSE*, 4 (1899–1901), 202–19.

Davis, M.D., *Hebrew Deeds of English Jews before 1290* (London, 1888).

Douie, D.L., and H. Farmer, eds, *Life of St Hugh of Lincoln*, 2 vols (Oxford, 1985).

Eidelberg, S., tr., *The Jews and the Crusaders: the Hebrew Chronicles of the First and Second Crusades* (Madison, 1977).

Fleming, L., ed., *Chartulary of the Priory of Boxgrove* (Sussex Record Society, 59, 1960).

Greenway, D., and J. Sayers, tr., *Jocelin of Brakelond: Chronicle of the Abbey of Bury St Edmunds* (Oxford, 1989).

Hardy, T.D., ed., *Rotuli Chartarum, 1199–1216*, vol. Ii (London, Record Commission, 1837).

—— ed., *Rotuli de Oblatis et Finibus in Turri Londinensi asservati, temp. Regis Johannis* (London, Record Commission, 1835).

—— ed., *Rotuli Litterarum Clausarum in Turri Londiniensi asservati*, I (1204–24); II (1224–27) (London, Record Commission, 1833–4).

—— ed., *Rotuli Litterarum Patentium in Turri Londiniensi asservati, 1201–1216*, 2 vols (London, Record Commission, 1835).

Howlett, R., ed., *Chronicles of the Reigns of Stephen, Henry II and Richard I*, 4 vols (RS 82, London, 1884–9).

Hungeston, F.C., ed., *Johannis Capgrave Liber de Illustribus Henricis* (RS, London, 1858).

Jacobs, Joseph, *The Jews of Angevin England: Documents and Records from Latin and Hebrew Sources* (London, 1893).

James, M.R., and Augustus Jessop, eds, *Thomas of Monmouth: The Life and Miracles of St William of Norwich* (Cambridge, 1895).

Labande, E., ed. and tr., *Guibert de Nogent: Autobiographie* (Paris, 1981).

Luard, H.R., ed., *Annales Monastici*, 5 vols (RS 36, London, 1864–9).

Matthew Paris, *Chronica Majora*, 7 vols (RS, London, 1872–84).

McGurk, P., ed. and tr., *The Chronicle of John of Worcester*, vol. III (Oxford, 1998).

Michel, F.X., *Hugues de Lincoln, receuil des balades anglo-normande et écossoises relatives au meurtre de cet enfant commis par les juifs en MCCLV* (Paris, 1834).

Mynors, R.A.B., R.M. Thomson and M. Winterbottom, eds and tr., *William of Malmesbury: The History of the English Kings*, I (Oxford, 1998).

Neubauer, A., and M. Stern, eds, *Quellen zur Geschichte der Juden in Deutschland* (Berlin, 1892).

Owen, H., ed., *The Description of Pembrokeshire by G. Owen of Henllys* (London, 1892–1906).

Patent Rolls of the Reign of Henry III, 1216–25 (London, 1901); *1225–32* (London, 1903).

Patterson, R.B., ed., *Original Acta of St Peter's Abbey, Gloucester, c. 1122–1263* (Bristol and Gloucs. Archaeological Society, Record Section, 1998).

Pipe Rolls: J. Hunter, ed., *Magnum Rotulum Scaccarii vel Magnum Rotulum Pipae 31 Henrici Primi* (London, 1833, repr. 1929); J. Hunter, ed., *The Great Rolls of the Pipe for the 2nd, 3rd and 4th Years of the Reign of Henry II* (London, 1844, repr. 1930). Pipe Rolls Society volumes: *The Great Roll of the Pipe for the 5th Year of the Reign of Henry II* (London, 1884, repr. 1966); *The Great Roll of the Pipe for the 6th Year of the Reign of Henry II* (London, 1884, repr. 1966); *The Great Roll of the Pipe for the 16th Year of the Reign of Henry II* (London, 1892); *The Great Roll of the Pipe for the 19th Year of the Reign of Henry II* (London, 1895); *The Great Roll of the Pipe for the 21st Year of the Reign of Henry II* (London, 1897); *The Great Roll of the Pipe for the 23rd Year of the Reign of Henry II* (London, 1905); *The Great Roll of the Pipe for the 30th Year of the Reign of Henry II* (London, 1912); *The Great Roll of the Pipe for the 34th Year of the Reign of Henry II* (London, 1925); D.M. Stenton, ed., *The Great Roll of the Pipe for the 2nd Year of the Reign of Richard I* (London, 1925); D.M. Stenton, ed., *The Great Roll of the Pipe for the 3rd and 4th Years of the Reign of Richard I* (London, 1926); D.M. Stenton, ed., *The Great Roll of the Pipe for the 10th Year of the Reign of Richard I* (London, 1932); D.M. Stenton, ed., *The Great Roll of the Pipe for the 13th Year of the Reign of King John* (London, 1953).

Potter, K.R., tr., *Gesta Stephani* (London, 1955, repr. Oxford, 1976).

Powicke, F.M., and C.R. Cheney, eds, *Councils and Synods with other Documents relating to the English Church*, vol. 2, parts i (1205–65) and ii (1265–1313) (Oxford, 1964).

Rigg, J.M., ed., *Select Pleas, Starrs and other Records from the Rolls of the Exchequer of the Jews A.D. 1220–1284* (London, 1902).

Robertson, J.C., ed., *William fitz Stephen: Life of St Thomas of Canterbury* (RS 67, London, 1878).

Rokeah, Zefira Entin, ed., *Medieval English Jews and Royal Officials: Entries of Jewish Interest in the English Memoranda Rolls, 1266–1293* (Jerusalem, 2000).

Rothwell, H., ed. and tr., *English Historical Documents*, III (London, 1975).

Sapir Abulafia, Anna, and G.R. Evans, eds, *The Works of Gilbert Crispin, Abbot of Westminster* (London, 1986).

Sayles, G.O., ed., *Select Cases in King's Bench: Edward 1st*, II (London, 1936–9).

Shirley, W.W., ed., *Royal and other Letters of the Reign of Henry III*, 2 vols (RS 27, London, 1862–8).

Stapleton, T., ed., *De Antiquis Legibus Liber: Cronica Maiorum et Vicecomitum Londoniarum* (London, Camden Society, orig. ser. 34, 1846).

[The] Statutes of the Realm, I (London, 1810).

Stubbs, W., *Historical Introduction to the Rolls Series* (London, 1902).

——ed., *Roger de Howden: Chronicle*, 4 vols (RS 51, London, 1868–71).

Stubbs, W., ed., *Chronicle of the Reigns of Henry II and Richard I (attributed to Abbot Benedict of Peterborough)*, 2 vols (RS 49, London, 1867).
—— ed., *Chronicles of the Reigns of Edward I and Edward II*, vol. I (RS, London, 1882).
—— ed., *Gervase of Canterbury: Historical Works*, 2 vols (RS 73, London, 1879–80).
—— ed., *Ralph de Diceto: Historical Works*, 2 vols (RS 68, London, 1876).
Thomas Elmham: History of St Augustine's Abbey, Canterbury (RS 8, London, 1858).
Treharne, R.F., and I. J. Sanders, eds, *Documents of the Baronial Movement of Reform and Rebellion* (Oxford, 1973).
Tübach, Friedrich, *Index Exemplorum: a Handbook of Medieval Religious Tales* (Helsinki, 1969).
Vaughan, R., ed. and tr., *The Chronicle of Matthew Paris: Monastic Life in the Thirteenth Century* (Gloucester, 1984).

3 Secondary Reading on the Jewish Community

Abrahams, B. Lionel, 'The debts and houses of the Jews of Hereford in 1290', *TJHSE*, 1 (1893–4), 136–59.
—— 'The expulsion of the Jews from England in 1290', *JQR*, 7 (1894), 75–100, 236–58, 428–58. (Also published as an essay, Oxford, 1895.).
—— 'Condition of the Jews of England at the time of their expulsion in 1290', *TJHSE*, 2 (1894–5), 76–105.
—— 'The economic and financial position of the Jews in medieval England', *TJHSE*, 8 (1915–17), 171–89.
Abrahams, I., *Jewish Life in the Middle Ages* (London, 1896).
Abrahams, Moses, 'Leaf from an English *Siddur* of the twelfth century', *Jews' College Jubilee Volume* (London, 1906), pp. 109–13.
Abulafia, David, *Frederick II: A Medieval Emperor* (London, 1988).
Adler, Michael, 'History of the "Domus Conversorum"', *TJHSE*, 4 (1899–1901), 16–75.
—— 'The Jews of Canterbury', *TJHSE*, 7 (1911–14), 19–96.
—— 'Jewish tallies of the thirteenth century', *MJHSE*, 2 (1935), 8–24.
—— 'Inventory of the property of the condemned Jews, 1285', *MJHSE*, 2 (1935), 56–71.
—— *The Jews of Medieval England* (London, 1939).
Alderman, G., *Modern British Jewry* (new edn, Oxford, 1998).
Alexander, Mary, 'A possible synagogue in Guildford', in G. de Boe and F. Verhaeghe, eds, *Religion and Belief in Medieval Europe: papers of the Medieval Europe 1997 Conference, Brugge*, IV (Bruges, 1997).
Anderson, M.D., *A Saint at the Stake: the Strange Death of William of Norwich, 1144* (London, 1964).
Anglo-Jewish Historical Exhibition, Royal Albert Hall, 1887. Catalogue (London, 1887).
Art et archéologie des juifs en France médiévale (Toulouse, 1980).
Asaria, Z., ed., *Die Juden in Köln* (Köln, 1959).
Ashe Lincoln, F., *The Starrs: their Effect on Early English Law and Administration* (London, 1939).
Bachrach, Bernard S., *Early Medieval Jewish Policy in Western Europe* (Minneapolis, 1977).
Baer, Y., *A History of the Jews in Christian Spain*, 2 vols (Philadelphia, 1961).
Bale, Anthony P., 'Framing antisemitic *exempla*: locating the Jew of Tewkesbury', *Mediaevalia*, 20 (2001), 19–47.
—— 'Richard of Devizes and fictions of Judaism', *Jewish Culture and History*, 3 (2001), 55–72.
—— '"House devil, town saint": antisemitism and hagiography in medieval Suffolk', in Sheila Delany, ed., *Chaucer and the Jews: Sources, Contexts, Meanings* (New York, 2002).

Baron, Salo W., 'The Jewish factor in medieval civilisation' [1941], reprinted in Robert Chazan, ed., *Medieval Jewish Life* (New York, 1976), pp. 3–50.
—— 'Who is a Jew?' [1960], reprinted in A. Hertzberg and L.A. Feldman, eds, *History and Jewish Historians* (Philadelphia, 1964) pp. 5–22.
—— 'Newer emphases in Jewish history' [1963], reprinted in A. Hertzberg and L.A. Feldman, eds, *History and Jewish Historians* (Philadelphia, 1964), pp. 90–106.
Bartlet, S., 'Three Jewish businesswomen in thirteenth-century Winchester', *Jewish Culture and History*, 3 (2000), 31–54.
Barzel, Y., 'Confiscation by the ruler: the rise and fall of Jewish lending in the Middle Ages', *Journal of Law and Economics,* 35 (1992), 1–13.
Baskin, J. R., 'Jewish women in the middle ages', in J.R. Baskin, ed., *Jewish Women in Historical Perspective* (Detroit, 1991), pp. 94–114.
Baumgartner, I., 'The other Rome: national minority groups and the Jewish community between the middle ages and the renaissance', *Historisches Jahrbuch*, 118 (1998).
Beinart, H., ed., *Atlas of Jewish History* (New York, 1992).
——, 'The expulsion from Spain: causes and results', in id., ed., *The Sephardi Legacy*, 2 vols (Jerusalem, 1992), II, pp. 11–42.
Biale, David, *Power and Powerlessness in Jewish History* (New York, 1986).
Blair, I., J. Hillaby, I. Howell, R. Sermon and B. Watson, 'The discovery of two medieval *mikva'ot* in London and a reinterpretation of the Bristol *mikveh*', *JHS*, 37 (2002), 32–4.
Blumenkranz, Bernhard, *Le juif médiéval au miroir de l'art chrétien* (Paris, 1966).
Böcher, O., *Die alte Synagoge zu Worms* (Worms, 1960).
Botticini, M., 'A tale of "benevolent" governments: private credit markets, public finance and the role of Jewish lenders in medieval and renaissance Italy', *JEH*, 60 (2000), 164–89.
Brand, Paul R., 'Jews and the law in England, 1275–1290', *EHR*, 115 (2000), 1138–58.
Browe, Peter, SJ, *Die Judenmission im Mittelalter und die Päpste* (Rome, 1973).
Burns, R.I., *Jews in the Notarial Culture: Latinate Wills in Mediterranean Spain, 1250–1350* (Berkeley, 1996).
Cabaniss, A., 'Bodo-Eleazar: a famous Jewish convert', *JQR*, 42 (1952–3), 313–28.
Camporesi, Piero, 'The consecrated Host: a wondrous excess', in Michael Feher, Ramona Nadaff and Nadia Tazi, eds, *Zone 3.1: Fragments for a History of the Human Body* (New York, 1989), pp. 220–38.
Chazan, Robert, *European Jewry and the First Crusade* (Berkeley, 1987).
—— *Daggers of Faith: Thirteenth-Century Christian Missionizing and Jewish Response* (Berkeley, 1989).
—— 'Ephraim ben Jacob's compilation of twelfth-century persecutions', *JQR*, 84 (1994), 397–416.
—— *In the Year 1096 . . . The First Crusade and the Jews* (Berkeley, 1996).
Chew, H.M., 'A Jewish aid to marry, A. D. 1221', *TJHSE*, 11 (1924–7), 92–111.
Christian Hebraism: the Study of Jewish Culture by Christian Scholars in Medieval and Early Modern Times (Cambridge, MA, 1988).
Cluse, Christoph, ' "Fabula ineptissima": die Ritualmordlegende um Adam von Bristol nach der Handschrift London, British Library, Harley 957', *Aschkenas*, 5 (1995), 293–330.
Cohen, Jeremy, *The Friars and the Jews: the Evolution of Medieval Anti-Judaism* (Ithaca, 1982).
—— *Living Letters of the Law: Ideas of the Jew in Medieval Christianity* (Berkeley, 1999).
Cohen-Harris, E., 'Where did medieval Jewish women stand? Visual sources, halakhic writings and architecture', *Conservative Judaism*, 52 (2000), 3–13.
Davies, R., 'The medieval Jews of York', *Yorkshire Archaeological Journal*, 3 (1875), 148–97.

de Bouard, M., 'L'affaire de la synagogue de Rouen', *L'Histoire*, 48 (1982).
Dobson, R. B., *The Jews of Medieval York and the Massacre of March 1190* (Borthwick Papers, no. 45, York, 1974).
—— 'The decline and expulsion of the medieval Jews at York', *TJHSE*, 26 (1974–8), 34–52.
—— 'The role of Jewish women in medieval England', in D. Wood, ed., *Christianity and Judaism* (= *SCH* 29, Oxford, 1992), pp. 145–68.
—— 'The Jews of medieval Cambridge', *JHS*, 32 (1990–2), 1–24.
—— 'A minority within a minority: the Jewesses of thirteenth-century England', in S.J. Ridyard and R.G. Benson, eds, *Minorities and Barbarians in Medieval Life and Thought* (= *Sewanee Medieval Studies*, 7, 1996), 27–48.
Dundes, Alan, *The Blood Libel Legend: a Casebook in Antisemitic Folklore* (Madison, 1991).
Edwards, John, 'Religious faith and doubt in late medieval Spain: Soria *circa* 1450–1500', *Past and Present*, 120 (1988), 3–25; reprinted in John Edwards, *Religion and Society in Spain c. 1492* (Aldershot, 1996), III.
—— 'Religious faith, doubt and atheism [with a contribution by C. John Sommerville]', *Past and Present*, 128 (1990), 152–61; reprinted in Edwards, *Religion and Society in Spain*, no. IIIa.
—— *The Jews in Western Europe, 1400–1600* (Manchester, 1994).
—— 'The Church and the Jews in English medieval towns', in T.R. Slater and Gervase Rosser, eds, *The Church in the Medieval Town* (Aldershot, 1998), pp. 43–54.
Einbinder, S.L., 'Pulcellina of Blois: romantic myths and narrative conventions', *Jewish History*, 12 (1998), 29–46.
—— 'Meir ben Elijah of Norwich: persecution and poetry among medieval English Jews,' *JMH*, 26 (2000), 145–62.
—— *Beautiful Death: Jewish Poetry and Martyrdom in Medieval France* (Princeton, 2002).
Elman, Peter, 'Jewish finance in the thirteenth century with special reference to royal taxation', *BIHR*, 15 (1938), 112–13.
—— 'The economic causes of the expulsion of the Jews in 1290', *Economic History Review*, 7 (1936–7), 145–54.
Emanuel, R.R., 'The Society of Antiquaries' sabbath lamp', *Antiquaries Journal*, 80 (2000), 308–15.
—— and M.W. Ponsford, 'Jacob's Well, Bristol: Britain's only known ritual bath (*mikveh*)', *Transactions of the Bristol and Gloucestershire Archaeological Society*, 112 (1994), 73–86.
Epstein, I., 'Pre-expulsion England in the responsa', *TJHSE*, 14 (1935–9), 187–205.
Erb, Reiner, ed., *Die Legende vom Ritualmord: zur Geschichte der Blutbeschuldigungen gegen Juden* (Berlin, 1993).
Fabre-Vassas, Claudine, *The Singular Beast: Jews, Christians and the Pig*, tr. Carol Volk (New York, 1997).
Flint, Valerie, 'Anti-Jewish literature and attitudes in the twelfth century', *JJS*, 37 (1986), 39–57 and 183–205.
Friedman, Lee M., *Robert Grosseteste and the Jews* (Cambridge, MA, 1934).
Gartner, Lloyd P., 'Cecil Roth, historian of Anglo-Jewry', in Dov Noy and Issacher ben-Ami, eds, *Studies in the Cultural Life of the Jews of England* (Jerusalem, 1975), pp. 69–86.
Gilbert, M., ed., *Atlas of Jewish History* (5th edn, London, 1976).
Glassman, B., *Antisemitic Stereotypes without Jews: Images of the Jews in England 1290–1700* (Detroit, 1975).
Glick, Leonard B., *Abraham's Heirs: Jews and Christians in Medieval Europe* (Syracuse, 1999).
Goitein, S.D., 'What would Jewish and general history benefit by a systematic

publication of the documentary Geniza papers?', *Proceedings of the American Academy for Jewish Research*, 23 (1954), 29–39.

Golb, N., *The Jews in Medieval Normandy: a Social and Intellectual History* (Cambridge, 1998).

Grabois, A., 'Les écoles de Narbonne au XIIIe siècle', in *Juifs et Judaisme de Languedoc* (Centre d'Études Historiques de Fanjeaux, Toulouse, 1977), pp. 141–57.

Grayzel, S., *The Church and the Jews in the XIIIth Century*, ed. K.R. Stow, 2 vols (New York and Detroit, 1989).

Greatrex, Joan, 'Monastic charity for Jewish converts: the requisition of corrodies by Henry III', in D. Wood, ed., *Christianity and Judaism* (= *SCH* 29, Oxford, 1992), pp. 133–45.

Gregg, Joan Young, *Devils, Women and Jews: Reflections of the Other in Medieval Sermon Stories* (Albany, 1997).

Grossman, A.M., 'Medieval rabbinic views on wife-beating, 800–1300', *Jewish History*, 5 (1991), 53–62.

Guttentag, G.T., 'The beginnings of the Newcastle Jewish community', *TJHSE*, 25 (1973–5), 1–24.

Hassig, Debra, *Medieval Bestiaries: Text, Image, Ideology* (Cambridge, 1995).

Heer, Friedrich, *God's First Love: Christians and Jews Over Two Thousand Years*, tr. Geoffrey Skelton (London, 1970).

Henriques, H.S.Q., *The Jews and the English Law* (London, 1908).

Hilberg, Raul, *The Destruction of the European Jews* (revised and definitive edition, New York and London, 1985).

Hillaby, J., 'Hereford gold: Irish, Welsh and English land. The Jewish community at Hereford and its clients, 1179–1253, Part 1', *TWNFC*, 44 (1984), 358–419; 'Part 2', *ibid.*, 45 (1985), 193–270.

—— 'A magnate among the marchers: Hamo of Hereford, his family and clients, 1218–1253', *JHS*, 31 (1988–90), 23–82.

—— 'The Hereford Jewry, part 3: Aaron le Blund and the last decades of the Hereford Jewry, 1253–1290', *TWNFC*, 46 (1990), 432–87.

—— 'The Worcester Jewry 1158–1290: portrait of a lost community', *Transactions of the Worcestershire Archaeological Society*, 3rd series 12 (1990), 73–122.

—— 'London: the thirteenth-century Jewry revisited', *JHS*, 32 (1990–2), 89–158.

—— 'Colonisation, crisis management and debt: Walter de Lacy and the lordship of Meath', *Ríocht na Mídhe*, 8 (1992/3), 1–50.

—— 'The London Jewry: William I to John', *JHS*, 33 (1992–4), 1–44.

—— 'Beth miqdash me'at: the synagogues of medieval England', *JEH*, 44 (1993), 182–98.

—— 'The ritual child murder accusation: its dissemination and Harold of Gloucester', *JHS*, 34 (1994–6), 69–109.

—— 'Testimony from the margin: the Gloucester Jewry and its neighbours, c. 1159–1290', *JHS*, 37 (2002), 41–112.

Hilton, C., 'St Bartholomew's Hospital and its Jewish connections', *JHS*, 30 (1987–8), 21–50.

Honeybourne, M.B., 'The pre-expulsion cemetery of the Jews in London', *TJHSE*, 20 (1959–61), 145–59.

Hsia, R. Po-Chia, *The Myth of Ritual Murder: Jews and Magic in Reformation Germany* (New Haven and London, 1988).

—— and H. Lehmann, eds, *In and Out of the Ghetto: Jewish–Gentile Relations in Late-Medieval and Early-Modern Germany* (Cambridge, 1995).

Huesca, Pedro Alfonso, *Diálogo contra los judíos*, introduction by John Tolan (Huesca, 1996).

Hühner, L., 'The Jews of Ireland', *TJHSE*, 5 (1902–5), 226–42.

Hunter, G., et al., eds, *Clifford's Tower Commemoration, York, 15–18 March 1990: a Programme and Handbook* (York, 1990).

Hyams, P.R., 'The Jews in medieval England, 1066–1299', in A. Haverkamp and H. Wollrath, eds, *England and Germany in the High Middle Ages* (Oxford, 1986), pp. 174–92.

Hyamson, Albert M., *A History of the Jews in England* (London, [1908] 1928).

Hyman, L., *The Jews of Ireland* (Shannon, 1972).

Isserlin, R.M.J., 'Building Jerusalem in the "Islands of the Sea": the archaeology of medieval Anglo-Jewry', in S. Kadish, ed., *Building Jerusalem: Jewish Architecture in Britain* (London and Portland, 1996), pp. 34–53.

Jacobs, J., 'Aaron of Lincoln', *TJHSE*, 3 (1896–8), 157–79.

Jeffrey, K., *Clifford's Tower and the Jews of Medieval York* (English Heritage, 1995).

Jenkinson, Sir Hilary, 'The records of exchequer receipts from the English Jewry', *TJHSE*, 8 (1915–17), 19–54.

Johnson, W., 'Textual sources for the study of Jewish currency crimes in thirteenth-century England', *British Numismatic Journal*, 66 (1996), 21–32.

Jones, Michael, ' "The place of the Jews": anti-Judaism and theatricality in medieval culture', *Exemplaria*, 12 (2000), 327–59.

Jones, Siân, Tony Kushner and Sarah Pearce, eds, *Cultures of Ambivalence and Contempt: Studies in Jewish/non-Jewish Relations* (London and Portland, 1998).

Jordan, W.C., *The French Monarchy and the Jews: from Philip Augustus to the Last Capetians* (Philadelphia, 1989).

Kadish, S., ed., *Building Jerusalem: Jewish Architecture in Britain* (London and Portland, 1996).

Kaplan, Yosef, and David Katz, eds, *The Expulsion of the Jews from England in 1290 and its Aftermath* (Jerusalem, 1992).

Katz, David S., *Philo-Semitism and the Readmission of the Jews to England, 1603–1655* (Oxford, 1982).

——'Marginalization of English modern Anglo-Jewish history', in Tony Kushner, ed., *The Jewish Heritage in British History: Englishness and Jewishness* (London, 1992), pp. 60–77.

Katz, S., 'Pope Gregory the Great and the Jews', *JQR*, n.s., 24 (1933–34), pp. 113–36.

Kauffman, C. M., 'Art and popular culture: new themes in the Holkham Bible picture book', in D. Buckton and T.A. Heslop, eds, *Studies in Medieval Art and Architecture* (Stroud, 1994).

Kisch, G., 'The yellow badge in history', *Historia Judaica*, 4 (1942), 95–144.

——*The Jews in Medieval Germany: a Study of their Legal and Social Status* (Chicago, 1949).

Krautheimer, R., *Mittelalterlicher Synagogen* (Berlin, 1927).

Kushner, T., 'James Parkes, the Jews and conversionism: a model for multi-cultural Britain?', in D. Wood, ed., *Christianity and Judaism* (= *SCH* 29, Oxford, 1992), pp. 451–61.

Lange, Nicholas de, 'James Parkes: a centenary lecture', in Siân Jones, Tony Kushner and Sarah Pearce, eds, *Cultures of Ambivalence and Contempt: Studies in Jewish/non-Jewish Relations* (London and Portland, 1998), pp. 31–49.

Langmuir, Gavin, ' "Judei nostri" and the beginning of Capetian legislation', *Traditio*, 16 (1960), 203–39.

——'The Jews and archives of Angevin England: reflections on medieval anti-semitism', *Traditio*, 19 (1963), 183–244.

——'The Knight's Tale of young Hugh of Lincoln', *Speculum*, 47 (1972), 459–82.

——'Thomas of Monmouth: detector of ritual murder', *Speculum*, 59 (1984), 820–46.

——*Toward a Definition of Antisemitism* (Oxford and Berkeley, 1990).

——'The faith of Christians and hostility to Jews', in D. Wood, ed., *Christianity and Judaism* (= *SCH* 29, Oxford, 1992), pp. 77–92.

Lilley, J.M., 'Jewbury update', *Archaeology in York, Interim*, 17 (1992), 25–33.
——et al., *The Jewish Burial Ground at Jewbury* (Archaeology of York 12/3, York, 1994).
Lindo, E.H., *The History of the Jews of Spain and Portugal* (London, 1848).
Lipman, Vivian D., 'The Roth "Hake" manuscript', in John M. Shaftesley, ed., *Remember the Days: Essays in Honour of Cecil Roth* (London, 1966), pp. 49–71.
——*The Jews of Medieval Norwich* (London, 1967).
——'The anatomy of medieval Anglo-Jewry', *TJHSE*, 21 (1962–7), 64–77.
——'Jews and castles in medieval England', *TJHSE*, 28 (1981–2), 1–19.
Loewe, Raphael, 'The mediaeval Christian Hebraists of England: the *Superscriptio Lincolniensis*', *HUCA*, 28 (1957), 205–52.
Maccoby, Hyam, *Judaism on Trial: Jewish–Christian Disputations in the Middle Ages* (Rutherford, 1982).
McCulloh, John, 'Jewish ritual murder: William of Norwich, Thomas of Monmouth and the early dissemination of the myth', *Speculum*, 72 (1997), 698–740.
Mellinkoff, Ruth, *Outcasts: Signs of Otherness in Northern European Art of the Late Middle Ages*, I (Berkeley, 1993).
Menache, Sophia, 'The king, the Church and the Jews: some considerations on the expulsions from England and France', *JMH*, 13 (1987), 223–36.
Mentgen, Gerd, 'Die Vertreibungen der Juden aus England und Frankreich im Mittelalter', *Aschkenas*, 7 (1997), 11–53.
Miyazaki, M., 'Misericord owls and medieval anti-semitism', in Debra Hassig, ed., *The Mark of the Beast: the Medieval Bestiary in Art, Life and Literature* (New York, 1999), pp. 23–50.
Moore, R.I., *The Formation of a Persecuting Society: Power and Deviance in Western Europe* (Oxford, 1987).
——'Antisemitism and the birth of Europe', in D. Wood, ed., *Christianity and Judaism* (= *SCH* 29, Oxford, 1992), pp. 33–57.
Mundill, Robin R., 'Anglo-Jewry under Edward I: credit agents and their clients', *JHS*, 31 (1988–90), 1–21.
——'English medieval Ashkenazim: literature and progress', *Aschkenas*, 1 (1991), 203–10.
——'Lumbard and son: the businesses and debtors of two Jewish moneylenders in late thirteenth-century England', *JQR*, 82 (1991), 137–70.
——'The Jewish entries from the Patent Rolls, 1272–1292', *JHS*, 32 (1990–2), 25–88.
—— *England's Jewish Solution: Experiment and Expulsion, 1262–1290* (Cambridge, 1998).
——'The medieval Anglo-Jewish community: organization and royal control', in *Proceedings of christliche und jüdische Gemeinden in kulturräumlich vergleichender Betrachtung. Trier 1999* (forthcoming).
Myers, David N., and David B. Ruderman, eds, *The Jewish Past Revisited: Reflections on Modern Jewish Historians* (New Haven and London, 1998).
Newman, A., 'The historiography of Anglo-Jewry, 1892–1992', *JHS*, 33 (1992–4), 215–18.
Nirenberg, David, *Communities of Violence: Persecution of Minorities in the Middle Ages* (Princeton, 1996).
Olszowy-Schlanger, Judith, 'The knowledge and practice of Hebrew gammar among Christian scholars in pre-expulsion England: the evidence of "bilingual" Hebrew–Latin manuscripts', in Nicholas de Lange, ed., *Hebrew Scholarship and the Medieval World* (Cambridge, 2001), pp. 107–28.
Pakter, Walter, *Medieval Canon Law and the Jews* (Ebelsbach, 1988).
Parkes, James, *The Jew and his Neighbour: a Study of the Causes of Antisemitism* (London, 1930).
——*The Conflict of the Church and the Synagogue: a Study in the Origins of Antisemitism* (London, 1934).

Parkes, James, *The Jew in the Medieval Community: a Study of his Political and Economic Situation* (London, 1938, 2nd edn, New York, 1976).

—— *Voyage of Discoveries* (London, 1969).

Pearce, Sarah, 'Attitudes of contempt: Christian anti-Judaism and the Bible', in Siân Jones, Tony Kushner and Sarah Pearce, eds, *Cultures of Ambivalence and Contempt: Studies in Jewish/non-Jewish Relations* (London and Portland, 1998), pp. 50–71.

Pepper, G., 'An archaeology of the Jewry in medieval London', *London Archaeologist*, 7 (1992), 3–6.

Peters, Edward, 'Jewish history and Gentile memory: the expulsion of 1492', *JH*, 9 (1995), 9–34.

Prynne, William, *A Short Demurrer to the Jewes long discontinued barred remitter into England, comprising an exact and chronological relation of their first admission into, their ill deportment, oppressions, and their final banishment out of England, collected out of the best historians and records. With reasons against their readmission to England* (2nd edn, London, 1656).

Rabinowitz, L., 'The London *get* of 1287', *TJHSE*, 21 (1962–7), 314–22.

Richardson, Henry G., 'The Chamber under Henry II', *EHR*, 69 (1954), 596–611.

—— *The English Jewry under the Angevin Kings* (London, 1960).

Richmond, Colin, 'Englishness and medieval Anglo-Jewry', in Tony Kushner, ed., *The Jewish Heritage in British History: Englishness and Jewishness* (London, 1992), pp. 42–59.

—— 'Parkes, prejudice and the Middle Ages', in Siân Jones, Tony Kushner and Sarah Pearce, eds, *Cultures of Ambivalence and Contempt: Studies in Jewish/non-Jewish Relations* (London and Portland, 1998), pp. 205–46.

Rigg, J.M., 'The Jews of England in the 13th century', *JQR*, o.s., 15 (1903), 5–22.

Roberts, M., 'A Northampton Jewish tombstone, c.1259 to 1290, recently rediscovered in Northampton Central Museum', *Medieval Archaeology*, 36 (1972), 173–8.

Rokeah, Zefira Entin, 'Some accounts of condemned Jews' property in the Pipe and Chancellor's Rolls: part 1', *Bulletin of the Institute of Jewish Studies*, 1 (1973), 19–42; part 2, *ibid.*, 2 (1974), 59–82; part 3, *ibid.*, 3 (1975), 41–66.

—— 'Crime and Jews in late 13th-century England, part 1', *HUCA*, 55 (1984), 95–158.

—— 'The state, the Church and the Jews in medieval England', in Shmuel Almog, ed., *Antisemitism through the Ages* (Oxford, 1988), pp. 99–125.

—— 'Money and the hangman in late thirteenth-century England: Jews, Christians and coinage offences alleged and real: part 1', *JHS*, 31 (1988–90), 83–109; part 2, *ibid.*, 32 (1990–2), 159–218.

—— 'A Hospitaller and the Jews: Brother Joseph de Chauncy and English Jewry in the 1270s', *JHS*, 34 (1994–6), 189–207.

—— ed., *Medieval English Jews and Royal Officials: Entries of Jewish Interest in the English Memoranda Rolls, 1266–1293* (Jerusalem, 2000).

Roth, Cecil, 'Jewish history for our own needs', *The Menorah Journal*, 14 (1928), 419–33.

—— *Medieval Lincoln and its Jewry* (London, 1934).

—— *The Jews of Medieval Oxford* (Oxford, Oxford Historical Society new series no. 9, 1945–6).

—— 'The intellectual activities of medieval English Jewry', *British Academy Supplemental Papers*, 8 (London, 1948).

—— 'Jews in Oxford after 1290', *Oxoniensia*, 15 (1950), 63–80.

—— *Essays and Portraits in Anglo-Jewish History* (London and Philadelphia, 1962).

—— *History of the Jews in England* (Oxford, 1941, 2nd edn, 1942, 3rd edn, 1964).

—— 'Why Anglo-Jewish history?' *TJHSE*, 22 (1968–9), 21–9.

Ruben, A., *The History of Jewish Costume* (London, 1973).

Rubin, Miri, *Corpus Christi: the Eucharist in Late Medieval Culture* (Cambridge, 1991).
—— 'The Eucharist and the construction of medieval identities', in D. Aers, ed., *Culture and History, 1350–1600* (Hemel Hempstead, 1992), pp. 43–63.
—— *Gentile Tales: the Narrative Assault on Late Medieval Jews* (New Haven, 1999).
Saltman, A., *The Jewish Question in 1655. Studies in Prynne's Demurrer* (Bar-Ilan U.P., 1995).
Saperstein, Marc, 'Jews and Christians: some positive images', *Harvard Theological Review*, 79 (1986), 236–46.
Sapir Abulafia, Anna, 'An attempt by Gilbert Crispin, abbot of Westminster, at rational argument in the Jewish–Christian debate', *Studia Monastica*, 26 (1984), 55–74.
—— 'Jewish carnality in twelfth-century Renaissance thought', in D. Wood, ed., *Christianity and Judaism* (= *SCH* 29, Oxford, 1992), pp. 59–75.
Sartre, Jean-Paul, *Anti-Semite and Jew*, tr. G.F. Bleeker (New York, 1965).
Schulz, Magdelene, 'The blood libel: a motif in the history of childhood', *Journal of Psychohistory*, 14 (1986), 1–24.
Seidmann, G., 'Jewish marriage rings', *Jewellery Studies*, 1 (1983–4), 41–4.
Seror, Simon, 'Les noms des femmes juives en Angleterre au moyen age', *REJ*, 154 (1995), 295–325.
Shain, Milton, *Antisemitism* (London, 1998).
Shreckenberg, H., *The Jews in Christian Art: an Illustrated History* (London, 1996).
Sinanoglou, Leah, 'The Christ child as sacrifice: a medieval tradition and the Corpus Christi play', *Speculum*, 48 (1973), 491–509.
Skerner, D.C., 'King Edward I's articles of inquest on the Jews and coin-clipping', *Historical Research*, 72 (1999), 1–26.
Stacey, Robert C., 'Royal taxation and the social structure of medieval Anglo-Jewry: the tallages of 1239–1242,' *HUCA*, 56 (1986), 175–249.
—— *Politics, Policy and Finance under Henry III, 1216–1245* (Oxford, 1987).
—— 'Recent work on medieval English Jewish history', *Jewish History*, 2 (1987), 61–72.
—— '1240–1260: a watershed in Anglo-Jewish relations?', *Historical Research*, 61 (1988), 135–50.
—— 'The conversion of the Jews to Christianity in thirteenth-century England', *Speculum*, 67 (1992), 263–83.
—— 'Jewish lending and the medieval English economy', in R. Britnell and B.M.S. Campbell, eds, *A Commercialising Economy: England 1086 to c. 1300* (Manchester, 1995), pp. 78–101.
—— 'Parliamentary negotiation and the expulsion of the Jews from England', in R.H. Britnell, R. Frame and M.C. Prestwich, eds, *Thirteenth-Century England VI* (Woodbridge, 1997), pp. 77–101.
—— 'From ritual crucifixion to Host desecration: Jews and the body of Christ', *Jewish History*, 12 (1998), 11–28.
—— 'Crusades, martyrdoms, and the Jews of Norman England, 1096–1190', in A. Haverkamp, ed., *Juden und Christen zur Zeit der Kreuzzüge* (Sigmaringen, 1999), pp. 233–51.
—— 'Anti-Semitism and the medieval English state', in J.R. Maddicott and D.M. Palliser, eds, *The Medieval State: Essays Presented to James Campbell* (London, 2000), pp. 163–77.
Starr, Joshua, 'The mass conversion of the Jews in southern Italy, 1290–1293', *Speculum*, 21 (1946) 203–11.
Stephenson, D., 'Colchester: a smaller medieval English Jewry', *Essex Archaeology and History*, 16 (1985), 48–52.
Stocker, D., 'The shrine of Little St Hugh', in T.A. Heslop and V. Sekules, eds, *Medieval Art and Architecture at Lincoln Cathedral* (British Archaeological Association Transactions 7, 1986), pp. 109–17.

Stokes, H.P., 'Records of mss and documents possessed by the Jews in England before the expulsion', *TJHSE*, 8 (1915–17), 78–97.

Stow, K.R., 'The Jewish family in the Rhineland in the high middle ages: form and function', *AHR*, 92 (1987), 1085–92.

——ed., *The Jews in Rome*, 2 vols (Leiden, 1995–7).

Streit, K.T., 'The expansion of the Jewish community in the reign of King Stephen', *Albion*, 25 (1993), 177–92.

Tallan, C., 'Opportunities for medieval northern European Jewish widows in the public and domestic spheres', in L. Mirrer, ed., *Upon My Husband's Death: Widows in the Literature and Histories of Medieval Europe* (Ann Arbor, 1992), pp. 115–27.

Tanguy, J., *Le monument juif du Palais de Justice de Rouen* (Rouen, 1990).

Taylor, P., 'Brutal truth', *Heritage Today: the magazine of English Heritage* (June 2001), pp. 43–7.

Tovey, De Bloissiers, *Anglia Judaica* (Oxford, 1738).

Trachtenberg, J., *The Devil and the Jew* (New Haven, 1943).

Vincent, N., 'Jews, Poitevins, and the bishop of Winchester', in D. Wood, ed., *Christianity and Judaism* (= *SCH* 29, Oxford, 1992), pp. 119–32.

——'Two papal letters on the wearing of the Jewish badge, 1221 and 1229', *JHS*, 34 (1994–6), 209–44.

von Mutius, H.-G., ed., *Rechtsentscheide Mittelalterlicher Englischer Rabbinen* (Frankfurt am Main, 1995).

Wasserstein, David J., 'Grosseteste, the Jews and medieval Christian Hebraism', in James McEvoy, ed., *Robert Grosseteste: New Perspectives on his Thought and Scholarship* (Turnhout, 1995), pp. 357–76.

Watt, J.A., 'The English episcopate, the state and the Jews: the evidence of the thirteenth-century conciliar decrees', in P.R. Coss and S.D. Lloyd, eds, *Thirteenth-Century England II* (Woodbridge, 1988), pp. 137–47.

——'Jews and Christians in the Gregorian decretals', in D. Wood, ed., *Christianity and Judaism* (= *SCH* 29, Oxford, 1992), pp. 93–105.

Wood, D., ed., *Christianity and Judaism* (= *SCH* 29, Oxford, 1992).

Yuval, Israel Jacob, ' "Vengeance and damnation, blood and defamation": from Jewish martyrdom to blood libel accusations', *Zion*, 58 (1993), 33–90.

4 Secondary Reading on British and Irish History

Alexander, J.W., *Ranulf of Chester* (Athens, GA, 1983).

Allen, D.F., *A Catalogue of English Coins in the British Museum: the Cross and Crosslets (Tealby) Type of Henry II* (London, 1951).

Allen Brown, R., *Castles from the Air* (Cambridge, 1989).

Archibald, M.M., and B.J. Crook, *English Medieval Coin Hoards: I Cross and Crosslets, Short Cross and Long Cross Hoards* (British Museum Occasional Paper 87, London, 2001).

Ayers, B., *Book of Norwich* (London, 1994).

Barlow, F., *William Rufus* (London, 1983).

Bartlett, R., *England under the Norman and Angevin Kings* (Oxford, 2000).

Bassett, S., ed., *Death in Towns: Urban Responses to the Dying and the Dead, 100–1600* (Leicester, 1992).

Beckerman, J.S., 'The forty-shilling jurisdictional limit in medieval English personal actions', in Dafydd Jenkins, ed., *Legal History Studies* (Cardiff, 1975).

Biles, M., 'The indomitable Belle: Eleanor of Provence', in Richard H. Bowers, ed., *Seven Studies in Medieval English History and other essays presented to Harold S. Snellgrove* (Mississippi, 1983), pp. 113–31.

Blackburn, M., 'Coinage and currency', in E. King, ed., *The Anarchy of King Stephen's Reign* (Oxford, 1994).

Brand, P., *The Making of the Common Law* (London, 1992).

Brooke, C., and G. Keir, *London, 800–1216: the Shaping of a City* (London, 1975).

Brooke, G.C., *A Catalogue of English Coins in the British Museum: the Norman Kings*, 2 vols (London, 1916).

Campbell, J., 'Norwich', in M.D. Lobel, ed., *The Atlas of Historic Towns*, II (London, 1975), pp. 2–3.

Cathcart King, D., *Castellarium Anglicanum* (New York, 1983).

Cherry, J., and J. Goodall, 'A twelfth-century gold brooch from Folkingham Castle, Lincolnshire', *Antiquaries Journal*, 65 (1985), 471–2.

Clarke, H., and A. Carter, *Excavations in King's Lynn, 1963–1970* (London, 1977).

Collis, J., *Winchester Excavations, Volume 2, 1949–1960* (Winchester, 1978).

Colvin, H.M., ed., *History of the King's Works: the Middle Ages*, II (London, 1963).

Corner, D.J., 'The *Gesta Henrici Secundi* and *Chronica* of Roger, parson of Howden', *BIHR*, 56 (1983), 126–44.

Crouch, D., *William Marshal: Court, Career and Chivalry in the Angevin Empire, 1147–1219* (London, 1990).

—— *The Reign of King Stephen, 1135–1154* (London, 2000).

Dalton, P., 'Ranulf II Earl of Chester and Lincolnshire in the reign of Stephen', in A. Thacker, ed., *The Earldom of Chester and its Charters* (= *Journal of the Chester Archaeological Society*, 71, 1991), 109–32.

—— '*In neutro latere*: the armed neutrality of Ranulf II of Chester in king Stephen's reign', *ANS*, 14 (1992), 39–59.

Davies, R.R., *The Age of Conquest: Wales 1063–1415* (Oxford, 1991).

Davis, H.W.C., 'London lands and liberties of St Paul's, 1066–1135', in A.J. Little and F.M. Powicke, eds, *Essays in Medieval History presented to Thomas Frederick Tout* (Manchester, 1925), pp. 45–59.

Davis, R.H.C., *King Stephen* (London, 1967).

Davison, B.K., 'The late Saxon town of Thetford: an interim report on excavations 1964–66', *Medieval Archaeology*, 11 (1967), 189–208.

Dixon-Smith, S.D., 'The image and reality of alms-giving in the great halls of Henry III', *Journal of the British Archaeological Association*, 152 (1999), 79–96.

Dolley, M., *Anglo-Norman Ireland, c. 1100–1318* (Dublin, 1972).

Drury, P.J., 'Aspects of the origins and development of Colchester Castle', *Archaeological Journal*, 139 (1982), 302–419.

Dunning, G.C., 'The Saxon town of Thetford', *Archaeological Journal*, 106 (1951), 72–3.

Flanagan, M.T., *Irish Society, Anglo-Norman Settlers, Angevin Kingship: Interactions in Ireland in the Late Twelfth Century* (Oxford, 1989).

Foard, G., 'The early topography of Northampton and its suburbs', *Northamptonshire Archaeology*, 26 (1995), 109–22.

Grimes, W.F., *The Excavation of Roman and Medieval London* (London, 1968).

Harvey, Barbara, *The Short Oxford History of the British Isles: the Twelfth and Thirteenth Centuries* (Oxford, 2001).

Hatcher, John and Mark Bailey, *Modelling the Middle Ages: the History and Theory of England's Economic Development* (Oxford, 2001).

Hill, J.W.F., *Medieval Lincoln* (Cambridge, 1948).

Hillen, H.J., *History of the Borough of King's Lynn*, 2 vols (Norwich, 1907).

Hines, J., 'The Becoming of the English; identity, material culture and language in early Anglo-Saxon England', *Anglo-Saxon Studies in Archaeology and History*, 7 (1994), 49–59.

Hinton, D.A., *Medieval Pottery of the Oxford Region* (Oxford, 1973).

Holt, J.C., *The Northerners: A Study in the Reign of King John* (Oxford, 1961).

Howell, M., *Eleanor of Provence: Queenship in Thirteenth Century England* (Oxford, 1998).

Johnson, C., and A. Vince, 'The south bail of Lincoln', *Lincolnshire History and Archaeology*, 27 (1992), 12–16.

Jupp, P.C., and C. Gittings, eds, *Death in England: an Illustrated History* (Manchester, 1999).

Keene, D., *Survey of Medieval Winchester* (Oxford, 1985).

Knowles, D., et al., *Heads of Religious Houses: England and Wales, 940–1216* (Cambridge, 1972)

Lewis, E.A., *The Medieval Boroughs of Snowdonia* (London, 1912).

Liebermann, F., ed., *Gesetze der Angelsachsen*, I (Halle, 1894).

Lloyd, Simon, *English Society and the Crusade, 1216–1272* (Oxford, 1988).

Maddicott, J.R.,'The crusade taxation of 1268–1270 and the development of Parliament', in P.R. Coss and S.D. Lloyd, eds, *Thirteenth-Century England II* (Woodbridge, 1988), pp. 93–117.

—— and D.M. Palliser, eds, *The Medieval State: Essays Presented to James Campbell* (London, 2000).

Madox, T., *The History and Antiquities of the Exchequer* (London, 1769).

Miller, Edward, and John Hatcher, *Medieval England: Towns, Commerce and Crafts, 1086–1348* (London, 1995).

Moore, J.S., 'The Anglo-Norman family', *ANS*, 14 (1992), 185–94.

Nightingale, P., 'Some London moneyers, and reflections on the organisation of the English mints in the eleventh and twelfth centuries', *Numismatic Chronicle*, 142 (1982), 34–50.

Ormrod, W.M., 'Royal finance in thirteenth-century England', in P.R. Coss and S.D. Lloyd, eds, *Thirteenth-Century England V* (Woodbridge, 1995), pp. 141–64.

Otway-Ruthven, A.J., *A History of Medieval Ireland* (2nd edn, London, 1980).

Owen, D.M., 'Bishop's Lynn: the first century of a new town?', *ANS*, 2 (1980), 141–53.

—— ed., *The Making of King's Lynn* (Oxford, 1984).

Palgrave, F., *The Rise and Progress of the English Commonwealth*, II (London, 1832, 2nd edn, 1922).

Partner, Nancy, *Serious Entertainments: The Writing of History in Twelfth-Century England* (Chicago, 1977).

Platt, Colin, *The English Medieval Town* (London, 1979).

Pollock, F., and F.W. Maitland, *The History of English Law before the Time of Edward I*, 2 vols (2nd edn, Cambridge, 1898).

Postles, D., 'Personal pledging: medieval "reciprocity" or "symbolic capital"', *Journal of Interdisciplinary History*, 26 (1996), 419–35.

Prestwich, M., *The Three Edwards: War and State in England 1272–1377* (7th edn, London, 1980).

—— et al., eds, *Thirteenth-Century England VII* (Woodbridge, 1999).

Rackham, B., *Medieval English Pottery* (London, 1957).

Rawcliffe, C., *Medicine and Society in Later Medieval England* (Stroud, 1997).

Rees, W., *South Wales and the March 1284–1415* (Oxford, 1924).

Reeves, A.C., *The Marcher Lords* (Llandybi, 1983).

Reynolds, S., *An Introduction to the History of English Medieval Towns* (Oxford, 1977).

Rigby, S.H., *English Society in the Later Middle Ages* (Basingstoke, 1995).

Roberts, C.A., et al., eds, *Burial Archaeology: Current Research, Methods and Developments* (BAR British Series 211, Oxford, 1989).

Round, H., *Geoffrey de Mandeville* (London, 1892).

Rutledge, E. and P., 'King's Lynn and Yarmouth: two thirteenth-century surveys', *Norfolk Archaeology*, 37 (1980), 92–114.

Salzman, L.F., *Edward I* (London, 1968).

Schama, Simon, *A History of Britain: at the Edge of the World? 3000B.C.–A.D.1603* (London, 2000).

Schofield, J., and R. Leech, eds, *Urban Archaeology in Britain* (CBA Research Report 61, London, 1987).

Shoesmith, R., *A Short History of Castle Green and Hereford Castle* (Hereford,1980).

——ed., *Hereford City Excavations Volume 3: The Finds* (CBA Research Report 56, London, 1985).

Southern, R.W., 'St Anselm and Gilbert Crispin, abbot of Westminster', *Medieval and Renaissance Studies*, 3 (1954), 78–99.

Stevenson, J.H., 'The castles of Marlborough and Ludgershall in the Middle Ages', *Wiltshire Archaeological and Natural History Magazine*, 85 (1992), 70–9.

Swanson, R.N., *Church and Society in Late Medieval England* (Oxford, 1989).

Turner, Ralph V., *King John* (London and New York, 1984).

Urry, W., *Canterbury under the Angevin Kings* (London, 1967).

Wade Labarge, M., *Gascony: England's First Colony, 1204–1453* (London, 1980).

Ward-Perkins, B., 'Why did the Anglo-Saxons not become more British?', *EHR*, 115 (2000), 513–33.

Wareham, A., 'The motives and politics of the Bigod family', *ANS*, 17 (1995), 233–42.

Warren, W.L., *The Governance of Norman and Angevin England, 1066–1272* (London, 1987).

Williams, J.H., 'From "palace" to "town": Northampton and urban origins', *Anglo-Saxon England*, 13 (1984), 113–36.

Index

Printed and bound by CPI Group (UK) Ltd, Croydon, CR0 4YY

13/04/2025

14656520-0001